LBJ
The Way He Was

LBJ
The Way He Was

FRANK CORMIER

DOUBLEDAY & COMPANY, INC.

GARDEN CITY, NEW YORK

1977

ISBN: 0-385-04825-4

Library of Congress Catalog Card Number 76–18338

For
Elizabeth, John, William, and Michael
who knew him when . . .

. . . they were very young.

Contents

Preface

When Lyndon Johnson dedicated the library that bears his name and now honors his memory, he declared:

"It is all here: the story of our time—with the bark off. There is no record of a mistake, nothing critical, ugly or unpleasant, that is not included in the files here. We have papers from my forty years of public service in one place for friend and foe to judge, to approve or disapprove."

It is in that spirit that I have written this book, trying always to see beneath the covering, the veneer, the bark of the public man to the extraordinary human being underneath. I have sought to portray the Lyndon Johnson I knew and liked and often admired. To do so, I felt obliged to make the picture complete, to deal with his follies and foibles as well as with his many strengths and triumphs. It is not a work of biography but rather an informal portrait—sketch, perhaps—of the most unforgettable personality I ever encountered.

To the extent of my knowledge, my notes from the period, and my memories, "it is all here . . . with the bark off."

FRANK CORMIER

LBJ
The Way He Was

1

"I Need Your Help"

Out the bus window I saw a dozen pigeons take wing, as if startled, from roosts in a small park. The bus stopped, then moved ahead past a drab brick building, past a lawn that sloped toward railroad tracks above. A policeman on a three-wheeled motorcycle jumped a curb and headed up the green embankment. Someone shouted from the front, "We've lost the motorcade!"

Ahead, somewhere, was a custom-fashioned Lincoln convertible carrying John F. Kennedy toward a luncheon crowd of Texas Democrats at the Dallas Trade Mart. Or so we thought. But what was the policeman doing and wasn't the highway ahead ominously empty?

By the time our bus, labeled "White House Press Bus ✕1" on a windshield placard, moved into a service drive at the Trade Mart, I think we all knew instinctively that we would not find Jack Kennedy there. A political trip begun in high spirits a day earlier had ended tragically as frightened pigeons wheeled into the cloudless sky above Dealey Plaza.

For me it was the end of a reporting assignment that had begun a year earlier: to cover John F. Kennedy's activities on a full-time basis as White House correspondent of the Associated Press, a venerable newspaper-owned co-operative serving editors and broadcasters around the globe. It also marked the beginning of a new assignment, with a President I had never met.

To me, at that hour, Lyndon B. Johnson was a very successful Texas politician whose manner and skills had been frequent targets of derision and whose tenure as Vice-President was associated in my mind with globe-trotting and the entertainment of a Pakistani camel driver.

However, I didn't know Jack Kennedy either when I was first assigned to the White House "beat." We had been introduced aboard Air Force One. That meeting with Kennedy and an early conversation with Johnson aboard the same plane leap to mind as revealing much about the contrasting styles and the differing problems and priorities of the two Presidents.

Indian Springs Air Force Base on the Nevada desert is nobody's idea of Camelot but the nondescript airstrip assumed a measure of unlikely glamor when Kennedy stopped there on December 8, 1962. The occasion was an inspection tour of a nearby nuclear weapons test area that was even more desolate. For Kennedy, the stopover held special significance because it followed by barely a month the nerve-jangling crisis triggered by the discovery of Soviet missiles in Cuba. The missiles had been taken away but the young President wanted to dramatize his commitment to a strong national defense effort and give thanks, at Indian Springs and elsewhere along his route, to the airmen and weapons makers who had given him the nuclear muscle to stare down Nikita Khrushchev.

The journey was equally significant from my standpoint because it was the first of hundreds of trips, covering hundreds of thousands of miles, as a White House reporter.

I was an unseasoned air traveler at the time, and a nervous one, but my fears were eased a bit at Indian Springs when I left the commercial airliner chartered for the White House press corps and boarded Air Force One for the first time. Surely, I reasoned, this was the world's safest and most pampered ship of the sky. I was on board as one of four members of a rotating "pool" of reporters who accompanied Kennedy everywhere aboard his glittering jet in order to relay to colleagues on the press plane any noteworthy happenings aloft.

Since then I've been aboard the blue, white and silver jet, or its near-identical successor with a different tail number, on flights to Peking, Moscow, Saigon and points between. No flight, however, can quite equal the first one from Indian Springs, Nevada, to Palm Springs, California, where Kennedy was to spend the weekend at the desert estate of old crooner Bing Crosby.

As Air Force One was configured at the time, reporters sat at a small table at the forward end of the main passenger cabin. That's where I was, strapped in tightly and gripping the arms of my chair, when the jet angled sharply aloft.

The plane was in a steep climb—"Fasten Seat Belts," read the illuminated warning—when Press Secretary Pierre Salinger climbed the sloping deck with admirable nonchalance and, leaning close to my ear, said, "Follow me."

Unbuckling with considerable trepidation, I managed to get out of my seat and defy basic laws of physics all the way down the canted aisle to the door bearing the presidential seal. Salinger opened it and motioned me through.

Kennedy sat facing me across a small desklike table. Salinger introduced me as a newcomer who had been covering economic and financial affairs. After a smile, a handshake and a quick pleasantry, Kennedy looked up—I was standing in front of him still battling for equilibrium—and asked, "How would you compare Bob Roosa and Julian Baird?" Just like that.

The President's reputation as a brain-picker had preceded him, yet I was startled to hear him asking *me* to appraise the relative merits of Robert V. Roosa, his Under Secretary of the Treasury for Monetary Affairs, and Baird, the white-haired, twinkle-eyed Minnesota banker who had held the same position in the Eisenhower administration.

"Mr. President," I responded, "Bob Roosa has a better grasp of international monetary problems but Julian Baird did a great job of managing the national debt under difficult circumstances."

Kennedy nodded and remarked that he had heard good things about Baird. Then he came back with another question: "What do you think should be done about the balance of payments problem?"

I told him I assumed he was not about to shut down overseas

bases, cut off foreign aid or adopt a protectionist trade policy. Therefore, I said, "I don't see any alternative but to clamp down on the export of long-term investment capital."

In retrospect, the suggestion may have had little merit. No matter. Kennedy didn't think much of it. "We can handle that by jiggering interest rates," he said, then wished me well and sent me on my way.

It was a no-nonsense encounter and I assume the President was more interested in appraising me than in my appraisals. In any case, our subsequent exchanges were limited largely to pleasantries, as when Kennedy once remarked as we headed for Palm Beach, "Frank, this sure beats the Treasury, doesn't it?"

Far more protracted, and lively, was a conversation with Johnson on the evening of January 5, 1964, six weeks after the shattering experience of Dallas. The new President was flying back to Washington from Texas, where he and his family had spent a busy Christmas and New Year's holiday. The plane was hardly off the ground at Bergstrom Air Force Base, outside Austin, when LBJ appeared in the aisle beside our table and began to talk. When it became apparent he was warming up for a long stay, I persuaded him to take my seat and squatted in the aisle with James B. (Scotty) Reston of the New York *Times,* who was aboard as a special guest.

"I'm the only President you've got," Johnson told us, "and I intend to be President of all the people. I need your help. If I succeed, you succeed. We all succeed together or fail together. With your help, I'll do the best job that's in me for our country. I don't want Jack Kennedy looking down at me from heaven and saying he picked the wrong Vice-President. But I can't do the job alone. I need your help."

Leaning forward and speaking earnestly in a soft drawl, he promised we could become the best-informed reporters in Washington.

"I'll tell you everything," he vowed. "You'll know everything I do. You'll be as well informed as any member of the Cabinet. There won't be any secrets except where the national security is involved. You'll be able to write everything. Of course"—and this rather shocked those among us who weren't accustomed to his verbal excesses—"I may go into a strange bedroom every now and then that I won't want you to write about, but otherwise you can write everything."

Johnson told us he hoped to make himself more available to the press than any President, and to have the best press relations. But he made it clear he could wield a stick as well as a carrot, saying, "If you want to play it the other way, I know how to play it both ways, too, and I know how to cut off the flow of news except in handouts." But the carrot was predominant as he concluded:

"There's no reason why the members of the White House press corps shouldn't be the best-informed, most-respected, highest-paid reporters in Washington. If you help me, I'll help you. I'll make you-all big men in your profession."

I hoped one of my colleagues would say something, anything, to disabuse the President of the notion that he and the White House press corps could establish a mutual aid society. We simply don't work that way with any President. Surely, we want all Presidents to succeed. We deeply wished the best for Lyndon Johnson. But we couldn't cut a deal, transform ourselves into propagandists, and retain a shred of self-respect.

In the startled silence that followed Johnson's proposition, I turned to him and, trying to skirt a direct challenge, said, "Mr. President, don't you realize that sooner or later every reporter around this table is going to write something that'll make you mad as hell?"

Johnson frowned at me and replied, in a tone of incredulity, "Why, I never got mad at a newsman in my life, except for one NBC man, and he broke my confidence." The frown became a scowl and he invoked the name of Jack Bell, then chief political writer and head of the Senate staff of the AP, a veteran reporter known for his irreverent approach toward politicians of all persuasions. Pounding the table for emphasis, Johnson fairly shouted at me, "I don't even get mad at Jack Bell—and he writes *black Republican stories!*"

LBJ's bold and bald approach to the five of us reflected, I would imagine, his Capitol Hill experiences—not with newsmen like Jack Bell but with fellow Senators who accepted horse trading and back-scratching as part of the legislative game. As reporters, we were quite prepared to give the new President the benefit of almost every doubt, at least for a time. A honeymoon period between President and press corps has come to be regarded as traditional, but it always has its limits.

Peter Lisagor of the Chicago *Daily News,* appearing on a public television panel early in the Johnson administration, summarized the situation in this fashion: "I think he would like to make cheerleaders out of all of us, and we're fighting hard to preserve our virtue, because soon enough, I think . . . we'll all turn into our natural state, which is to be common scolds, and he'll have to deal with us then."

Johnson in fact wanted to make cheerleaders and devoted followers out of all Americans. In a dizzy whirl of meetings after Kennedy's murder, day after day and often long in the night, Johnson gave voice to emotional appeals for unity and support from a people traumatized by the assassination. He sought continuity of government without a faltering step, the enactment of the programs Kennedy had put before a skeptical Congress, and national unity in pursuit of both goals.

Even as Air Force One carried Kennedy's body and the new President from Dallas to Washington, Johnson sought out the Kennedy men aboard and appealed to them to remain at his side in the new administration. To cabinet members he declared, "I need you more than Jack Kennedy did." To the fifty Governors, "I need your heart and your hand." To a group of farm state legislators, "My ox is in the ditch and I need your help."

Whitney Young, national director of the Urban League, was sitting at home with his wife in New York City, watching the nonstop television coverage of the Kennedy tragedy, when Johnson called to pledge that he, the first Southern-born President since Woodrow Wilson, would fight—yes, fight—for Kennedy's civil rights bill.

Was Young coming to the funeral? The black man said he had been told he would receive an invitation but none had arrived; there had been a mix-up. Johnson called back twenty minutes later to say a White House driver would meet Young with an invitation at Washington National Airport.

In four weeks LBJ received in his office about four hundred individuals or small groups. He presided over forty large meetings. He placed or accepted well over a thousand telephone calls. The message never varied. "I need your help."

If the appeal occasionally lacked grammatical precision or elegant language, folks knew what he meant. To members of the prestigious Business Council, his appeal was homespun as he invoked the memory of his friend and fellow Texan, House Speaker Sam Rayburn:

". . . I remember Mr. Rayburn told me that, in his fifty years here, he believed the most frightened man that he ran into was the average American businessman. He said that he [the businessman] can go to bed at night . . . and wake up in the morning knowing that his property has not been confiscated out from under his pillow, he is still frightened. And if he can't scare himself enough, he will go hire a lawyer or a public relations man to keep him scared.

"So, gentlemen, I say banish your fear and shed your doubts and renew your hopes. We have much work to do together. We want you to roll up your sleeves and let's get about doing it."

It may not have been the sort of message the bankers and corporation presidents in Johnson's audience were accustomed to hear, but they chuckled dutifully and, more important, they bought it.

My first look at Johnson the President came at 4:45 P.M. on the day after Kennedy's murder when he stepped into a White House conference room to read a proclamation of mourning before radio microphones and television cameras. He was composed and solemn, even funereal. His manner befitted the occasion.

In the days that followed, Johnson displayed an instinct for doing the proper thing, for uttering the appropriate word. We saw him often as he was quietly assertive in sessions with Congress members, Governors, foreign leaders and influential private citizens, yet modest and self-effacing as he and his wife Lady Bird moved with the stricken Kennedys through the rites for the dead. He seemed almost unerring as he presided over an abrupt and difficult but astonishingly smooth period of transition. As reporters, as citizens, we were pleased and perhaps a bit surprised.

Johnson's initial approach to the press corps was open, even solicitous. When he delivered a Thanksgiving Day address to the nation within a week of the assassination, those of us who were members of the press pool were ushered to front-row folding chairs facing his desk, and right beside those of Mrs. Johnson and their daughters. We had never before been given such a choice vantage point for a presidential address.

A few days later Johnson sent for Philip Potter and Gerald E. Griffin of the Baltimore *Sun,* "my favorite newspaper," and took them to the Capitol in his limousine for a weekly luncheon of the House delegation from Texas. To legislators and reporters, he recalled Mr. Rayburn's advice to another instant President, Harry Truman: "Harry, there will be people that surround you, wall you off from others, and some of your aides will try to make you think you're the smartest man in the world. But you know and I know that's not true." Johnson said he was accepting the advice, then pulled out a ten-dollar bill and paid the lunch tab for himself and his two guests.

Nothing quite like it had happened since Truman himself, on his first morning in office, spotted the AP's Ernest B. (Tony) Vaccaro on the curb as he left his apartment and hauled him off to the White House. It was Tony's beat for the rest of Truman's tenure.

That the unorthodox might become commonplace in the Johnson administration became more evident on Saturday, December 7, 1963, when about thirty of us gathered in Salinger's office for what we presumed would be a routine news briefing.

"The President would like you to come in and have coffee with him," Salinger announced with a huge grin.

Trooping into the Oval Office, we found Johnson seated in a rocking chair that, except for cocoa-brown upholstery, was identical to the familiar one Kennedy had used. LBJ presumably was not averse to fostering this type of association-by-indirection with the fallen leader, but we subsequently determined that the rocker was more than a ploy. Dr. Janet Travell, Kennedy's back specialist, had prescribed the chair for Johnson when she gave him a checkup as Vice-President.

Crowding onto the room's two sofas and every available chair, we were served coffee by Navy stewards, a bit of hospitality that produced awkward moments after it became apparent this was to be LBJ's first news conference and we had to juggle coffee cups, saucers, pens and notebooks. When everyone was served except the President, Johnson looked at an empty table beside his chair and exclaimed, "Where the hell's my coffee?"

Merriman Smith of United Press International, doubtless relishing the prospect of a competitor's discomfiture, responded, "I believe you'll discover, sir, that Karl Bauman of the Associated Press drank it!"

While Bauman spluttered, a black-jacketed steward hastily produced the President's cup of Sanka; LBJ avoided straight coffee.

Mrs. Kennedy and her two children had just vacated the White House living quarters, so Johnson's first recorded exchange with the press corps began like this:

"This will be your first night here?"

"Yes."

"How do you feel about it?"

"I feel like I have already been here a year."

Hardly an inquisition, although the questioning became a bit more pointed as we began exploring the dimensions of the forthcoming federal budget.

Hovering about the room as Johnson discoursed on fiscal matters was a small dark man we had come to recognize as the presidential shadow. The grandson of Sicilian immigrants and husband of a former LBJ secretary, Mary Margaret Wiley, Jack Valenti proved himself a man for all chores, "a valuable hunk of humanity," as Johnson kept him hustling:

". . . Jack, give me that sentence that I asked you to get for my next speech. I think it rather explains my view on the budget . . . Jack, if you will get me that figure, I would like to have it. It's right on my desk, on the budget, on the top . . . There is a one-line note on the top of my desk, Jack, from the Director of the Budget, that has the chart on it. . . ."

Although Johnson was retaining the Kennedy staff, as reporters we were getting acquainted with a new group of men, most of them Texans, who owed a particular loyalty to the new President. Valenti was the most visible and accessible of these at the start, a gregarious man who had written a newspaper column in Houston and took pleasure in interpreting his boss for our benefit. He was a good source because, as LBJ phrased it, "He gets up with me every morning. He stays up with me until I go to bed at night, around midnight, and he is the only one who can really take it. The rest of these fellows are sissies."

Walter Jenkins, LBJ's top aide of long standing, was too retiring and reticent to be of much help, at least to most of us. More useful, and more detached than the supremely loyal Valenti, was Horace Busby, another transplanted Texan who had been a newspaperman, newsletter writer, consultant and off-and-on Johnson employee.

We learned weeks after the fact about Busby's curious vigil at LBJ's bedside on the night after Kennedy's murder, an episode that strongly suggested the new Chief Executive was assailed by inner uncertainties. At Johnson's behest, Busby had waited in the darkened room for the President to fall asleep. When he finally felt able to edge quietly toward the door, he was brought up short by a rather plaintive call from the bed: "Buz . . . Buz, are you still there?" Twice more this happened until Busby made his escape after four hours of silent waiting.

Although men like Valenti and Busby became valued sources, LBJ himself was the ultimate informant. Presidents normally keep a considerable distance between themselves and the men and women who report their activities. Exceptions like Charles Bartlett and Benjamin Bradlee, in the case of Kennedy, "knew him when." This also was true of Johnson's closest reporter friend, William S. White. As an AP reporter covering the Texas Congressional delegation before World War II, White convinced the young Representative Johnson that he could get his name in more papers back home by talking to the AP than by talking to other Texas reporters; most newspapers in the state received White's reports while most competitors filed to a single paper. White never came close to monopolizing LBJ as a news source, however, and Johnson as President seemed prepared to embrace us all.

Flying to New York City on December 17, 1963, to address the United Nations General Assembly, Johnson displayed a new approach toward press pools. Four of us were aboard in our usual seats, but little else was the same. Kennedy had made it a practice to walk through the plane, shaking hands, engaging in brief exchanges of little substance, then vanish into his private compartment. When Johnson appeared, it was to invite us—Alvin Spivak of UPI, Tom Wicker of the *Times,* Sid Davis of Westinghouse Broadcasting, and myself—to join him in his bedroom-sitting room aft to discuss economy in government.

Johnson was determined at the time to win early enactment of a Kennedy-sponsored tax-cut bill that had been languishing in Congress. His experience on the Hill convinced him, however, that he would get nowhere unless he made a convincing show of holding down federal spending. Emerging as his champion economizer was Secretary of Defense Robert S. McNamara, who was closing down "surplus" military bases with the President's enthusiastic support.

"I have found the myth of McNamara to be true," Johnson declared, and promised to support him in still further base closings. In time, of course, LBJ had to back off a bit since even the most obscure base has its own Congressional constituency. By then, however, Johnson had made his point, with McNamara's help.

Although the President occasionally referred to his Pentagon chief as "that fellow with the Stacomb in his hair," and even mimicked his quick and precise patterns of speech, I never heard him utter a truly unkind word about him, even after McNamara began to question American policy in Vietnam. I suspect LBJ was awed by McNamara's intelligence (he sometimes referred to him as "Professor" McNamara), which he celebrated with stories that may even have contained a germ of truth:

"He [McNamara] treats me just like he treats everybody else. I called him up at the Pentagon one morning about seven o'clock after I had read in the papers something I thought ought to be checked out. He answered the phone himself. When I told him who I was, he said, 'Yes, Mr. President, I know what you're calling about. I've already got my people investigating it. When I get some answers, I'll call you. Thank you for calling, Mr. President.' Then he hung up on me."

We learned very early that you could put yourself in peril if you always accepted LBJ's pronouncements at face value. Hyperbole was a natural feature of his conversational style, especially when he was in a storytelling mood.

In our initial contacts with Johnson, we also learned that Secretary of State Dean Rusk ranked high among his cabinet favorites. Johnson called him "Dean" and told us Rusk had always taken great care to make certain Vice-President Johnson was briefed fully and often on foreign affairs, a kindness that others in government did not always extend. Kennedy, who addressed Rusk as "Mr. Secretary," often circumvented his chief diplomat and reportedly was ready to dump him in a second term.

As Johnson talked with us informally in those first weeks and months, he returned repeatedly to the theme that the presidency was an office he never wanted.

"You folks who think I'm power-hungry may not believe it, but I never wanted this job for a minute," he insisted. "I already had a satisfyin' job as Senate majority leader. I had all the honors I could want. And I'm reaching the age where I'd like nothing better than to sit on my ranch on the Pedernales and watch the deer and the antelope play. What's more, I never believed a Southerner ever would be elected President in my lifetime."

I must confess I doubted him then, and I remain unconvinced that this man of enormous appetites, vaulting ambition and large if somewhat fragile ego never aspired to be President. I do suspect, however, that LBJ's inner uncertainties caused him to question his own ambition and to acknowledge that the presidency was a position he was unlikely to achieve—much as he might want it—through the direct process of nomination and election.

On the single occasion, in 1960, when Johnson was an announced candidate for the Democratic nomination, he entered the race just six days before the convention—hardly the timing of a confident contestant.

Johnson told us, and repeated in his memoirs, that he agreed to challenge Kennedy in Los Angeles only because Sam Rayburn and Philip Graham, then publisher of the Washington *Post,* argued that Kennedy would be labeled the tool of big-city Roman Catholic bosses—and lose the election to Richard Nixon—if he were allowed to sail through the convention without a serious challenge. According to LBJ, Rayburn detested Nixon because he felt Eisenhower's Vice-President had accused him and Harry Truman of treason, something Nixon always denied.

LBJ himself once stated publicly, in 1964, that he agreed reluctantly to be Kennedy's 1960 running mate because "I just knew in my heart that it was not right for Dick Nixon ever to be President of this country."

When Rayburn heard a rumor that Johnson would be offered second place on the ticket, LBJ delighted in recounting, the House

Speaker told his fellow Texan he would be "idiotic to accept." Next morning, however, Mr. Sam offered contrary advice and declared, when Johnson demanded an explanation, "I'm a damn sight wiser man this morning than I was last night."

One friend who did not doubt that LBJ contracted the presidential fever during his high-flying Senate years told an AP colleague in 1963: "You know, a man who aspires to the presidency must have a liberal coating of egotism. But Lyndon has been double-dipped."

Evidence of the Johnson ego was omnipresent. After a month in office he had Salinger convene a White House meeting of top government public affairs officers so he could complain they weren't earning their pay.

"You're not getting my picture on the front page the way you did Kennedy's," Johnson lamented.

Ego, a sense of history and good political practice combined to produce in LBJ an obsessive interest in photographs. After our first Air Force One flight to New York with him, each of us in the press pool received matted, autographed photos of us sitting on two sofa beds facing the President, whose left profile was exposed to the camera. In the years that followed, I received a stack of others; Johnson handed out pictures like peanuts—and I never knew anyone who wasn't pleased to get them.

His concern about being photographed only from his "good side" always remained a puzzle to me. I thought his face was reasonably symmetrical. When an AP photographer, Charles Gorry, sneaked around to LBJ's right during a news conference, the President was furious—until he saw the pictures on page one; then he requested a dozen sets of prints.

Johnson surely was history's most photographed President. He often boasted of compiling a complete photographic record of his administration. One of his first acts in office was to make certain Assistant Press Secretary Malcolm Kilduff arranged for photos and a voice recording of his oath taking in Dallas.

The President's favorite photographer, who never annoyed him with lights or flash bulbs, was Yoichi Okamoto, a United States Information Agency employee who had been assigned to film LBJ's 1961 mission to the newly constructed Berlin Wall. As President, Johnson quickly added "Okie" to Salinger's Press

Office Staff. But Washington television commentator Richard Harkness soon reported Okamoto was snapping thousands of pictures while LBJ talked about saving tax dollars. *Newsweek* mentioned 11,000 negatives. Okamoto was sent back to USIA.

The new Chief Executive showed equal enthusiasm for reading about himself, with unpredictable results. A colleague was dictating bulletin copy from his press-room phone booth when Salinger rapped on the glass door and announced, "The President says to tell you you've got the wrong emphasis in your lead." Another newsman who had reported a forthcoming state visit by the West German Chancellor got a call direct from Johnson. Said the President, "That's not Adenauer who's coming to see me, it's Erhard!"

Not all presidential reaction was negative, either. After Cecil Holland wrote about Johnson's economy-in-government campaign in the Washington *Star,* LBJ serenaded him with a half hour of telephonic praise.

Women reporters shared equally in Johnson's near-smothering embrace of the press corps. He surprised them following a treaty-signing ceremony by taking them on an escorted tour of his living quarters, into rooms most of them had never seen. But this proved to be only a warm-up for December 23, 1963, the day black bunting was stripped from the White House and replaced by Christmas decorations.

All members of Congress were invited that evening to a holiday party at which LBJ climbed on a gilt chair under a sprig of mistletoe to thank them for their labors and urge fresh endeavors in 1964. The festivities also featured an upstairs tour that included a display of pajamas laid out on the beds.

As the guests were leaving, Johnson intercepted four women reporters—Frances Lewine of the AP, Dorothy McCardle of the *Post,* Isabelle Shelton of the *Star* and broadcaster Hazel Markel—and hustled them back inside to pose with him and Lady Bird on a marble staircase.

The President then led them downstairs and through the florist's room and swimming pool to the empty Cabinet Room where, he said, he would hang a portrait of Franklin D. Roosevelt, "the ablest man we ever had in this town."

In a small room "where I come to sit and think," next to the Oval Office, LBJ pointed to a framed letter in which Dwight D.

Eisenhower expressed delight at Johnson's recovery from his severe heart attack of July 2, 1955. "I earnestly hope for your sake," the letter read, "that you will not let your natural bent for living life to the hilt make you try to do too much too quickly." The letter, dated September 23, 1955, was unsigned because, Johnson explained, Eisenhower himself suffered a heart attack before he could sign it.

On the wall with the letter were photographs of Eisenhower, Kennedy, Rayburn and the President's father, Sam Ealy Johnson.

Taking the women into the Oval Office, "where I have to sign seven hundred documents a day," Johnson impulsively picked up a telephone and, despite the late hour, placed a call to Jacqueline Kennedy, "a very special favorite of mine," who was in Palm Beach. The ladies were more than a little embarrassed as they listened to him convey best wishes of the holiday season to the young widow.

Before the reporters left, Johnson fetched up four family portraits and signed one for each, "With warm regards from her friends, the LBJ's."

"You're as good as the men reporters, maybe better," the President told them, "and I want your bosses to know it." Then, in a confidential tone, he related that the military wanted an additional nine billion dollars in the next budget. "Nobody has written it, you've got it," he said.

The President neglected to mention that he was not about to honor the money request. The "leak" to the ladies simply was a single piece in a much larger mosaic Johnson was creating so he could emerge in election year 1964 as a heroic foe of runaway federal spending. If his antics sometimes appeared madcap, there often was method to them.

2

"My Rich Inheritance"

Christmas Eve, 1963, was a happy time for Lyndon Johnson and I was pleased to share it with him. Returning to his native "hill country" in central Texas for the first time as President, he behaved like a youngster turned loose from school.

Ever since he bought the LBJ Ranch from an aunt in 1951, its four hundred acres on the banks of the Pedernales River had claimed an increasing share of his affection, particularly after the weeks he spent there recuperating from his heart attack. Good friends were convinced the seizure gave him his first intimations of mortality, redirecting more of his thoughts toward the site of his birth just down the river road, close by the one-room school of his childhood and the walled family graveyard sheltered by gnarled and stately live oaks.

"It's one place where they know if you're sick and care if you die," he told us as Air Force One headed toward Austin, state capital and population center of his old Congressional district, sixty-five miles from the ranch.

Reminiscing once at the White House about walking barefoot along the Pedernales to visit his granddaddy, LBJ made evident his love for the land where his roots were firmly planted:

   . . . Those hills, and those fields, and that river were the only world that I really had in those years. So I did not know how much more beautiful it was than that of many other boys, for I could imagine nothing else from sky to sky. Yet the sight and the feel of that country somehow burned itself into my mind.

We were not a wealthy family, but this was my rich inheritance. All my life I have drawn strength, and something more, from those Texas hills. Sometimes, in the highest councils of the nation, in this house, I sit back and I can almost feel that rough, unyielding, sticky clay soil between my toes, and it stirs memories that often give me comfort and sometimes give me a pretty firm purpose.

Small wonder that Secretary of Agriculture Orville Freeman emerged from one of his first conferences with the new President to exclaim: "He is an agrarian populist. You could almost feel the soil running through his fingers."

Johnson's first trip home as "President of all the people" would have been a happy occasion under almost any circumstances. It was made happier by a victory in Congress that very day that could be viewed as a major milestone along the road to what later came to be called the imperial presidency. Almost from the first day of the Johnson administration, President and Congress had wrestled over an effort by conservative Republicans to block the sale of grain to the Soviet Union and Eastern Europe by legislating a ban on federal guarantees of loans intended to finance such trade. The issue remained in doubt until an unusual 7 A.M. House session on December 24 at which Johnson's forces prevailed.

"At that moment," he wrote in his memoirs, "the power of the federal government began flowing back to the White House."

Within two hours of the House vote, the Johnsons and their daughters were bound for home, stopping briefly in Philadelphia for a Democratic House member's funeral.

The press pool for the flight was invited on this occasion into the office compartment of Air Force One, where I had met John Kennedy. Johnson was troubled by a problem he felt sure we could solve to his satisfaction: what dateline should be used by reporters covering his holiday-season activities in Texas? He urged upon us the choice of Johnson City.

"It's my home," he insisted. "My granddaddy founded it before the Civil War. I grew up there and first ran for Congress from there. It's my legal residence and most of my mail is addressed there."

We were sympathetic to his request, realizing that it reflected his pride in the family name. We had several problems with his recommendation, however. For one thing, the press corps was being housed in Austin's venerable Hotel Driskill and much of our copy would emanate from daily news briefings there. Would it be fair to readers to use a dateline scores of miles from the city where we'd be writing? Moreover, tiny Stonewall ("Peach Center of Texas/Home of LBJ") and the village of Hye, both with rural post offices, were ten miles or more closer to the LBJ Ranch than Johnson City. We decided that honesty required us to use an Austin dateline when writing from there, using Johnson City only when we actually traveled to the hill country. I'm certain the President was not pleased, but I never heard him mention the subject again.

Flying west, the President also discoursed on the budget, on his pledge to economize, on new programs "to create jobs," on an effort—kept secret until then—to encourage a role for private investors in Latin American development, and on plans for a family Christmas. He also talked about himself.

"I've been workin' sixteen hours a day for the past month," he reported, "but I never felt better. I only require four or five hours' sleep a night, and I fall asleep easily. School friends used to say, 'Ole Lyndon will never commit suicide; he'd fall asleep thinkin' about it.' But I've been an early riser all my life. My daddy used to come in my bedroom at four-thirty in the morning when I was workin' on the highway gang, right out of high school [pronounced hah-school], and he'd twist my big toe, real hard so it hurt, and he'd say, 'Git up, Lyndon, every other boy in town's got a half hour's head start on you.'"

The President told us, "The doctors wanted me to keep my weight down to 190 pounds after I had my heart attack, but I thought I looked like a scarecrow. I weighed 205 pounds this morning, and I'm satisfied with that."

The talk, actually a monologue spurred on only by our occasional questions, continued:

"When we get to Austin, Lady Bird and I are going to stop by and pay our respects to Governor Connally. John and Nellie are among our dearest and oldest friends. Of course, the Governor could meet us at Bergstrom, but we don't think that's the right thing to do."

At the Governor's Mansion, a beautiful plantation-style, Greek Revival home near the Capitol, Connally greeted his friend from

Washington with a left-handed grip, his right arm still in a sling from the serious wounds he suffered while riding in the Kennedy death car. Mrs. Connally and two Connally children were there, as were Lynda and Lucy Johnson, the latter still several weeks away from calling herself Luci. It was a family affair with kisses, coffee and conversation and, among the men, country tales.

The President recalled being routed from bed by his daddy to race to a neighbor's still in the family Model A and help dispose of evidence before revenue agents could get there. Guffawing loudly, Johnson reported the mission was a success but that the harried neighbor "shit all over himself" in the process.

If our Christmas Eve exposure to Lyndon Johnson had ended there, it would have represented unprecedented press pool socializing with an incumbent President. LBJ was not through with us, however; he whisked us off by helicopter to a bare-dirt landing strip at the remote Round Mountain ranch of A. W. Moursund, a Johnson City lawyer known as "A.W." or "Judge," for yet another holiday reunion.

Moursund, a pleasant, round-faced man who never seemed to get used to reporters, had been designated recently as a trustee for the first family's sizable fortune, to serve so long as Johnson remained in office. He also merited Johnson's highest tribute as "a good man to go to the well with."

"When the Indians were in these hills, raidin' and scalpin', during my granddaddy's time," the President explained, "you had to have somebody you could depend on go with you when you had to draw water from the well. The Judge is that kind of man."

The country in which we found ourselves lent credence to Johnson's frontier reference. The hills were sere and bleak, if strangely beautiful, and the soil was thin and chalky. Cacti and scrub growths of evergreen Mexican cedar and Spanish oak abounded. The first animal to greet us, lumbering improbably around rocks and hummocks, was a nine-banded armadillo, and we were warned about rattlesnakes.

A Johnson we had never seen emerged at the Moursund ranch. Gone were the low shoes, conservative necktie and tailored dark suit. In their stead were tooled leather boots, open-neck khaki shirt and matching Western pants, and a light-colored five-gallon hat set at a rakish angle upon the familiar head.

We expected to be dismissed at the landing strip but the President announced: "The Judge and I are goin' to do a little deer huntin' and you-all can tag along if you want to."

We four reporters crowded into a station wagon that Secret Service agents had expected to have to themselves. Ahead were LBJ and Moursund in the Judge's brown Lincoln Continental sedan.

In minutes we were driving across a field dominated by a structure unlike any I had ever seen, an elevated cabin, on stilts, from which a hunter could take aim at deer feeding below. It was called a hunting tower. Johnson and Moursund did not stop, which was fine with me. I found the tower offensive, even after I learned that the hill country has been overpopulated with deer ever since mountain lions, bobcats, wolves, black bear and other large predators vanished from the region. That kind of hunting didn't seem like sport to me.

Our two vehicles lurched ahead, bumping over rutted trails that wound and dipped through gullies walled by eroded limestone. Then the big Lincoln stopped and a Secret Service agent ran forward to inquire if something was wrong. Nothing was; LBJ simply wanted us reporters to join him in the sedan, which didn't seem so big after the four of us jammed ourselves into the back seat.

With Moursund at the wheel, Johnson kept busy pointing to white-tailed deer in the rough growth along the trail, most often spotting them long before we could. He even spied a dead one in a rocky gully and told the Judge he ought to have it removed. Then, with a grunt, he directed Moursund to stop again. An agent was beside us quickly.

"Damn it," the President snapped at him, "I don't want you tailgatin' me! Now, you keep that wagon back outta sight or I'm gonna shoot out your tires!"

I felt sorry for the agent, especially because his job had not been made easier by the tragedy of a month earlier. However, the driver of the station wagon fell back and, from time to time, it was hidden from our view.

Johnson demonstrated genuine if somewhat sporadic affection for some agents like Rufus Youngblood, who had shielded him with his body in the Dallas motorcade, and Lem Johns. However, for reasons that never were evident to me, the President could also be perversely cruel toward his faithful bodyguards. Perhaps he felt hemmed in by the inescapable requirements of security. On the other hand, we quickly learned he had a short fuse with all subordinates.

In an off-the-record talk at the White House a few weeks earlier, Johnson had shocked me by exploding: "If I ever get killed, it won't be because of an assassin. It'll be some Secret Service agent who trips himself up and his gun goes off. They're worse than trigger-happy Texas sheriffs."

When LBJ's threat to shoot out the tires was reported later in a national magazine, he was furious, incorrectly concluding that an agent had talked out of turn. His anger coincided with irritation at an internal Secret Service memo that reported a drop in agent morale after Dallas and an increase in the number of veteran agents seeking transfers away from the White House. Youngblood wrote in his memoirs, *20 Years in the Secret Service,* that Johnson called him at home one evening and declared, "If the Secret Service wants to go back to counterfeiting, then I'll get [J. Edgar] Hoover to assign me a couple of men to stand by my side without all this damn fuss!"

As our Christmas Eve hunt continued, I confess I was disturbed by the sight of an American President sitting in a limousine with his arms cradling a rifle with a telescopic sight. Memories of Dallas were too fresh. I was more disturbed when Johnson raised it through the open window at his side and lined up on a doe innocently grazing fifty yards away. Slowly, however, he lowered the weapon and, turning toward the back seat, drawled, "I haven't got the heart to kill her."

The "hunt" ultimately ended without a shot being fired, but Johnson nevertheless had enjoyed it in full measure. He was happy just being home.

"I've only been here an hour," he declared, "and I feel better already."

For the ebullient President, Christmas Day itself was joyous and busy. He arose at 6:30 A.M. and soon was out in, for the hill country, glorious winter weather. Temperatures climbed into the seventies, a marked contrast with freezing weather in Washington where six inches of snow blanketed the ground.

With Moursund, Johnson drove around his own ranch inspecting white-faced Herefords that had been added to the LBJ herd since his last visit. Then the President and Mrs. Johnson made a tour of the rural neighborhood, distributing poinsettia plants to friends. LBJ also telephoned greetings to Eisenhower, Truman and Herbert Hoover, the only living former Presidents. And he talked by phone "two or three times" with Secretary Rusk about an eruption of violence on Cyprus.

Johnson even found time to sign papers leasing forty acres of land across the Pedernales from his four hundred acres.

"We had to get some extra stomping ground," he explained.

For the press corps, the holiday brought us our first look at the LBJ Ranch. In buses and rented autos we drove out from Austin for what was supposed to be a brief picture-taking session with the Johnsons and their kin on the lawn outside the ranch house. LBJ's unpredictability asserted itself, however, as he took us in tow and seemed bent on showing us everything—all this despite the fact that we already had been invited to return two days later for a full tour.

The smiling host greeted us in khaki shirt and ranch trousers, green and brown striped tie, green and brown checked sports jacket and orange-colored boots. Gathered around him were twenty-seven relatives, including a second cousin, E. H. Johnson of Stover, Missouri, who ventured: "There's always been quite a few of us. Since Lyndon became President a good many more kinfolk have showed up."

Lady Bird told us there were so many kin they had to be invited in shifts. "If you're wondering whether I have kinfolk," she chirped, "they're coming later"—for New Year's.

Very much the country gentleman impresario, Johnson introduced us to everyone, sometimes in teasing, playful fashion.

"Tex and Sam Houston, you come over here first," he commanded, taking obvious delight in the regional names. Then to white-haired Huffman Baines:

"Uncle Huff, how old are you?"

Frowning, the old man replied, "I don't know."

"A very sensible answer," said Mrs. Johnson, trying to mask the embarrassment of the old man's forgetfulness. Someone else reported that Mr. Baines was seventy-nine.

We also met Oreole Bailey, the President's spry "Cousin Oreole," who lived about a quarter mile down the river road toward the family graveyard.

"We visit her every night," said Johnson, "and we get a nice little walk. It keeps us physically fit, and when we visit her we must be mentally awake."

Lynda Bird was wearing a Christmas gift from her father, a tentlike red shift purchased during a recent vice-presidential trip to Finland. When she sidled up, LBJ reached out and bunched together the folds of fabric that hung loosely about her middle and assured us with a grin that she was not in a family way. She blushed, and so did some of us.

Most of his gifts to the family were clothes, Johnson told us, and had been purchased on his behalf by a volunteer shopper because he couldn't get out to the stores himself. The volunteer was Betty Fulbright, wife of the chairman of the Senate Foreign Relations Committee.

Overflowing with energy, the President hopped up on a stone wall to survey the rough winter-brown grass that sloped down to the placid Pedernales, widened by a concrete dam he had erected on the property. The AP's Sid Moody once wrote of the river, "George Washington could have thrown a paper dollar across it against a brisk headwind." But Johnson assured us it could become a rampaging torrent. It rose to the front steps of the house at the time Mrs. Johnson lost a baby by miscarriage and "we had to take her out the back way." That's why the Johnsons decided to build their own landing strip right behind the house, he said. An undulating ribbon of asphalt equipped with lights and other navigation aids, it was designated as the area's official airport and thus eligible for federal aid.

With long strides, the President led us to the family hangar, behind an equipment shed, to admire a new brown and white twin-engine prop plane purchased by a family corporation. Outside the hangar was a luxuriously equipped jet helicopter, paid for by us taxpayers.

The impromptu tour inevitably included a livestock pen and loading chute. Pointing to the chute, Johnson joked, "That's where the cattle go out and the money comes in." He added that there were only about one hundred cattle on the LBJ Ranch but nearly a thousand more on other family lands nearby.

On the front lawn LBJ ambled over to a three-hundred-year-old live oak and pointed to a spotlight high in the branches. "It's a beacon that guides us home at night," he said. Then he flipped a

switch attached to the trunk and lively music came from speakers
hidden in the foliage, all part of an elaborate ranch communications system labeled "Big Brother." Indicating the concrete
apron around his heated swimming pool, which was covered with
a green plastic sheet "to keep the leaves out," he said it was fine
for dancing "by the younger folk."

By now we'd seen just about everything in the immediate vicinity except the twelve rooms of the two-story frame and limestone
house, and a woman reporter asked if we could do that. Johnson
thought it was an excellent idea but his wife, mindful of hungry
guests, thought otherwise. After looking sweet daggers at the
newswoman who had made the suggestion, she turned to her husband.

"I'd just give them a wonderful tour when they come back Friday," she reminded him. "The turkey and dressing are not getting
any better—but, as you say, darlin'."

Off we trooped into the President's paneled office, dominated
by, if you exclude the owner, an eight-foot Christmas tree of native cedar, heavy with decorations and surrounded by unopened
gifts. Then upstairs to a door that wouldn't open.

"Mrs. Johnson has locked the bedroom on me," he joked. The
door was opened from the inside by the First Lady, whom we suspected of taking refuge there from the throng of strangers marching through her home.

We exited from the comfortably furnished house past a deer-
head hatrack with a piece of red felt fitted over the nose, then out
the front door decorated with a big wreath of pine cones, acorns,
seed pods and native greens. Beneath our feet was a worn mat
bearing an appropriate legend: "All the World is Welcome Here."
It was time to leave.

"I've got something for you-all if you'll wait a minute," LBJ announced as we started across the lawn. With a word, he sent a
couple of retainers hurrying away. They returned with two large
cardboard cartons packed with ashtrays. One contained enameled
metal ones proclaiming the location of the LBJ Ranch on a map
of Texas. The other was filled with crystal ones on which were
etched the presidential seal and Johnson's autograph.

"I bought these in Norway on my last trip," he said, which
caused me to do a double take until it occurred to me the etching
must have been done in the United States during the past month.

"You-all can have either one you want," said the President, "but only take one. And, in case you're worried about it, they only cost a few cents apiece and come under the Paul Douglas rule." He referred to the Illinois Senator's stringent stricture against the acceptance of costly gifts by public officials. I don't believe anyone refused Johnson's gifts. I took a glass one.

"Merry Christmas," the presidential Santa Claus called out as we walked toward our vehicles over concrete slabs in which, when they were wet, prominent ranch visitors like John F. Kennedy had used spikes to inscribe their signatures. It was called the "friendship walk."

Our final view was of our Chief Executive stooping to retrieve ashtray wrappers that some of our number had thoughtlessly dropped on the lawn.

Driving to and from the ranch that day, we could see some of the changes being wrought by virtue of Johnson's abrupt change of status. A freshly covered trench paralleled U. S. Highway 290 for mile after mile; we could only guess what it contained. Shiny new wires hung from poles along the route and more were being installed. We saw Bell System trucks from as far away as Wisconsin.

A President requires dependable communications, and one as wedded to the telephone as Lyndon Johnson needed more than most. Years later, after federal largesse in upgrading Richard Nixon's properties became an issue, we learned that the government's investment in communications at the LBJ Ranch came to about $3,573,000.

The entire Stonewall-Hye-Johnson City area benefited. The President's nearest neighbor, Harvey Jordan, had to contend with a ten-party phone line before the trucks came. "The service couldn't be worse in Mexico," he complained. Of course, LBJ never shared Jordan's problem. Long before becoming President, he enjoyed such amenities as a specially grounded telephone that he could use while floating in his swimming pool.

So many changes were being made at the ranch, however, that Mrs. Johnson told us when we returned two days after Christmas, "I hardly recognize my own home." She pointed to a small white guardhouse put up by the Secret Service and said, "This little thing here is one of the changes and I hope the neighbors don't mind it." One got the impression she could have done without it.

About two hundred of us, reporters and photographers from Austin as well as Washington, rode to the ranch in five intercity buses for Mrs. Johnson's day as tour guide. When we arrived, LBJ was nowhere to be seen.

Mrs. Johnson greeted us warmly—"I'm Lady Bird Johnson, you-all"—and said we'd have to divide up into three busloads, to correspond with the number of guides: herself, Lynda Bird, and the ranch foreman, Dale Malechek. The First Lady suggested those with a particular interest in animal husbandry accompany the foreman. Needless to say, hers was the most crowded bus.

She told us that the LBJ Ranch was part of the lands that the President's grandfather had divided among his nine children, and that she and her husband had bought the place, then in very dilapidated condition, from one of those children, Aunt Frank Johnson Martin.

"My first act was to get the tree surgeon," she recalled, to save the ancient live oaks. She said her husband's first priority was to dam the river.

While we were enjoying the tour, we saw LBJ riding around in a white Lincoln convertible with Secretaries Rusk and Freeman. In *A White House Diary,* Mrs. Johnson wrote:

. . . Later on he said, "Why didn't you tell me you were going off with the newsmen?" Well, I thought five Greyhound buses loaded with press were fairly easy to spot, so I didn't see why it was necessary to alert him.

Of course, it was *her* tour, and I suspect the President felt slighted on the sidelines.

Bus microphone in hand, Mrs. Johnson talked knowledgeably to us about farming and provided thorough and lively answers to questions about ranch operations and the Johnson ancestry. Much of the LBJ acreage, we learned, was devoted to oats, barley, alfalfa, coastal Bermuda grass and Sudan grass that was used as feed for the cash crop of Herefords. The gently rolling fields were irrigated with water pumped from the Pedernales and distributed through thirty-foot lengths of movable aluminum pipe. Toting the pipe was "the roughest job" on the ranch, she reported.

Mrs. Johnson cited farm roads and rural electrification as "the greatest things that happened to this country." She reminded us that they had a strong advocate in her husband's first great political hero, Franklin D. Roosevelt, and got in a good word for LBJ by declaring that his "happiest days" were spent as a young Congressman fighting for rural electrification.

Pointing to five earthen pools built to catch rain water—and as a home for catfish raised for eating—she remarked that she was glad Secretary Freeman was there, so he could see how ranch folks depend on Agricultural Extension Service agents "who help us out telling where to build tanks and terraces."

When the bus frightened a flock of sheep and one leaped high in the air, she explained they were an African strain. As one lamb threatened to dart in front of the vehicle, she expressed hope it wouldn't get killed because "it's too valuable."

The First Lady said she was sorry we were seeing the land in its winter colors, "sere, dry and gray," but noted that our visit coincided with the calving season. Pointing, she said, "There is a sweet sight—a pretty, fresh-looking calf."

We drove past the site of the President's birthplace and stopped at the graveyard where lie Johnsons, Buntons, Forsyths and members of other interrelated families. The graves of the President's parents were marked by identical monuments of red granite from Texas quarries. His mother, Rebekah Baines, had written his father's epitaph: "Of purest gold from the Master's hand/a man who loved his fellow man."

Directly in line with a church steeple across the river, the graveyard wall had been breached to accommodate an iron gate Mrs. Johnson told us she had found and installed. To afford an unobstructed view of the church, a swath had been cut through the trees on the other side of the Pedernales.

It was a delightful tour and it ended in a field on the riverbank where Walter Jetton, the "barbecue king" from Fort Worth, awaited us with great quantities of barbecued chicken and ribs, hot coffee and Pearl beer.

For many of us an outdoor barbecue was an entirely new experience and we attacked the smoky, greasy meat with relish. It was delicious. But our fun ended all too soon. The President arrived and stood on a bale of hay, ostensibly to introduce Rusk and Freeman, and held a full-scale press conference—while we tried in vain to cope simultaneously with ribs, beer, pens and notebooks. It had been Mrs. Johnson's tour but *he* had the final word.

During this first trip to Texas we came to feel like shuttlecocks as we moved repeatedly between Austin and the LBJ ranch. Just two days after Mrs. Johnson's tour and his news conference, we were back to share in festivities attending one of the most bizarre yet successful state visits of a foreign leader.

West Germany's rotund, pink-cheeked Chancellor, Ludwig Erhard, had been scheduled to meet with Kennedy at the White House on November 24. Instead he came for the assassinated leader's funeral and was invited back by Johnson for a summit conference at the new Chief Executive's ranch.

The Erhard visit easily could have proved a disaster but it did not, thanks in good measure to the bountiful hospitality of the Johnsons.

Erhard's arrival meant finding beds for more than twenty-five extra people in the Johnson home and other houses on the property. The First Lady surrendered her bedroom to make office room for two secretaries. LBJ gave up his office to his guest. The Johnson daughters moved out of their rooms. Foreman Malechek and his family shared their home with speech writers. Members of the White House kitchen staff shared chores with ranch cooks.

Somehow it worked.

The area around the ranch was settled in the 1840s by German emigrants led by Baron Hans von Meusebach. That the Germanic heritage survived was made evident to us on Sunday, December 29, when the Johnsons took Erhard by helicopter to the small city of Fredericksburg, about fifteen miles west of the ranch, for church services.

"The Chancellor must have felt pretty much at home," wrote my AP colleague, Douglas B. Cornell. "He heard scarcely a word of English."

Mayor Sidney Henke welcomed Erhard in German. The pastor of Bethany Lutheran Church prayed and sermonized in German. The choir sang in the same language. LBJ was one of the few, it seemed, who had no choice but to talk Texan.

The Fredericksburg visit was merely the first event of a festive day unique in the annals of American diplomacy. No one who was there is likely to forget the state dinner the Johnsons gave for their guest that afternoon.

The site was the weathered clapboard gymnasium of the Stonewall High School less than three miles from the ranch. A somewhat rickety building, it had gotten fresh white paint in the most noticeable places. Bunting in the German national colors helped disguise its other shortcomings. Inside were bales of hay, western saddles, lariats, lighted red lanterns and tables covered in red-checked cloth. Plus a fine grand piano that seemed in danger of sinking through the floor.

The very idea of holding a state dinner in Stonewall, Texas, was daring—and refreshing. Barely a hamlet, Stonewall had just eight business establishments: three service stations, a cafe-motel, two grocery stores, a garage and a button factory. Even that listing makes it seem bigger than it really is.

More than three hundred guests were invited to the dinner and there weren't enough tables to accommodate everyone. Many of us ate buffet style, sitting in the removable bleachers used for Stonewall High's basketball games.

Also unique, for a state dinner, was the menu. We consumed four hundred pounds of beef, three hundred pounds of ribs, more than one hundred pounds of German potato salad, one hundred pounds of cole slaw, twenty-five gallons of ranch beans, seventy gallons of beer and ample amounts of coffee and soft drinks.

The entertainment was catholic in scope. There was hillbilly music, singing by a choir of schoolgirls ("Deep in the Heart of Texas" was sung in German), and a recital of Brahms and Bach by the Texas-born Van Cliburn.

Johnson and Erhard, the latter seeming to chain-smoke large cigars, had a grand time, as did everyone else with the possible exception of Pierre Salinger.

In a playful mood, the President called on his press secretary to follow Van Cliburn to the keyboard. Reddening, Salinger responded, "Do you think it's fair to put me on after Van Cliburn?" Johnson insisted that the White House spokesman, who had been something of a piano prodigy as a child, entertain. Salinger made the best of it by announcing he would try to forestall criticism by playing a number no one would recognize, "something I wrote myself." He got rave reviews.

After handing out Texas hats to every German in sight, including a score of German reporters, LBJ made it clear that newsmen from Washington would have to settle for a presidential jibe.

"Mr. Chancellor," he said, "in a few moments now I am going to turn you over to the American press, and then I think you will know how the deer feel."

Next day we were spared the long drive to the ranch—but we were kept busier than ever as Johnson came to Austin and set a frenetic pace for us to follow. Here is how I reported it at the time:

President Johnson came by helicopter to the big city from the Hill Country today and:
—Went to a funeral.
—Got his hair cut.
—Stopped for a cup of coffee.
—Signed some bills.
—Strolled a while.
—Dedicated a synagogue building.
—And tried out his political handshake.

It all started with a flying trip from the LBJ Ranch to attend the funeral of a family friend, Mrs. Tom Miller, and to speak at the dedication of an Austin synagogue.

The President made it an outing. He looked up old friends, poked his head into downtown stores for a handshake, and then invited about forty friends to come up and see him in his twelfth-floor Commodore Perry Hotel suite.

Before that, with another old friend, barber Gus Elderman, he got caught up on Austin doings and had his hair cut.

One of Johnson's stops was at the Hotel Driskill. He got his coffee at the coffee shop counter and then went upstairs to make a few phone calls in a fourth-floor suite.

He signed the bills in the brief time he was there, too.

Finally, Johnson decided to move his operations to the Commodore Perry, where he was supposed to go all along.

He walked the few blocks between the two hotels and was accompanied by Gene Sanderford, about seventy, of Austin, whom he has known since the days when Johnson was state director of the National Youth Administration in the 1930s.

"He's a mighty good Democrat," Johnson declared, "one of the best."

A motorcycle escort trailed along the street beside Johnson as he walked.

When a Secret Service agent suggested the direction the stroll should take, Johnson said he knew the town better than the agent and went his own way. . . .

The President returned to Austin the next day, for New Year's Eve, and attended four parties, one of which we of the press corps threw at a private club in the Driskill. LBJ sat down at a table by the bandstand and talked up a storm, all the while enjoying Cutty Sark and soda. Around midnight he made his way across the lobby and into the Headliners Club, where he grabbed up the startled but immensely pleased wife of a member and took a turn around the dance floor. It was early morning when he returned to the ranch, after enjoining us to eat black-eyed peas on the first day of 1964 if we wanted luck throughout the year. He also confessed he'd finally shot two deer, both of them bucks.

Mrs. Johnson had not joined her husband for the strenuous round of partygoing. She had stayed home watching movies with relatives.

During the eleven days Johnson spent in Texas, he saw one Chancellor, half of the ten cabinet members, all of the Joint Chiefs and a great many reporters. The four of us who went "hunting" with him on Christmas Eve were but the vanguard of a small army.

Tom Wicker of the *Times,* Douglas Kiker of the New York *Herald Tribune* and Phil Potter of the *Sun* were invited to a fish fry. Hugh Sidey of *Time* got a boat ride and a chicken dinner. Marianne Means of the Hearst newspapers, a very attractive young woman, sat beside Johnson at dinner one evening, at his insistence: he had an eye for the ladies. As many as six reporters at one time stayed overnight at the ranch.

Potter wrote about a large group of reporters following the President on foot one evening to Cousin Oreole's place. Holding a flashlight, LBJ kept tossing loose stones off the road and complaining that heavy traffic during his stay had kicked them up.

Ms. Bailey surveyed the press contingent and expressed reservations about them, saying a woman reporter recently had called on her late at night and asked why she was barefooted. "I don't go to bed with my shoes on," the old woman huffed.

Cousin Oreole's home was small and consisted mainly of a combination bedroom-sitting room. Red plastic birds sat atop her television set and on the walls were a colored portrait of LBJ as a House member and a poster from his first, unsuccessful, Senate campaign. The poster heralded such slogans as "Dependable and Experienced" and "Roosevelt and Unity."

Johnson spotted a White House telephone on the floor and demanded, with mock seriousness: "What are you doing with that phone? If you pick it up you might get Khrushchev!"

When a reporter inquired about her age Ms. Bailey would only say, "Old enough to have been here when Lyndon was born."

There was much banter during the visit. The President told his cousin he'd picked up a rumor she'd been "courtin' a neighbor."

Ms. Bailey was a member of the Christadelphian sect that believes death means a speedy journey to hell, there to await the resurrection and a final judgment of salvation or damnation. She asked the President if he'd received a Christadelphian tract from Australia that she wanted him to read. He hadn't seen it. She said she gave it to "that FBI man"—her term for Secret Service agent.

Then she picked up an astrological magazine and, kissing Johnson on top of the head, announced: "The magazine has your horoscope. It says you'll be a good President but won't be re-elected." LBJ laughed.

An oil fire heated the room and Potter calculated that Johnson, who liked fresh air, got up at least a half dozen times to open the front door. Cousin Oreole shut it each time.

One of the most amusing happenings associated with Johnson's assiduous wooing of the press during the holiday season involved Bill Mauldin, the Pulitzer Prize-winning editorial cartoonist.

Mauldin was at the ranch when Scotty Reston telephoned Johnson to say he would be passing through Texas and would like to stop by for a visit. LBJ readily agreed that both Reston and his wife should come, promising to send a plane to Dallas to pick them up.

A licensed pilot, Mauldin flew the Johnson family's new Beechcraft Queen Air to Dallas and back, making himself agreeable by personally carrying the Restons' baggage and responding with "yes sirs" and "no sirs" to every word from the eminent journalist.

Reston did not make the connection between his pilot-baggage handler and the prominent cartoonist until they faced each other across the Johnson breakfast table the next morning.

When Republican Barry Goldwater made a televised announcement that he would seek his party's presidential nomination in 1964, LBJ was nowhere near a TV set. He, Mrs. Johnson and Moursund were conducting motorboat tours for reporters at yet another family ranch, this one located where the Llano River becomes a man-made lake, which was soon to be renamed Lake Lyndon B. Johnson.

It was called the Heywood Ranch and its history says something about the intricacies of Johnson's land dealings. Moursund and an entity called the LBJ Company had purchased the 4,718 Heywood acres from Texas Christian University in 1961 for $500,000. A day after the purchase Johnson personally took over the LBJ Company's interest in the property and, with Moursund, sold 242.7 acres of the shoreline land to the Comanche Cattle Company, which the Judge headed, for $328,661 in notes. This land in turn was subdivided into Comanche Rancherias and Comanche Ranchettes advertised for sale at $6,000 to $7,000 a lot.

In the presence of the relaxing newsmen, Moursund joked that Johnson was trying to escape capital gains taxes by giving away lots to women age eighteen to thirty-five with appropriate measurements, and thus also assuring himself of having interesting neighbors.

"Now don't you believe that fantasy," Mrs. Johnson cautioned.

Although the President did not watch Goldwater live, he cut short the lake outing so the entire party could return to the LBJ Ranch by helicopter in time for NBC's Huntley-Brinkley Report. He used a wrist alarm to remind him of major newscasts.

Watching a filmed report on the Goldwater announcement, Johnson wondered aloud why the Arizona Senator had elected to do it on a Friday, because "he'd get more space in the Monday morning papers."

The President broke into a broad, warm smile when the broadcaster continued, "At the LBJ Ranch, meanwhile, the nation's business went forward."

While Mrs. Johnson passed appetizers of smoked deer meat, Gulf shrimp and Cheddar cheese, a newsman asked the President if he thought Richard Nixon might also make a race for the presidency.

"I don't know," Johnson replied. "I don't even know whether I will."

3

"Let Us Continue"

When Lyndon Johnson first went before Congress as President, his appeal for unity in a time of trouble was combined with a plea that the legislative branch join with him in enacting, as memorials to the slain Kennedy, the many administration bills that had been languishing before it for many months.

"Let us continue," he said as he pressed particularly for passage of Kennedy's tax reduction and civil rights measures, a challenging agenda that many felt was beyond early accomplishment. They did not know their new President, however; did not appreciate his firmness and determination and, indeed, had yet to learn that the knowledge he had gleaned during a lifetime of work on Capitol Hill could, when coupled with presidential power, produce legislative miracles.

"I don't want to be remembered as a can't-do man," Johnson told us. Grinning, he echoed a rallying cry uttered in House debate years earlier by Magnus Johnson of Minnesota: "The only thing to do is grab the bull by the tail and look the situation in the face."

Georgia's Richard Russell, one of Johnson's closest Senate friends, had said when LBJ was Democratic leader: "Lyndon Johnson hasn't got the best mind in the Senate. He isn't the best orator. He isn't the best parliamentarian. But he is the best combination of those qualities."

Sharp as they were, Johnson's legislative skills may have been matched by intangible personal resources that appeared at times to border on the occult. His father, who served several terms in the Texas legislature before and during the First World War, used to tell him that a good politician could walk into a crowded room and know at once who would support him and who would not. When LBJ recalled this for us, it seemed implicit that he was claiming such powers for himself—and we were not much inclined to doubt him; sometimes I suspected he could read minds.

Even if the Johnson qualities that seemed near mystical were nothing more than mythical, he unquestionably had a capacity for tireless striving and a thorough working knowledge of human nature. He knew how to get along with diverse types of people and, in the process, get ahead.

LBJ often recalled that when he was a young schoolteacher he and a colleague who was the baseball coach were reprimanded by the principal for smoking in the presence of their students. Johnson said he heeded the warning but the other man insisted that it was his right to smoke wherever he chose. Result: Lyndon Johnson soon found himself teaching *and* coaching. The story was told so often that the President seemed bent on convincing us that in teaching, in politics and just possibly in journalism you sometimes must go along if you want to get along.

Another of his favorite recollections concerned his adoption of a quotation from Isaiah, "Come now, and let us reason together," as symbolizing his approach to the legislative process. Here is how he told it at a 1964 breakfast ceremony in Portland, Oregon, that celebrated a link-up of two power transmission systems, one public and the other private:

"I am going to interpolate for a moment here to tell you of an experience I had as a young man trying to reconcile the views of the leaders of public and private power in my state.

"We had a great man who happened to be a spokesman for the Electric Bond and Share, who was president of one of our great power companies, and he looked just like a Methodist deacon; a very attractive man, very cautious in what he said.

"I had negotiated with him for three days and I never made a dent in his armor. He was looking after those stockholders and he looked at me with what I thought was contempt.

"Finally I got up in my youthful enthusiasm, and some impulsiveness that I am very much against these days, and I said, 'So far as I am concerned, you can take a running jump and go straight you know where.' . . . All of my REA people and public power people applauded me and said it was a great speech. I started out of the room and they all stood.

"As I walked out the door, I saw an old man there that was the general counsel of the water district. He was an ex-Senator. I said, 'Senator, how did you like my speech?' He said, 'Come by the office and I would like to talk to you about it.' . . . So I went by and he said, 'You are in public life. You are a young man just starting out and I want to see you move along and do well. But,' he said, 'the first thing you have to learn, son, is [that] to tell a man to go to hell and to make him go there are two different propositions. . . . Mr. Carpenter doesn't want to go. . . .' He said, 'It took me two months to get this group together and now you bust it up in two minutes. I will have to work now until we can get together and follow the advice of the prophet Isaiah, "Come now, let us reason together." ' "

For those of us in the press corps, an initial exposure to LBJ's heavy reliance on psychology in furtherance of his legislative ends left us feeling a good deal like Mr. Carpenter. Johnson did not tell us to go to hell, but he did not please us either. We became unwitting partners in promoting his strategy of winning a tax cut by convincing Congress he was not among the big spenders.

Budget Director Kermit Gordon had been scheduled to meet with President Kennedy on November 27, 1963, to present a new federal budget of $101.5 billion, although we did not know the figure at the time. With a presidential election approaching, it is safe to assume that Kennedy would have insisted that the total be trimmed below $100 billion. Up to that point, the record had been $98.3 billion during the 1945 fiscal year when World War II swelled the total.

On December 3, Press Secretary Salinger told us, with LBJ's approval, that the first Johnson budget would range between $98 billion and $103 billion. Then came the President's *kaffeeklatsch* news conference of December 7 at which he emphasized prospective spending increases required by law. Although Johnson promised he would pare away every cent possible, he told us it would

Democrat, was summoned to the Oval Office for a wooing, he found a shiny dime on the rug in front of Johnson's desk.

"I thought there was a kind of a tight situation down here in the expenditure of money," chided Haley, "yet I find this dime lying in front of your desk."

The President asked to inspect the coin. He looked it over carefully, then put it in his pocket, which prompted Haley to declare, "I wish I'd kept my mouth shut. I would have been a dime ahead."

Johnson's parsimony was not entirely feigned. As late as 1965 some White House offices still were using his vice-presidential stationery for non-official mail. And the President's brother, Sam Houston Johnson, reported that LBJ had been after him for thirty years to turn off unnecessary lights, saying, "Sam Houston, are you working for me or the power company?"

Electricity was a relatively rare and precious commodity during their hill country boyhood and Lyndon Johnson, as an early advocate of rural electrification, may have valued it more than most men. As President he returned often to the Johnson City headquarters of the area's rural electric co-operative and pointed with pride to a bronze plaque by the door that commemorated his role in its founding.

Most of us reporters were skeptical, nevertheless, when Johnson began turning off lights around the White House. Having been burned so recently, we were not prepared to accept his claim that he had been able to cut the monthly electric bill to $3,000 from $5,000, especially after his press secretary declined to produce evidence to support it.

That the White House was darker than ever before, and remained so as long as Johnson was President, was plainly evident. When we had to walk from the West Wing, which housed the old press room as well as the Oval Office, to the East Wing after dark, we complained that we should be given flashlights. We learned that electricians had been ordered to dismantle switches that automatically turned on closet lights when the doors were opened. Occasionally we'd see the President himself prowl down the corridor near Salinger's office, open a rest-room door and switch off the light inside.

Officials at the Treasury Department, next door to the White be exceedingly difficult to get the total below $102 billion. It was the biggest news out of the press conference.

We continued to write about the $102 billion budget until LBJ met with us over drinks in Austin on New Year's Eve. It was then that he related, off the record, that although he had expected the budget to be $102 billion to $103 billion he just might be able to cut it by "a billion or two." Asked whether the total would be closer to $100 billion or $101 billion, he paused, then said, "One hundred billion." At our urging, which he doubtless had anticipated, he agreed that we could write about the "brighter" budget prospects, but only if we did not reveal him as our source.

When the final figure subsequently proved to be $97.7 billion, below even the lowest figure first mentioned by Salinger, we felt we had been misused so that LBJ could posture as a fiscal miracle worker. Without a doubt, this was the first fissure in what eventually became known as Lyndon Johnson's credibility gap. He had made important points with Congress, but at a cost; few among us ever accorded him unquestioning trust thereafter.

Of course, Johnson did deserve credit for putting a lid on spending. Kennedy probably would not have worked at it so singlemindedly. Presidential head-knocking was required, and Johnson approached the task with relish. When Director James E. Webb of the National Aeronautics and Space Administration demanded more money than the new President was willing to provide, Webb was reminded that he once had served as Truman's Budget Director. If he could not control NASA spending, Johnson warned, he could find himself back in the Bureau of the Budget.

LBJ well knew, of course, that it was difficult for Webb or any other appointee to argue with a President beyond a certain undefined point. After the Joint Chiefs visited the LBJ Ranch to discuss their budget, Johnson told Phil Potter: "They're like men in a football huddle, each proposing different plans. But when the quarterback says, 'I think I'll go around end this time,' they all shift over to the right side."

Unlike the Joint Chiefs, members of Congress do not serve at the pleasure of the President. To win them over and keep them won, he had to keep plugging away at the economy-in-government theme long after the success of his budget ploy.

When Representative James A. Haley, a conservative Florida

House, were acutely aware that Johnson could see their building from his living quarters. With him in mind, although another motive was professed, they issued a directive to all employees:

In addition to the practical aspects of economy, there is a psychological factor . . . the public takes a critical view of buildings which are brilliantly lit at such times as it would be quite evident they are not being occupied by the working tenants. . . . Where it is necessary that certain lights be burned at night . . . it would be helpful if the Venetian blinds were lowered and then the slats tilted to close them.

When Johnson addressed the 1964 convention of the Chamber of Commerce of the United States, he boasted, "You can go home and tell your friends that you have an independent, taxpaying, light-bill-saving President in the White House!" Three months after he took office, the Harris poll showed that eighty-one per cent of the public approved of Johnson's handling of federal spending.

Still LBJ was not satisfied. The press, he believed, was not doing enough to publicize his economizing. This led to a comic scene aboard Air Force One after LBJ got aboard dripping perspiration, having made an outdoor speech in bright sunlight. Heading for his bedroom to change clothes, he enjoined the press pool to follow. I recall that William J. Eaton, then of UPI, and Jerry Greene of the New York *Daily News* were with me.

As we sat on the beds, Johnson stood between us and fairly bellowed, while he removed his shirt and trousers: "Every time I hold a press conference I talk about economy in government, and every time I talk about it you bury it back with the truss ads!" By this time he'd shucked off his underwear and was using a large white towel to dry himself.

"Mr. President," I said, "you talk about other things besides economy in government at press conferences, things that are 'hot and spot,' that are newsier and have greater immediate interest. Naturally, they get filtered up to the top of our stories and economy in government gets filtered down, because you talk about it all the time."

Standing buck naked and waving his towel for emphasis, the President exploded. "Well, I'll tell you one thing: I'm gonna keep talkin' about it until you vomit it up!"

LBJ wanted everybody to jump on his wagon and help build living memorials to Jack Kennedy—and Lyndon Johnson. No one was excluded; there was room for all.

For a few months, at least, women were one of his prime target groups, appealed to through a campaign for the recruitment and promotion of women in government. Addressing the Women's National Press Club on February 3, 1964, Johnson declared, "This Administration is not running a stag party." A month later he honored six career women in government service at a White House ceremony and said, "I believe a woman's place not only is in the home, but in the House and Senate and throughout government." To a group of Democratic women he offered this message: "I don't want the male members of our party to be worried. They will always have a place in the federal government as long as there is no woman to fill the job."

Johnson exaggerated, of course. His campaign did expand the number of women in government, and it did lead to promotions to some of the higher civil service ranks. But women never remotely approached parity with men in the Johnson administration, or in any other. The statistics churned out to record what really were minor advances made good election-year reading, however, for millions of women voters, only a few of whom heard Johnson tell jokes that today would be labeled sexist. An example, when a group of foreign students visited the White House in the spring:

"I am glad Mrs. Johnson asked me to speak. I thought of the story of the man and his wife who were having an argument. The man's neighbor said to him, 'I understand you and Mary had some words.' He said, 'Yes, I had some, but I didn't get to use mine.'"

No segment of the population, no interest group, was immune to Johnson's blandishments. Business, labor, young people, intellectuals—all were courted.

Johnson was proud of the young people on his staff, like Bill Moyers, and bragged about them. Even when he joked at their expense, it was in a good-natured way. He related, for example, that one youthful aide, when instructed to get busy on the farm bill, replied: "I don't have a file on it. I will look it up but I think you ought to tell them, if we owe it, we will pay it."

When twenty-four-year-old Richard Nelson moved quickly to

fetch some papers Johnson wanted to show to a group of us, the President observed, "That young man is going to make a fine public servant—when he gets some maturity." LBJ meant it as a compliment.

On Nelson's recommendation, Johnson recruited Eric Goldman, the Princeton University historian, as his ambassador to the intellectual community. It was the first White House position created by LBJ and it was announced with fanfare. Goldman was charged with keeping the President in touch with specialists who otherwise would have no contact with government, and to serve as relay man for ideas submitted by thinkers, writers and academicians. An intriguing assignment, it expired of frustration in the early stages of America's direct involvement in the Vietnam War.

LBJ valued, if sometimes grudgingly, his association with those who could claim academic accomplishments. Addressing the 1964 annual luncheon of the Associated Press in New York, the President interjected in rather gratuitous fashion:

"This is the kind of a distinguished gathering that reminds me of a meeting in the Cabinet Room the other day. Around that table sat three Harvard men, two Yale men, Dean Rusk and three other Rhodes scholars, and one graduate of Southwest Texas State Teachers College."

It was a reflection of Johnson's nagging sense of inadequacy at lacking Ivy League credentials, at being stamped, or so he thought, as a Texas bumpkin. It was a feeling that never left him no matter how high his popularity ratings soared. His record might surpass his predecessor's, but Jack Kennedy had been a Harvard man and Johnson was envious. With a group of state university presidents who met with him, LBJ's grasp for learned coattails was particularly pathetic:

". . . when you find someone who is unusually objective and judicious and able and talented and dedicated that could profit from his experience here, and that we could learn from, I would like for you to drop a note to Dr. Ralph Dungan over here, who is on my staff. Stand up, Ralph. . . .

"I want you to go back and train some more Dr. [Donald] Hornigs for me—my science adviser; some more Dr. [McGeorge] Bundys, some more Dr. [Walter] Hellers, some more Dr. Dungans. Dr. Cater over there, I jerked him out of school. Stand up

here, Doug. This is Douglass Cater, a young man on my staff that
I brought out of school up here."

This was hogwash. Hornig and Heller were the only certified
doctors in the lot. Although Bundy was a former dean of the Fac-
ulty of Arts and Sciences at Harvard, his highest degree was a
B.A. from Yale. Cater had an M.A. degree from Harvard but was
best known as a Washington journalist who happened to be serving as a visiting professor at Wesleyan University when LBJ hired
him. Dungan had an M.S. from Princeton.

Of the group, Heller perhaps ranked highest in Johnson's esteem. He told us that Heller was the one man in government who
could state a case briefly and concisely "so I can get it right off."
The President credited the distinguished economist with using
one-syllable words, eight-word sentences and three-sentence para-
graphs.

Unlikely as it may seen, Jack Valenti was among Johnson's candidates for intellectual canonization. "He's a Harvard man,"
Johnson boasted. "He's got more Harvard degrees than Mac
Bundy." The President respected Valenti because, among other
things, he was a reader and a graduate of the Harvard Business
School, with a master's degree. "He reads all the time," said the
admiring President. "He even takes two books with him into the
bathroom—props them up alongside his mirror and reads while
he shaves."

Valenti might seem an unlikely choice to be cast as an intellectual but his friends could argue, with justification, that he was
learned. A group of us, including Valenti, argued once about the
source of a Kennedy quote: "There are three things which are
real/God, human folly and laughter/The first two are beyond our
comprehension/So we must do what we can with the third."
Valenti was alone in correctly ascribing the quotation to Aubrey
Menen's translation of the Ramayana, an epic poem of India.

In zealously soliciting the allegiance of women, young people
(the eighteen-year-old vote was coming ever closer to reality) and
the intellectual community, Johnson did not expend a fraction of
the effort he devoted to the representatives of big business and big
labor. In his first months in office he was extraordinarily successful, considering that he was a Democrat, in capturing the fancy of
businessmen. Perhaps equally remarkable was his success with

union chiefs, many of whom had opposed his nomination for the vice-presidency.

With representatives of both groups he was totally at ease, displaying none of the inferiority feelings that academicians seemed to arouse in him. He shared the social welfare goals of labor leaders and the acquisitive instincts of corporation presidents. He sympathized with the aspirations of "the folks" and could read a profit and loss statement with as much understanding as the board chairman of General Motors.

When he recalled, for members of the Business Council, Sam Rayburn's claim that businessmen were beset by fear, Johnson was not entirely joking. He believed they were fearful men and he played upon that theme in appealing to them to join with him in improving the lot of less fortunate Americans. To the Chamber of Commerce, he said:

". . . if you don't remember anything else that I say to you today, remember this because it is in the interest of each of you, regardless of what party you belong to and regardless of your balance sheet: . . . if a peaceful change of these conditions is impossible, a violent change is inevitable. I am just as sure of that as I sit here."

A conciliator by instinct and legislative training, Johnson also seized opportunities to emphasize the community of interests shared by management and labor, and to say a good word about each group when talking to representatives of the other. Inviting business leaders to a White House dinner during his first springtime in office, the President told them:

"Next week the key labor leaders of the country will come to see me here. . . . And I will lay the cards out just as straight for them as I do for you.

"That way everybody will know the score—like the conversation at the card table when one of the boys looked across the table and said, 'Now, Reuben, play the cards fair. I know what I dealt you.'

"I know what I dealt *you*—an honest appeal to help give this country years of unparalleled prosperity."

Johnson's rapport with business and labor paid spectacular dividends in 1964 when he succeeded in averting a paralyzing rail strike scheduled over a long-festering work rules dispute. Calling negotiators from both sides to the White House, he enjoined them to "put your Bible in your hip pocket and your demands in the other and come in this room and . . . let us reason together."

A witness to LBJ's intervention later told Walter Mears of the Associated Press: "You don't forget that he's President—and you don't forget that this is a very tough guy. He just hangs on and hangs on until he gets what he's after."

For all their seriousness, the negotiations produced moments of humor, as when a railroad executive turned to Johnson and, inspired by the President's folksiness, began, "I'm just a country boy—"

"Hold on there," Johnson interrupted. "Wait a minute. When anyone approaches me that way I know I'm going to lose my wallet."

For the benefit of the railroad men, and their fears, LBJ twice talked about a Texas friend whose 2,000-acre ranch in Cuba had been seized by the Castro government; his listeners sensed in this an oblique threat that stalemate and a nationwide strike might lead to government seizure of their properties.

When Charles Luna, president of the Brotherhood of Railway Trainmen, complained that talk in Congress of compulsory arbitration was like fixing a noose around labor's neck, the President suggested the issue might be avoided if the unions were to postpone their strike deadline for fifteen days to permit further negotiations.

"Now, Charlie, you're a Texan and I'm a Texan," he said, "and it's not like one of those damnyankees asking you to do this."

The union men continued to balk and Johnson led them out of the Cabinet Room to a bathroom near the Oval Office for what he later referred to as "my outhouse meeting." There they capitulated. LBJ led them back to the Cabinet Room, stood over them as they worked out final details with management representatives and finally turned off the lights as the weary negotiators filed out.

Eager to spread the good news, Johnson sent word to the TV networks that he wanted to make an immediate live appearance. Told it would take at least an hour to set up cameras, he drove through rush-hour traffic to station WTOP where, flanked by the chief negotiators from both sides, he enjoyed a moment of triumph during the prime evening news slot.

The long ride to WTOP rankled, however, and prompted John-son to ask the networks to set up a permanent television studio in the White House. This was done, in the East Wing theater, at great cost to the networks, which kept a producer and camera crew on duty all day every day whether the President appeared or not.

Johnson particularly savored his triumphs, then and later, be-cause he questioned their permanence. In the same month that a rail strike was avoided, the President went to a dinner party at the home of columnist Max Freedman, where a group of prominent editors had gathered, and, after displaying euphoric ebullience at the dinner table, became morose as he later drove Eugene Patter-son of the Atlanta *Constitution* to his hotel. Although I heard him express similar sentiments on several occasions, I never heard at one time the entire litany of woe he poured out to Patterson, as recounted by Richard Harwood and Haynes Johnson in their in-formal biography, *Lyndon:*

The Kennedy crowd and the intellectuals and the fancypants were never going to accept him as President of the United States, he said. They would never let him up, they would never give him a chance. They would cut him to pieces because of his speech, his mannerisms, his Southern origins. It was inevitable, he said, and no matter what he accomplished in the days and years to come, he never would be appre-ciated by the "Eastern crowd." They were mad that he was in office, and they were going to get him one way or the other. Just watch. He knew his education would never qualify him in the eyes of the Ivy League; knew that his backwoods accent would gain him the nickname "Cornpone" in the smart Georgetown salons; knew the liberal redhots would never trust his background; knew most of his fellow South-erners would never forgive his demands for black rights and knew many blacks would never fully trust him for being Southern. He could read the trouble coming.

"You just wait," he said, "and see what happens when I put one foot wrong."

Such doubts were submerged on the evening that Johnson delivered his first State of the Union address to Congress. Leaving the podium, he was mobbed by old colleagues offering congrat-ulations.

"Yeah," he whispered to one startled Senator, "I was inter-rupted by applause eighty times!"

The faithful Valenti customarily compiled such statistics and he never was known to err on the low side. But the press corps count of seventy-nine interruptions was more than adequate to set a record.

During his first hundred days in office LBJ frequently drew comparisons between his batting average on Capitol Hill and the one compiled by his hero FDR during the period that became celebrated as the First Hundred Days of the New Deal. Although Johnson genuinely cherished his memories of Roosevelt ("He was like a daddy to me"), he took pleasure in trying to claim a superior statistical record.

Presumably it was not by happenstance that Johnson, during those early months, often wore the type of soft felt hat that Roosevelt had favored. In any event, once LBJ's own legislative record was established the hat rarely was seen—much to the vocal dismay of Alex Rose, president of the Hatters Union.

Politically, Johnson was a creature of the New Deal. When his home Congressional seat fell vacant in 1937, Mrs. Johnson borrowed $10,000 from her well-to-do father to finance her husband's campaign on an uncompromising pro-Roosevelt platform. The field was crowded and few observers saw much hope for the Johnson candidacy, if only because he backed FDR's proposal to enlarge, or "pack," the Supreme Court and thus overcome the conservative majority that was rejecting major New Deal programs as unconstitutional. The court plan proved to be disastrous politically, but not for LBJ. When he emerged from the pack as the winner, Roosevelt was cruising in the Gulf of Mexico. The President promptly invited the newest House member to join him in Galveston and ride the presidential train across Texas. They remained good friends ever after.

In dealing with Congress, as was the case with the rail negotiators, Johnson as President simply would not take "no" for an answer. When, for example, he was rebuffed upon calling his friend Richard Russell to ask that he serve on the Warren Commission that would investigate the Kennedy murder, LBJ had a ready response: "Well, Dick, this is going to be mighty embarrassing for me. We've already given the press an advance statement naming the members of the commission and you're on it. I hope you won't let me down." Of course, Russell didn't.

Two weeks after taking office, Johnson talked about the embattled tax bill with Harry Flood Byrd, Sr., the conservative Virginia Democrat who would have much to say about the measure's fate by virtue of his chairmanship of the Senate Finance Committee. The President walked Byrd arm in arm out of the Oval Office to the reception lobby, where we waited, and announced they were in "general agreement" on terms of the bill and procedures for handling it in the Senate. Byrd looked a bit uncomfortable but raised no protest. Once he got away from the White House, however, he told Jack Bell, "We didn't agree on a damned thing."

When Johnson assumed a posture of quiet reasonableness, which was most of the time in public, he liked to say: "We do not see everything alike. If we did we would all want the same wife—and that would be a problem, wouldn't it!" Where the fate of legislation was involved, Johnson usually was able to persuade a Congressional majority to see things his way, no matter what they thought about Lady Bird.

One morning Byrd's Senate committee adopted a series of tax bill amendments that would have repealed $455 million of excise levies. During the lunch hour LBJ worked the telephone and succeeded in reversing the decision on each amendment by a single vote.

"If he had opened the window of his office," said a Finance Committee Democrat, "I could have heard him."

When Johnson later was asked at a party to explain his dramatic success, he demurred, saying, "You already assume too much about my arm-twisting ability anyway."

According to those he telephoned, the President mostly confined himself to arguments that other approved tax cuts would become unbalanced, that excise reductions could lead to a time-consuming search for offsetting increases, and that interjection of the excise issue might jeopardize the entire bill.

Impatient at any delay, Johnson didn't even give his telephone a rest after the Finance Committee stamped its final approval on the tax bill. Twice he called a woman clerk to urge haste in preparing the document for presentation on the Senate floor.

The telephone also figured prominently in a successful presidential effort to ward off a $519 million cut in his 1964 foreign aid bill. Although the appropriation ultimately was reduced by

$200 million, this was small compared to the cutbacks that had been engineered year after year by aide foe Otto E. Passman of Louisiana. Outraged, Passman protested that Johnson had "worked tricks you couldn't even see in the circus."

Edmond LeBreton, head of the House staff of the AP, wrote about another instance in which LBJ used his telephone technique to good effect:

> Johnson hadn't been President very long. There was a vote coming up and it was close. A page came up to the Representative sitting next to me with a note that there was a call for him in the cloakroom. When he came back, I asked who was calling. "The President," he said, and he looked sort of glazed. Johnson knew just what point the debate had reached and who needed calling right then.

For Johnson, the telephone was an indispensable means of human contact, whence sprang his power. Any phone at hand became like a growth on his right arm.

At his desk, under the dining table, in all bathrooms were telephones for the President's use, some of them multi-button consoles that allowed him, with a mash of the finger, to reach without delay his key advisers and errand boys in the White House, at the State Department, or across the Potomac at the Pentagon or CIA. Liz Carpenter, Mrs. Johnson's remarkably effective press secretary, counted forty-two buttons on LBJ's Oval Office telephone, although perhaps she shared his gift for hyperbole; I thought there were only twenty-four. In any case, each time one was flattened a red light would glow somewhere in Washington, demanding immediate attention. It was called the POTUS light, for President of the United States.

When Mrs. Johnson was introduced to Frederick R. Kappel, then the board chairman of the American Telephone and Telegraph Company, she told him the Johnsons were among his best customers. The President was sensitive about his love affair with the telephone, however, and rarely allowed himself to be photographed with a receiver in his hand.

The LBJ telephone stories that circulated in Washington were only somewhat exaggerated. One that I presume was apocryphal featured his acquisition of a mobile phone for the limousine that was provided for him when he was Senate Democratic leader. It was said that Johnson's envious Republican counterpart, Everett McKinley Dirksen of Illinois, hastened to get a phone for his own Cadillac. Placing a car-to-car call to Johnson, Dirksen initiated this exchange:

"Lyndon, this is Everett. I wanted you to be the first to get a call from my new mobile telephone."

"Why, Ev, I think that's marvelous—I'd like to visit with you longer but my *other* phone is ringing!"

Said Dirksen a few months after LBJ entered the White House: "He called me up six times yesterday. I can't get my work done because he's always got me on the phone."

Democrat Hubert Humphrey voiced a remarkably similar complaint: "I've had ten calls from the man today. He has a new idea every thirty minutes and he calls me about it. I can't do anything he wants done because I don't have time to get going between calls."

White House aides *always* were expected to stay close to their telephones. When a wife apologized to Johnson because her husband was in the shower, he hung on until the man answered. "Are you dry?" he asked, "I wouldn't want you to catch cold." He was angry, not solicitous.

LBJ's assistants rarely ventured out of the White House at lunchtime, knowing they might be called at any moment and fearing their boss's wrath. Most of Kennedy's New Frontiersmen had gourmet tastes and enjoyed frequent leisurely lunches with reporters, affording us opportunities to eat well on the expense account and gather good stories in the process. In the five-plus years that Johnson was President, I succeeded only once in luring one of his men to lunch. Horace Busby and I walked two blocks to a seafood restaurant and had barely settled down to our martinis when Busby was summoned to the phone. Johnson had learned that he was having lunch with me and demanded he return to the White House at once to eat with him.

The President, I suppose, was a workaholic, deterred by the necessity neither to eat nor to sleep. As a Senator he tried using shifts of employees to operate his office around the clock, but it didn't work out. As President he kept five secretaries busy working two shifts. JFK had managed nicely with just two secretaries.

Even when he seemingly was at play, Johnson was likely to be working. Entertainment at the White House was included in his bag of tricks. To be wined, dined and danced with is to be lobbied, if in a most pleasant and unobjectionable way. A Representative with considerable seniority told Ed LeBreton:

"When my wife went home during the Kennedy administration, people would ask her what Mrs. Kennedy was really like. You know, the people at home assume if you're in Washington you're on easy terms with everybody. She had to say she had never met Mrs. Kennedy. That's a little hard on a Congressional wife. Now she can tell them what Lady Bird said the last time she was at the White House, what she wore and all that sort of thing."

Republicans were wooed as ardently as Democrats. At a January dinner dance the President sat next to Mrs. Barry Goldwater, whose husband already was acknowledged to be his most likely November opponent.

"May I have the first dance?" he asked her. "I want to get in good with you. I may want to be invited back here sometime."

When the first half dollars bearing Kennedy's image were minted, Johnson paid for and sent to each member of Congress a coin and a personal note.

"He's always giving you something," said a House member. "A pen, or a Kennedy half dollar, or some sort of gimmick or gadget. It's funny but you always keep those things, and you sort of like it."

It was all part of what had been called, in his Senate days, the Johnson Treatment, although most recipients of the Treatment found it to be more aural and tactile. It usually included, for example, the "laying on of hands," which the AP's Raymond J. Crowley described thusly:

First the handshake, with the left hand in action, too, pressing the subject's right elbow. Then the shift—one hand on the lapel, the other alternately encircling a shoulder and gesticulating close to the subject's nose.

If you happened to be seated within Johnson's reach, the hands part could involve rather painful variations. He often punctuated his conversation by jabbing you in the chest with a stiff forefinger or by pounding on your knee. I discovered you could get bruises that way. Perhaps that's why LBJ glanced up at House Speaker

John McCormack at a bill-signing ceremony to remark, "I believe he may think a bill a day will keep the President away."

Bills reached Johnson's desk with a dazzling frequency during the 1964 session and the President took a very personal and proprietary interest in the process, as he made evident at a July 18 news conference [my emphasis is added]:

"We have passed the tax bill. *We* have finally passed the civil rights bill. *We* have passed the farm bill. *We* have passed the International Development Act—the idea that had such great difficulty and was defeated on the first go-round.

"Before *we* adjourn, I hope to conclude many other bills that are now in conference."

A month later, with the presidential election campaign about to begin in earnest, all members of Congress were invited to a backyard evening reception at the White House. Using a bunting-draped stage set up on the lawn, singers and dancers put on a show that featured campaign songs of the past, from "Old Abe Lincoln Came Out of the Wilderness" to "I Like Ike." As a special tribute to the Eighty-eighth Congress, the troupe sang something called "Jump on the Wagon," with lyrics that promised, if everyone jumped on the wagon of the good old Eighty-eighth, "we'll all take a ride."

The star of the evening, naturally, was the genial, beaming, patriarchal President.

"This session of Congress," he declared, "has enacted more major legislation, met more national needs, disposed of more national issues, than any other session of this century or the last."

The superlatives perhaps were somewhat overdone, but a record of achievement nevertheless was there for anyone to see. LBJ and Congress had continued—in fact, had given a new life to—John F. Kennedy's New Frontier. And a lot of Americans were jumping on Lyndon Johnson's own wagon. It didn't have a name, but he soon remedied that.

4

"Do What Comes Naturally"

"No other President ever spent so much time with so many newsmen, and on terms of such personal intimacy," I once wrote. "If you were covering city hall in Anyplace, U.S.A., it's difficult to imagine you'd spend as much time with the mayor."

Besides hunting expeditions, lake cruises and fish frys, members of the press corps, and our bosses, were treated to cocktails and sherry in the family living room upstairs at the White House, luncheons in the family dining room, safaris around the back yard, and dips in the White House swimming pool.

Lyndon Johnson's informality was particularly in evidence around the pool. Trunks and suits of all shapes and sizes hung from hooks along one wall but the President preferred to skinny-dip, at least in male company.

There seemed to be little point in trying to guess what LBJ would do next, or where he might appear. When columnists Marguerite Higgins and Peter Lisagor gave a luncheon at her Georgetown home for Bill Moyers, Jack Valenti and Carl Rowan, who had recently been named director of the United States Information Agency, Johnson showed up unbidden, explaining, "You didn't think I was going to let these young men come over here and chat with old friends and leave me out, did you?"

The President turned up late one afternoon in the West Wing reception lobby, where we relaxed when we weren't at our desks in the crowded press room nearby, and caught one of our number dozing on a sofa. Prodding him awake, Johnson looked down and declared, "I'm mighty pleased to see that the Chicago *Tribune* is ever on the alert!"

Malcolm Kilduff, the assistant press secretary who had announced Kennedy's death at Parkland Hospital, was equally startled when Johnson strode into Kilduff's office and, eying the desk, barked, "I sure hope your mind isn't as cluttered as your desk!" Once the President was out of sight, a chastened Kilduff swept his desk top clean and kept it that way until LBJ returned a few days later to observe, "Mac, I sure hope your mind isn't as empty as your desk!"

Johnson could be an unmerciful tease, taking delight in his own thrusts in direct proportion to the degree of embarrassment displayed by his victim. But he was equally quick to show a warm heart and generous spirit, as my parents discovered when they went to the White House for a public tour on a May morning in 1964.

Quite naturally, they wanted to see where I worked so I arranged with the Press Office to have them admitted to the West Wing following the tour. After showing them my cramped quarters—a tiny cubicle with a single chair that three of us shared—and the reception room, I suggested they might want to hang around for a half hour and witness a bill-signing ceremony in the Cabinet Room. That would give them their first close-up look at a President in action. I knew it would be a real treat for a couple in their seventies from a New England town of just over five thousand who were visiting the White House for the first time.

When reporters and photographers were summoned for the event, my mother and father tagged along and the three of us stood waiting in a corner, well away from a patient assemblage that included House Speaker John McCormack, Senate Democratic Leader Mike Mansfield and a dozen other luminaries from Congress and the executive branch.

The appointed hour for the signing came and went without a

sign of Johnson. Then George E. Reedy, who had recently been appointed press secretary, rumbled in, sucking on his cherished pipe, and I introduced him to my parents. After chatting awhile, Reedy vanished into the adjacent office, between the Cabinet Room and the Oval Office, that housed the President's secretaries. A half hour passed as we shuffled from foot to foot. Johnson's frequent tardiness sometimes bordered on rudeness and I had to feel sorry for busy men like McCormack and Mansfield.

Suddenly Valenti shot through the door behind which Reedy had disappeared and, spotting me, snapped, "Where are they, Frank?" Taking Valenti's cue, I intercepted the President, who had entered the room behind him, and introduced my parents to LBJ.

In a quiet voice, Johnson began talking as if he had nothing else on his mind, reminiscing at length about his own mother ("one of the best friends I ever had") while mine beamed in wonderment and appreciation. I thought of the waiting dignitaries and the bill to be signed. Johnson turned to me: "Bring them into the office afterwards. I want to visit with them some more." Then he turned to the business at hand. I whispered to my mother that she should not count on the promised office visit because Johnson doubtless had many other things to do.

While we watched and listened, the President read a five-minute speech about the wonders of the law he was signing—the Pesticide Act amendments inspired by Rachel Carson and her *Silent Spring*. One of the television film cameramen had trouble with his equipment and so informed Johnson at the end. The President, whose patience often was limited, obligingly reread the entire speech. Then he grabbed up a handful of pens inscribed, "The President—The White House," and began signing his name one letter at a time, distributing pens as he used them to McCormack, Mansfield and some of the others.

"Miz Cormier!" Johnson said in a loud voice. It was a command and my mother stepped up to the cabinet table to accept a pen. With that, the President rose from his high-backed black leather chair, shook a few hands and stepped briskly toward the door.

"Bring 'em along, Frank," he said as he passed. We dutifully followed him into the adjoining office where several secretaries seemed very busy.

"Clean up these desks!" snapped Johnson. "The place looks like a pigsty." Of course, it didn't look at all bad. I suppose he was just letting everybody know who was boss, or maybe he had a thing about desk tops.

The President's own desk in the Oval Office was clear of papers when we stepped into the room in his hustling wake.

Directing us to a cushiony sofa in front of the fireplace, LBJ plopped down in his Kennedy-style rocker and mashed a button on the coffee table between us. Appearing almost instantly was a black-jacketed Filipino steward, assigned to the Navy-operated mess downstairs, who was dispatched to bring us three cups of coffee and one of Sanka.

Johnson wanted to know where my folks were from and what my dad did for a living. Informed that my father had been a Ford dealer in Orange, Massachusetts, for more than fifty years but was semi-retired because of heart trouble, LBJ recalled his own heart attack and the two men began comparing notes.

Then the President leaned toward my mother, his expressive face shining with seeming sincerity, and declared grandly:

"Miz Cormier, your son is in a critical position at a critical time in our nation's history. He's in a job where he could make lots of mistakes—but he doesn't make very many!"

I thought my mother might swoon. For myself, I was mindful that it was an election year and that we were being exposed to the vaunted Johnson Treatment. Obviously the President was entertaining us only because I was a White House correspondent whose favor he coveted. Even more obvious was his gross exaggeration of my importance. Yet his hospitality and even his excursion into hyperbole were kindnesses that came easy to him. Perhaps more than most Presidents, he liked people as individuals—"p-e-e-p-u-l," as he spelled it out in some public speeches—and not simply people as a vague abstraction. He could be as comfortable as a well-worn shoe with just about anybody.

When Johnson would hunker down on the porch of a mountain shanty in Appalachia, there was a large element of political hokum in his staged chat with the impoverished householder. Still, he had known such individuals all his life and could relate to them. If the man turned out to be a moonshiner, as one did, he could only chuckle with country-bred affection for country folkways. After he once halted a city motorcade so he could exchange pleasantries with some ladies gathered on the sparse lawn of a large, decaying house, we learned it was the kind of house that is not a home. Had Johnson known it, he wouldn't have cared.

His easy rapport with people, with individuals, was manifested, a few months after our Oval Office visit, when he emerged from his limousine in a working-class neighborhood in Milwaukee to greet an overweight, beery-looking man in a plaid mackinaw.

"You goin' to vote Democratic next Tuesday?" asked the President after some preliminary conversation.

The man looked at him scornfully: "You know goddamn well I am, Lyndon!"

Smiling, the President reached into his coat and pulled out a ballpoint pen bearing a facsimile of the Johnson autograph. Accepting it without so much as a thank-you, the man said, "Lyndon, how about givin' me another one of them for my wife?" Lyndon did.

Although he was exceedingly mean on occasion, excesses being a part of his nature, Johnson could bestow kindnesses with unaffected pleasure. When Bill Costello, who was White House correspondent for the Mutual Broadcasting System, suffered a heart attack during a Johnson trip to the LBJ Ranch, the President surrendered one of his Lincoln Continentals for Mrs. Costello to use as long as her husband was hospitalized in Texas. Johnson also visited the hospital himself.

The broadcaster made a promising recovery from subsequent open heart surgery but LBJ worried about him. He wanted to do more, so he made Bill Ambassador to Trinidad and Tobago, where sunshine was plentiful and official duties were less than onerous. Johnson did not do this in exchange for a fat campaign contribution but because Bill Costello was one of the p-e-e-p-u-l he liked.

It was difficult to divorce political considerations from anything that Johnson did. But he did a lot of things because they gave him, and others, pleasure. I like to think there was an element of that in our family gathering at the White House.

While talking with my parents that morning, Johnson mashed another button on the coffee table, summoning up the answering voice of a secretary from a small speaker on the table.

"Bring me in one of those big colored pictures," Johnson ordered. Within seconds he was signing a matted presidential portrait: "To Mr. and Mrs. E. Edmund Cormier—With warm regards and memories of a pleasant visit at the White House. Lyndon B. Johnson. 5/12/64. Washington, D.C."

The President looked at his watch as he wrote out the inscription and my father later told me, "I thought he was putting down the time of day." It was a calendar watch and LBJ was checking the date.

Getting out of his rocker, Johnson had a further treat in store for his visitors. "We've got to show 'em the Rose Garden," he told me. Moving through french doors onto the canopied walk that extends from the Oval Office to the living quarters, we found the garden aglow with flowering trees and springtime flowers of many varieties. Johnson loved the garden and used it for ceremonies as often as possible in good weather, something that would have disturbed Jack Kennedy, who was so proud of the big rectangle of grass in the center that he rarely let people walk on it.

"Have you seen the house yet?" asked Johnson. I assured him that my parents had enjoyed a complete tour. That wasn't entirely true but I was becoming uncomfortable about taking up so much of his morning; but had I said otherwise, I suspected he was quite prepared to conduct his own tour of private corners closed to the public.

So we returned to the Oval Office where Johnson rummaged through a desk drawer and came up with a small cardboard box. Holding it out with a flourish, he said with great solemnity:

"Miz Cormier, this is for *you* from the thirty-sixth President of the United States!"

Inside was a presidential medallion with Johnson's profile in bas-relief on one side.

Feeling like someone who has just met Santa Claus and is imposing on his time, I tried to excuse us, with appropriate thanks. "Don't go yet," said Johnson, "we've got to show 'em where I do my quiet thinking." He ushered us into his small hideaway office, which contained a desk, sofa and a couple of armchairs. Offering expansive explanations, he pointed proudly to the autographed portraits of his political heroes that he had shown to the four women reporters some months earlier. Then he turned to a wall-mounted hardwood case, inscribed as a gift from the National Geographic Society, and rolled down a map of Texas.

"Frank, I don't see the fine print too good," he confessed. "Show 'em where Johnson City is." I did as directed and he declaimed on the glories of his native hill country.

Johnson next escorted us into yet another office where some of his assistants worked. At the far end of the room was Dave Powers, who had been Kennedy's closest "pal," a title the amiable Powers was quick to bestow on anyone he met.

"Dave," shouted the President, "have you met Frank Cormier's daddy?" There were handshakes all around, followed by our expressions of gratitude for the President's hospitality. My parents walked away clutching their gifts, certain that Lyndon Johnson was everything Jack Valenti claimed him to be: "a sensitive man, a cultivated man, a warmhearted man." The one and only POTUS, a man of many surprises.

Some of our earliest surprises stemmed from Johnson's unorthodox approach to press conferences. Eleven days after coffee-in-the-office evolved into a conference, he had us back for one without coffee. As before, it began with us trouping unsuspecting into Pierre Salinger's office to hear that "the President will conduct the briefing today."

As we walked the few yards to Johnson's office, Salinger came up beside me and said, "Frank, you ask the first question." Inasmuch as I had only a few seconds in which to compose my thoughts, I'm not embarrassed about the exchange that followed:

Q.: Mr. President, could you give us any exposition of your attitude toward perhaps an early meeting with Premier Khrushchev?
A.: I am willing to meet with any of the world leaders at any time there is any indication a meeting would be fruitful and productive. When there are such indications, I will be glad to make a decision and inform you of it.

Another newsman wondered if this was to be "the type of press conference you intend to hold . . . or is this just an interim press conference?" We were accustomed to the televised sessions Kennedy had held in the State Department auditorium but Johnson's first two had come unannounced and unbroadcast.

"I would say," replied Johnson, "that we are going to maintain an adequate flow of information to the press at all times in the best manner that we can. We will do what comes naturally. Maybe it will be a meeting of this kind today, maybe a televised meeting tomorrow, with maybe a coffee session the next day. We don't want to be too rigid. We always want to be flexible."

It didn't take us long to realize that Johnson would "do what comes naturally" on virtually every occasion. Had I gone around the world with him when he was Vice-President, his ad hoc habits would have been no surprise at all.

According to one man who was there, the relatively few reporters who accompanied Johnson were getting restive by the time the party reached Bangkok. Carl Rowan, who was Ambassador to Finland at the time and had been borrowed by LBJ to handle the press on the trip, suggested to the Vice-President that the reporters would be happier if they were kept busier. Rowan suggested a news conference and Johnson agreed to hold one in the Thai palace where he was staying.

At the appointed hour Rowan and the reporters gathered in a palace sitting room but the Vice-President did not appear. Worried, Rowan went to LBJ's bedroom where he found Johnson sitting on the bed in his underwear.

"Mr. Vice-President," he said, "it's time for the press conference."

"What in the hell do you think I'm sitting here waiting for!" Johnson exploded.

So the Vice-President met the press in his skivvies and Rowan was thankful that one reporter, Nancy Hanchman (later Dickerson), hadn't gotten the word.

Johnson's initial experiments with presidential news conferences were not uniformly applauded. We called them "quickies," a term that galled him, and complained that lack of advance notice precluded coverage by specialist reporters from the State Department, the Pentagon and other beats. In addition, the broadcasters were unhappy because LBJ had made no provision yet for radio or television coverage. That Johnson was irritated at our irritation became plain at an Oval Office conference on January 25, 1964, when he said, in a biting way:

"Don't run out of here if you have any questions you want to ask. Ask them. I will answer them. This is not a quickie news conference. I don't know what you call a formal one. I guess I ought to wear a white tie. I came to work this morning and I didn't think it was formal; I just thought I was supposed to be here. And if you are all here, I will give you anything I know at any time. . . .

"I have seen thirty or forty reporters who have asked to come in on special things that they wanted to do. Some of them wanted to write about Cousin Oreole. Some of them wanted to write about what I think of my wife. Some of them wanted to tell their editors that they saw me and here is what they think will happen in the wild blue yonder. I try to see all of them I can with my schedule, and I am very happy with them. I never enjoy anything more than polite, courteous, fair, judicious reporters, and I think all of you qualify."

The very next press conference, which was called on about two hours' notice in a fresh setting, the White House theater, had Johnson riled up for days because of a single critical question. More than one hundred of us were jammed into the long narrow room, many standing, more seated on folding chairs, and a few enjoying the relative luxury of upholstered chairs up front. Here is the exchange that set Johnson off:

Q.: Mr. President, many of us are wondering why you would hold a news conference in a cramped little room such as this . . . when you have facilities available to accommodate all newsmen, such as the State Department?

A.: I don't have an answer to that question of yours. I thought this would be ample to take care of your needs. I am sorry if you find yourselves uncomfortable. It was much more convenient to come here at the time that I could come, and I was attempting to satisfy the newsmen. . . .

The questioner was Tony Sylvester of WTOP, the son of Arthur Sylvester, who was Johnson's Assistant Secretary of Defense for Public Affairs. The President, bent on postponing for as long as possible an appearance in the State Department auditorium that would invite comparisons with Kennedy, was outraged at what he

regarded as the temerity of the younger Sylvester. With deep sarcasm and much emotion, he later exclaimed to some of us:

"Imagine that little pissant sitting there in *the President's chair* —the one I use when I watch the movies—and complaining that he wasn't comfortable!"

Johnson did not face live television cameras at a news conference until February 29, 1964, his one hundredth day in office. He did so at the State Department, but in the International Treaty Room rather than the larger auditorium. I thought he did quite well on TV, then and on most subsequent occasions, although he continued to shrink from the type of conference at which Kennedy excelled. Mrs. Johnson knew how he felt, as she confided in a 1964 entry in *A White House Diary:*

At 3:30 I watched one of his confrontations, a televised press conference, the sort of thing you must steel yourself to go through, almost as you would face a firing squad. I watched it on TV in my bedroom, every nerve aquiver with sympathy.

Johnson held only one conference in the old Kennedy setting, presumably to prove to himself that he could do it, and thereafter opted most often for the East Room of the White House when TV cameras were involved. There were other settings, too, especially for the "quickies." When we went to the New York World's Fair in May, LBJ decided on fifteen minutes' notice to hold a press conference in the small auditorium at the United States Pavilion. It was a stifling room, made the more so because Johnson, although forced to mop his face periodically with a handkerchief, ordered the fans turned off on grounds that they were "noisier than the correspondents." When a reporter mercifully ended the session, Mrs. Johnson, sitting on the stage near her husband, clasped her hands together and declared, "I'm with you!"

Just three days earlier, the President had held the most unusual of all his news conferences. In telling us beforehand what he had in mind, he said his sixteen-year-old daughter Luci had been so proud when he showed up for her crowning as queen of the Shenandoah Apple Blossom Festival, at Winchester, Virginia, that it occurred to him our youngsters might take as much pride in us. Therefore, he said, wives and children could attend his next press conference so they could see us in action.

My wife Margot wrote for the AP an account of our family's participation in what my colleague Arthur L. Edson described as "a crossbreeding of sober news and Disneyland":

WASHINGTON, MAY 7 (AP)—A whoop of joy came from 10-year-old Elizabeth, a hundred questions from 5-year-old John, a thoughtful silence from 4-year-old Billy.

My husband had just announced that "you're all invited to President Johnson's news conference." He suggested that even the baby, Michael, would want to go—but he was overruled.

Yesterday—the big day—I got shoes polished and Sunday School suits out. Billy's jacket was dirty and I had to borrow one.

Naptime was a shambles. No one would sleep.

We were in the car by 3:15 and on the drive into the city the boys rehearsed the greeting, "How do you do, Mr. President."

At the White House gate, a long line of mothers and children waited. It looked like Saturday afternoon at the neighborhood movie theater, except for everyone looking more dressed up.

Entry to the White House grounds brought a reaction of excitement mixed with relief that we had made it. The lawn was lush and green, the red-coated Marine Band was playing, and red-and-white striped awnings hung over the refreshment stands.

We found the best seats we could, well in the rear. While waiting for the President to appear [the conference was held on an outdoor stage], the children made two trips for cookies and punch. When they weren't eating or drinking, they kept asking, "Where's the President? Where's daddy?"

Johnson came into view and the boys jumped to stand on their folding chairs. John's chair seat collapsed and his latest cup of punch flew over the both of us.

As the President made his opening announcements, Elizabeth sat engrossed. The boys wriggled and squirmed. I didn't hear much of what he said.

The President recognized dad for a question and the boys stood on their seats again.

"Daddy's up now," John announced. We couldn't hear the question and then John added, "Daddy's down now."

For the boys, the news conference was over.

The children made another trip to the refreshment stand, although the conference continued. Then more wriggling and squirming—and questions: Where'd the band go? Is that the White House? What's that on top of it?

When the President invited all the youngsters to join him on the stage, Elizabeth took the boys in tow.

I saw them climb to the stage. Then they vanished in the throng.

I saw the President, looking somewhat like the pied piper, and scores of other children. My own were out of sight.

Reappearing finally, they made yet another trip to the refreshment tent.

Elizabeth managed to shake hands with Mrs. Johnson. And all the children got to pat the President's beagles, Him and Her.

Everyone was happy.

Asked if he'd do it again, Johnson paused, then said, "I haven't any plans to." But, he acknowledged, "I try to give you variety."

Part of the variety he referred to involved a Johnsonian exercise that we came to call the "walkathon," in which he would lead several dozen of us on stop-and-go hikes around the roughly circular driveway on the South Lawn of the White House. This practice prompted Phil Potter to suggest a variation on a Bible song as the press corps anthem: "He walks with us, and he talks with us, and he tells us we are his own."

It was a rough course for the women reporters with high heels, and for Press Secretary Reedy and his hammertoed feet. Secret Service agents had enough sense to work it in relays.

Actually, there were hazards for everyone. Pete Lisagor, while keeping his eye on LBJ instead of the road, walked into a lamppost and had to have his head bandaged. Others tripped over the long metal-chain leashes that Johnson used for his beagles. And whenever the President stopped—to emphasize the importance of what he was saying, or simply to drink from a water fountain— the entourage that followed was apt to perform a reasonable imitation of a chain-reaction crash on a foggy freeway.

There was another problem, too: unless you were close to Johnson's elbow, you could walk a couple of miles without hearing a word he said. Although he often talked off the record, he sometimes said something significant. That apparently was not the case when the AP's John Barbour reported that a thirty-five-minute hike "covered about two and a half miles—but very little else."

You might hear Johnson discussing the relative merits of com-

peting policy options. Or he might have nothing more substantive
on his mind than a complaint that he had been slandered by
Scotty Reston, who had written in the *Times* that Johnson
couldn't find anyone he could beat at golf.

"I guess it's possible to slander a person and still tell the truth,"
the President mused with a twinkle in his eyes. "What he said is
true. I can't break one hundred any more."

The walks tended to coincide with lunchtime, which caused
Mrs. Johnson to fret. She called him in the Oval Office as he was
about to lead a group of us to the South Lawn and appealed to
him to come upstairs and eat instead. Her voice came over a
speaker on his desk.

"I'll be up in a bit," he replied, quickly flipping a switch that cut
her off.

"Why didn't you let her answer?" snapped Potter, who never
was awed by the man, although he was one of Johnson's most
vocal admirers in the press corps. LBJ merely scowled at him and
headed for the driveway.

On another occasion Mrs. Johnson came out of the house to
fetch him for lunch. The President did one more lap with her,
then went inside. Later, however, he complained to us that he
would have set a new distance record of fourteen laps had she not
interrupted him.

After one walk, a reporter griped that he was having difficulty
keeping pace with Johnson's manifold activities, prompting this
exchange:

Johnson: What would you suggest—not do so much?
Reporter: Well, you might try to space things out a little bit.
Johnson: Why don't you-all appoint an advisory committee to
George Reedy?

The President took the walks, I'm sure, for fresh air and exercise. As he told us, "I subscribe to the view once expressed that if
you want to know if your brain is flabby you better feel of your
legs."

After hiking six laps he said he'd make one more circuit and
then maybe take a swim because "I need some exercise."

At a Rose Garden ceremony in 1965 honoring winners of Physical Fitness Leadership Awards, Johnson extemporized:

"You may not be able to tell it by just looking at them, but I want to give my personal testimony in behalf of the newspapermen and newspaperwomen, that they are doing very well in our own White House physical fitness training program on our daily walks. We have had very few casualties—we have lost one or two high heels, had one or two dropouts—but generally speaking, the marks are high. Give me a little more time and both the press and, I hope, the President will be in better shape."

For a time it seemed as though Johnson was dedicated to the physical conditioning of the entire tourist population in Washington, as he invited them inside to walk.

The first time it happened was April 11, 1964, while he was walking before lunch with Bill Moyers. Seeing people at one of the big iron gates, Johnson ordered them opened so that about one hundred strangers could make a circuit of the driveway with him.

"Do you cut this grass yourself?" a man asked.

"No, sir, I don't," the President replied, "but I'd probably feel better if I did."

Johnson spotted a White House reporter who had entered with the crowd.

"You don't belong here," he said. "If you want to march, join the Army."

"I've already done that," said the reporter, ducking into the throng.

Johnson escorted the visitors back to the gate through which they had entered and set up an impromptu receiving line, shaking hands with each departing tourist.

The event was so unprecedented that we ran an account of it on our main news wire under an "urgent" designation.

The novelty wore off the following week as the President greeted tourists at the gate three days running. But we continued to report his ebullient behavior as he prefaced his South Lawn tours with cracks like, "All of you ugly men get up front and all of you pretty girls come back here with me!"

Johnson walked for nearly an hour one day when the temperature was near ninety, stopping at the gate to exchange his gold LBJ tie clip with a man from Racine, Wisconsin, who had one with big lettering that spelled "Johnson." That's how the President acquired an advertisement for the Johnson wax company.

Another time he met a family from Falfurrias, Texas, and asked, "You-all know Mr. Percy Hunter down there?" When the response was affirmative, he said, "Well, tell him hello for me." Turning to us, he remarked, "That's where they have that good creamery butter."

After exchanging greetings at the gate during one walkathon, Johnson tried to explain his zest for handshaking. Recalling a tour of military bases that he made with Jack Dempsey during World War II, the President said the former heavyweight champion was forever throwing them off schedule by lingering to shake hands. Johnson said he asked why Dempsey did this and would never forget the reply:

"Congressman, it's been twenty years since I was champ. If the people still want to shake hands with me and get my autograph, I want to do it."

"I want to be the people's President," Johnson declared in a 1964 television interview, "and in order to do so, you have to see the people and talk to them and know something about them and not be too secluded.

"I think [the Secret Service] would feel better if the President kept one hundred yards distance from every human being, but that is not practical."

Not natural, either.

5

"Press Palms . . . Feel the Flesh"

Long before he became President, Lyndon Johnson explained his highly personalized approach to campaigning by declaring, "I have to press palms and feel the flesh." In the early months of 1964, with his popularity ascending as Americans admired the smooth transition engineered by the relative stranger who had become President by accident, and with election day approaching, Johnson was eager to be about the business of flesh-pressing.

Although he continued to harbor doubts about the wisdom of making a national campaign in his own name, Johnson's misgivings were close to subliminal. His instincts told him to start running, to mingle with people beyond the White House gates no matter what his bodyguards preferred.

In moving rather tentatively toward the posture of active campaigner, Johnson characteristically cloaked his true inclinations with statements of lofty purpose, pledging to concentrate almost exclusively on his official duties and limit his political appearances to those required to fulfill Democratic fund-raising commitments made by John F. Kennedy. Thus, on February 27, 1964, Johnson was bound for a Democratic dinner at Miami Beach's Fontainebleau Hotel, via Palatka, Florida, and the dedication of the Cross-Florida Barge Canal.

What followed was the most extraordinary cloak-and-dagger

aerial odyssey by an American President since the wartime travels
of Franklin D. Roosevelt. Security precautions for this, Johnson's
first avowedly political outing, were more stringent than any ever
seen in peacetime.

Those of us making the trip as members of the press pool on
Air Force One might have guessed that something was amiss from
the advance schedule provided by the Press Office. It contained
large gaps and failed to list many key arrival and departure times,
even some of the places we'd be going. We knew by this time,
however, that Johnson had a penchant for secrecy and were
prepared to attribute the odd-looking schedule to that.

When we got to Andrews Air Force Base, outside Washington,
to begin the flight, I had my first suspicions that something more
was involved than the President's predilections. Instead of boarding the regular Air Force One, which was nowhere to be seen, we
were steered toward an outwardly identical but slightly shorter
sister ship that normally bore the tail number 86970. But the
number wasn't there; it had been painted over.

Asking a crewman what had happened to the larger plane, I
was told that it was being overhauled. I could get no explanation
for the missing tail number.

Once we were aloft, all four members of the Johnson family
made themselves visible; I had expected the two daughters to be
in school. The Johnsons seemed affable and relaxed, however, and
certainly gave no hint that they had cause for concern.

More unusual was the presence of both James J. Rowley, chief
of the Secret Service, and Gerald Behn, the head of its White
House detail. For both men to make an ostensibly routine overnight domestic trip was highly unusual.

During most of our flight to our initial destination, the Jacksonville Naval Air Station, we were in heavy clouds. I took this to be
quite unusual, also, given the ability of a 707 to fly above most
cloud banks.

After a round trip by helicopter to Palatka, where the canal was
suitably dedicated in a driving rain, we returned to the substitute
Air Force One and took off for a destination that was not revealed
until we were airborne. We found we were headed for West Palm
Beach and would drive from there to the ocean-front home of the
paralyzed Joseph P. Kennedy for an unannounced presidential
visit.

We supposed we would continue to Miami by jet, as our schedule indicated, but now were given special instructions that made evident the extent, if not the precise nature, of the security considerations involved. Instead of reboarding the plane, we would make the sixty-seven-mile flight in a fleet of helicopters that would carry no markings to distinguish one from another.

Whenever the President boards a helicopter, it normally bears the presidential seal on its nose section and is further marked by a red numeral "1" by the front door. Other choppers making a flight carry similar numerals in sequence and members of the travel party are assigned by number to the various craft.

In this instance, we were told we could tell which helicopter to board by the color of a cloth ribbon that would be hanging from a railing built into the front door, which was designed to serve as a boarding ramp when lowered. This meant that when the door was raised and closed for take-off the ribbon would disappear inside the cabin.

We still did not know where we would land in the Miami area. Ultimately we set down on fairways of the Bayshore Country Club, where we saw further evidence of the extraordinary precautions being taken.

As the President's closed limousine headed for the Fontainebleau, an Army helicopter, with armed security agents aboard, hovered barely seventy-five feet above the car—much closer than is normal. More startling, however, were the military jets crisscrossing Miami Beach at low altitude. And only later did we learn about still other security measures:

—The White House Communications Agency, which is charged with keeping Presidents in touch with the world, had set up bases at Miami International Airport, Homestead Air Force Base, and at airports in West Palm Beach, Fort Lauderdale, and Key West, so flight plans could be changed more readily on short notice.

—Secret Service agents had made themselves conspicuous at Miami International, thus luring most of the Florida press corps there to await a presidential arrival that never happened.

—On the flight from Washington two planes identical to 86970, and with their tail numbers also painted over, had flown near us, unseen in the clouds. Moreover, there had been an escort of Air Force fighters out there, and Navy ships had been deployed in coastal waters below.

A few hours after we returned unscathed to Washington, having taken off in secret from an air base near Miami, Gene Miller of the Miami *Herald* reported the reason for the precautions. The Secret Service had received a tip, he wrote, that a suicide pilot might try to ram Air Force One, or it might become the target of a Cuban-based missile. Agent Rufus Youngblood subsequently revealed that the Federal Bureau of Investigation had passed along intelligence that a Cuban pilot might attempt to intercept the presidential jet and ram it or shoot it down.

After these many years, the incident continues to intrigue me because of Lee Harvey Oswald's Cuban connection and the persistent speculation, for which no evidence has been produced, that there could have been a link between Kennedy's death and plots by the Central Intelligence Agency to eliminate Fidel Castro. The strange episode certainly established the fact that, thirteen weeks after Dallas, American officials felt compelled to deal seriously with the idea that someone in Cuba might have had designs on the life of Lyndon Johnson.

Soon after the Florida trip the President told television interviewers that under no circumstances would he undertake active campaigning until after the Democratic National Convention had selected a nominee, whoever that might be. ABC's William H. Lawrence, having observed a good deal of disguised campaigning in his lifetime, wanted to know whether "we might see a few old-fashioned, non-political conservation tours or inspection tours."

"You will see them before and after the convention," Johnson replied. "They are part of the work of the President. I think part of the President's job is to get out and see the people and talk to them about what the government is doing and make reports."

Within days we were hearing that Johnson's "non-political" touring would be based on his rhetorical declaration of an "unconditional war on poverty." Asked at a March 28 news conference if a tour of poverty areas was in the offing, the President responded:

"Yes. I told one person about it the other day and it has been leaked all over Washington since. I want very much to go into some poverty areas when time will permit and we can arrange it. . . .

"I am sorry that it has had to be announced in advance because now we will have all the wires coming in from the various places and it will create more problems than it will solve. But I have seen reference to it. It is true."

Johnson's reluctance to acknowledge any plan or intention before he was firmly if not irrevocably committed to it created problems for the press corps throughout his administration. We never could plan on anything and we had to be prepared, as best we could, for the unexpected. I once flew to Texas without so much as a toothbrush, and we stayed there several days. The White House Transportation Office several times chartered airliners for press use on trips that never happened; our employers had to pay for them.

More disturbing, I felt, because it sometimes seemed to border on the aberrant, was Johnson's tendency to alter his plans if they became public knowledge sooner than he intended. During a trip to Texas, my co-worker Karl Bauman received a message from a newspaper in West Virginia asking if LBJ was going to dedicate a dam in that state. Bauman, who was heading for the ranch, took the message with him and showed it to Bill Moyers, hoping to get an answer. Johnson saw the slip of paper passing between the two men and demanded to have a look. After studying the message, the President turned to Bauman and said, "I'm hopin' and I'm plannin' to go, but if you write it, I won't go!"

At a 1964 news conference LBJ elaborated on some of the factors that inspired the secrecy that so often shrouded his travel plans:

". . . just where I will be at some certain day in October, I can't determine, and I don't want to announce, because then you have me canceling and adjusting my plans, things of that kind. That makes more of a story than my appearance would make, or maybe what I had to say makes."

On another occasion, Johnson offered yet another explanation, this time in the form of an analogy. When he was growing up, he related, his father had packed everyone into the family car and driven for miles to a country fair expecting to hear a speech by Dan Moody, then the Attorney General of Texas, but Moody failed to appear. The next week they trekked to another fair and, once again, a promised appearance by Moody failed to materialize.

"You know," the President told us, "that no Johnson ever voted for Dan Moody after that."

Johnson's penchant for secrecy was not confined to his travel plans, however, and it did not develop only after he reached the White House. He had displayed the same propensity as Senator and Vice-President.

Before Vice-President Johnson set off on an Asian tour for Kennedy, Spencer Davis of the AP reported that he would carry to Ngo Dinh Diem in Saigon an offer of twenty-seven million dollars in United States aid. Infuriated by the report, LBJ nagged at Davis all the way across the Pacific and, once they had reached Asia, summoned Carl Rowan to ask, "Carl, do I look like I'm wearin' glass pants?" Assured that his trousers appeared quite conventional, Johnson exclaimed, "Well, if I'm not wearin' glass pants, how in the hell can Spencer Davis see twenty-seven million dollars in my pocket!"

The amount involved turned out to be closer to twenty-five million.

Johnson's reaction was much the same in 1964 when the Washington *Post* reported that the President would announce, in addressing the annual Associated Press luncheon, that he was ordering a reduction of about forty-five per cent in United States production of weapons-grade fissionable materials. At a news conference the following day, Johnson told us: "My advice to you is to wait for the speech . . . and not to put much stock in what you get second or third hand. I am still working on it and the report is very inaccurate."

Delivering the speech a day later, LBJ announced plans for a four-year production cutback that, when coupled with other reductions he had recently ordered, "will mean an over-all decrease in the production . . . of enriched uranium by forty per cent."

In Johnson's own good time a series of poverty trips were announced. April saw him visiting pockets of unemployment in Indiana, Pennsylvania, West Virginia and Kentucky.

There were crowds at every turn, offering palms to press and flesh to feel. LBJ would wade into their midst, hat tipped on the back of his head, grinning broadly and shoving his right hand forward to afford someone a quick grasp. Simultaneously he would move his left hand over his right toward someone else, then repeat the process, hand over hand, almost endlessly. At the end of a long day of harvesting affection the backs of his hands would be scarred with cuts from rings and fingernails. Medical aides would cover them with bandages and a soothing cream.

Crowds can be dangerous in other ways, too, as the Johnsons discovered when their helicopter set down in a schoolyard in South Bend. Youngsters, joyous and squealing, pressed in upon them so relentlessly that Secret Service agents were forced to exert superior pressure in order to extricate the President and his wife. Several children were injured. I was caught up in the crush and, frankly, I found the experience rather frightening.

From the look on her face, Mrs. Johnson shared my apprehension, and was concerned for the safety of the children. Her husband seemed oblivious to everything except the attention and adulation, although on many other occasions I heard him speak sharply in cautioning well-wishers to protect the youngsters in their midst.

A lifetime in politics had never before brought the President such riches of acclaim. He not only savored it but often seemed to become intoxicated from it. Reluctant to turn away from any friendly crowd, he was constantly falling behind schedule.

"I'm runnin' late," he would apologize. "I am usually a dollar short and an hour late, but my intentions are good."

An April 24 trip to Pittsburgh marked the emergence of LBJ's true campaign style, all in the non-partisan cause of fighting poverty, of course. With throngs lining both curbs in a working-class neighborhood, Johnson violated an unwritten rule that had been observed since Dallas. Abandoning his enclosed, armored limousine, he stepped into the Secret Service convertible behind it and stood there waving and inviting his welcomers to move close enough to touch.

He next unveiled a new political weapon, the bullhorn. Every block or so, sometimes oftener, he would stop the cavalcade and, standing in the back of the open car, raise the battery-powered horn to his lips and express pleasure at seeing "so many happy, smiling faces."

As the convertible inched forward, Johnson displayed a wave that was to become another of his campaign trademarks. Called the "fishtail flutter," it involved a rapid undulation of the fingers of both hands, which were outstretched level with the shoulders.

At scheduled "speakin's" on bunting-draped outdoor platforms, in auditoriums and union halls, Johnson would rise from a brown-upholstered folding chair that accompanied him everywhere. Because the President had endured enough hard seats before reaching the political pinnacle, White House baggage handlers preceded him to every public platform with the special padded chair that they carried in a large canvas sack.

Also awaiting Johnson at each stop would be a bullet-resistant rostrum from which an aide would suspend a three-dimensional presidential seal at the precise moment of LBJ's introduction.

Once LBJ got from his chair to the rostrum, the folks out front would be treated to a down-home message that always seemed to please them. For example:

"The American people don't ask for much—a school for their children, a church for them to worship in according to the dictates of their own conscience, a picture on the wall, and a rug on the floor, and a little music in the house."

Even if some of the phrases had been borrowed from Phil Murray, the union chieftain, audiences seemed to find the message appealing, with its own plain eloquence. On rare occasions, however, Johnson would disappoint his listeners, if not baffle them, by resorting to a hokey, patronizing device, an alphabet trick, that he evidently thought was clever. This is how it went:

"I have talked to you about a six-point program. . . . Food—that is 'F.' Recreation—that is 'R.' Jobs and wages and income—that is 'I.' Education—that is 'E.' Increased Social Security, Medicare and nursing homes for the older folks—that is 'N.' And a strong nation that will defend us and help us get peace—defense—that is 'D.' . . . That spells 'friend.' "

One of Johnson's first poverty-tour stops was at Inez, Kentucky, a town of nine hundred in Hatfield and McCoy country with an unemployment rate of thirty-seven per cent. Accompanied by Mrs. Johnson, the President drove through the hollows to a rude cabin where the Tom Fletchers lived with their eight children. In his neatly pressed suit, LBJ "set awhile," meaning he squatted, on the rickety front porch and discussed with Fletcher, who wore khaki trousers and a tattered sports shirt, the challenges involved in raising a large family on an annual income of about four hundred dollars earned by scratching coal from the nearby hills.

The two men talked so intently that they never noticed when a gust of wind blew the door off the privy beside the cabin.

"Take care of yourself," said Johnson as he headed toward his car, "and don't forget now, I want you to put those boys back in school."

" 'By, chillun," said Mrs. Johnson.

The President and his wife were able to carry off their conversations without appearing even slightly ridiculous. They could have been chatting with Texas neighbors. The Fletchers displayed a natural dignity of their own.

Once Johnson got back aboard his plane, however, his own dignity deserted him as he sat across a table from me drinking a highball of scotch whisky. He commenced to indulge in a very bad habit of belching loudly, and without covering his mouth, after each healthy swallow. I saw him do this often and never could understand why he did it. Perhaps he wished to demonstrate that he was President and could be as uncouth as he pleased.

Whenever LBJ went into his belching act, I found myself fighting off the kind of laughter that brings tears to the eyes. I did not want to laugh in the President's face but, on this occasion, he quickly gave me an opportunity to do so without embarrassment.

Before leaving Inez, Johnson had greeted a man who had been wheeled out of his house on a bed. The invalid had been paralyzed from the waist down for more than six years.

"Did you see that little ol' boy on that litter?" Johnson asked me. "I want to tell you, when he looked up and saw his President, there was a satisfied man. It reminded me of my old daddy's definition of the satisfied man. He's the fellow that takes a good healthy shit every mornin'—and gets his newspaper on time!"

Lyndon Johnson was one of the best storytellers I ever met, and his fund of tales was rich. He would weave stories and amusing recollections into speeches and casual conversations in a way that was natural and pointed and gave an element of added zest to the whole.

"We like this democracy so much, this freedom so much," he told one political audience, "we want everybody to have a little taste of it. It is like the fellow who had a few too many drinks. He came home, and he got to sleep and woke up in the middle of the night. His mouth was burnin' and he said to his wife, 'Get me some ice water.' And she got the pitcher of ice water and brought it to him and he took a drink. Then he said, 'Honey, this is so good, go wake up the kids and give them some of it.'"

Introduced by Governor Frank G. Clement in Knoxville, Tennessee, Johnson responded, "I believe this introduction you just gave me is about the best introduction I have ever had in all my public life, except one that I had down in Texas one time when my county judge was supposed to introduce me and he didn't show up and I had to introduce myself!"

On other occasions he would begin a speech in this fashion: "I wish my mother and father might have been here to hear that introduction, because my father would have enjoyed hearin' what you said about me and my mother would have believed it."

Acknowledging an introduction in St. Louis by August A. Busch, Jr., the President began:

"I appreciate the introduction Gussie gave me. I am somewhat overawed by it. I am reminded of the frustrating experience that a preacher down in my country had when he went to his church one Sunday in a little rural area, and he found that his parishioners had presented him with a new Ford automobile as a present. He was so excited about the present . . . he got up and said, 'Well, I do deserve it, but I don't appreciate it.' Well, I do appreciate it, Mr. Busch, and I don't deserve it."

Johnson had a vast store of preacher stories, reflecting no doubt the God-fearing rural environment in which he was raised. One of his favorites, used in extemporaneous speeches, concerned a clergyman who dropped his sermon notes while heading for church and was unable to retrieve them before his dog chewed them up.

"When the preacher went into the pulpit," LBJ recounted, "he apologized to his congregation and said, 'I am very sorry, today I have no sermon. I will just have to speak as the Lord directs. But I will try to do better next Sunday.'"

Addressing the Friendly Sons of St. Patrick in New York, Johnson declared:

"It always makes me a bit wary to be the last speaker on any program. Even the most attentive can get a bit weary. I remember one time in my home country a preacher was vexed because one of his congregation always went to sleep in the midst of the sermon. One Sunday while he was giving the devil fits, sure enough his sleeping worshiper was snoring gently in the front row.

"The preacher determined he would fix this character and fix him once and for all. So in a whisper he asked the congregation, 'All who want to go to heaven, please rise.' As one man, they all got to their feet except the front-row dozer. He kept snoring on. Then the preacher shouted at the top of his voice, 'All those who want to be with the devil, please rise!' The sleepyhead came awake with a start. He jumped to his feet. He saw the preacher standing tall and angry in the pulpit, and he said, 'Well, preacher, I don't know what it is we are voting on, but it looks like you and me are the only ones for it.' "

Johnson also talked many times about a woman who telephoned her bank to arrange for the disposition of a thousand-dollar bond: "The clerk asked her, 'Madam, is the bond for redemption or conversion?' There was a long pause, and then the woman said, 'Well, am I talking to the First National Bank or the First Baptist Church?' "

As he traveled the country in 1964, Johnson usually found he could cite encouraging economic statistics even as he inveighed against the specter of poverty. Of course, he had a story to go with the statistics:

"Almost every day brings more good news about the economy. Some economists and some critics have reacted like the young father who was stationed in the Mediterranean. He received a telegram from his mother-in-law which read, 'Twins arrived tonight. More by mail.' He was surprised, and so have many people been surprised by what this free enterprise system is doing. It seems there is always more by mail."

Very occasionally, LBJ would suggest that one could get too much of a good thing, as he tried to illustrate with a tale involving Senator Tom Connally of Texas:

"The Senator was speaking down home and he started out talking about the beautiful piny woods of East Texas, and then he moved on through the bluebonnets and out to the plains and down through the hill country to the Gulf Coast and then he got back to the piny woods and started all over again. . . .

"And this little old fellow rose up in the back of the room and yelled out: 'The next time you pass Lubbock, how about letting me off?' "

The President's humor invariably was folksy, often involving himself or his family or some identifiable episode in his life. Addressing members of the Georgia legislature at a breakfast in Atlanta, he reported: "I had the great privilege last year . . . of having your Governor in my home. He and Senator Russell and Bobby Russell and Mr. [J. B.] Fuqua came down and stirred up my deer and chased them around for two or three days. I hope the Governor has a better aim in Georgia than he has in Texas."

At the fiftieth anniversary convention of the Amalgamated

Clothing Workers, Johnson declared: "As the husband of a wife and the father of two active daughters, I am happy to have this opportunity to meet with representatives of the clothing industry to which I owe much—literally. In the twenty-nine years of married life, I have learned that if clothes don't make the man, they certainly can break him."

In addressing Democratic gatherings, the President, projecting his own concern that regional prejudice might hurt him, often called for "a truly national party which is stranger to no region, an open party which is closed to none, which knows no color, knows no creed, knows no North, no South, no East, no West." On other occasions, however, he poked fun at such points-of-the-compass references:

"Of course, I do not want to go as far as the Georgia politician who shouted from the stump in the heat of debate, 'My fellow citizens, I know no North, I know no South, I know no East, I know no West.' A barefooted, freckle-faced boy shouted out from the audience, saying, 'Well, you better go back and study some geography!' "

Most of Johnson's stories were harmless and lacked a living target, which was appropriate because he had very limited tolerance for pointed humor at his own expense. This was illustrated by a mortifying experience that Pierre Salinger innocently brought upon himself.

During a visit to the LBJ Ranch, the press secretary was convulsed by an Art Buchwald column that zeroed in on some of the Administration's foibles, and he urged Johnson to read it. A few hours later Salinger encountered the President again and inquired if he'd read the column. LBJ said he had not yet done so. Lunchtime arrived and the President, his family and a group of White House aides, including Salinger, gathered in the dining room.

"Somebody get me the *Herald Tribune,*" Johnson ordered. "Pierre [pronounced "peer"] tells me that Art Buchwald has written a very funny column today."

The newspaper was brought to LBJ, who handed it down the table to Salinger.

"Read it out loud, Pierre, so we can all hear it," the President directed.

Salinger's reading was greeted by a heavy silence. When he was finished, Johnson looked around the table and inquired, "Any of you-all think that's funny?"

No one said a word.

"Pierre," the President continued, "I want to tell you a little story. Some years back, Drew Pearson was writin' a lot of ugly things about George Smathers. And each time, George would call up his brother Frank down in Florida and complain about the terrible things Pearson was doin' to him. But Frank kept tellin' him, 'Don't pay any attention, George. Nobody reads Drew Pearson anyway.' Then one day Pearson wrote a column about Frank Smathers. In no time at all, Frank was on the phone complainin' to George. You see, Pierre, it all depends on whose ox gets gored!"

LBJ could live without Buchwald's jibes. He craved affection and applause. On May 22 he reaped both as he visited the University of Michigan campus to deliver what became known as his "Great Society" speech. Afterward, as Air Force One left Willow Run Airport for Washington, the President stood in the aisle, disdaining both seat and seat belt in his eagerness to solicit our reaction.

"You had the crowd with you all the way, Mr. President," he was told by Charles Roberts of *Newsweek,* who added that the speech had been interrupted by applause twelve times.

"There were more than that," Johnson insisted, and sent for Jack Valenti. "How many applauses were there?" he asked his aide.

"Fourteen," Valenti replied.

We checked the markings Jack had made on his copy of the speech text and discovered he had included the cheers when the President was introduced and when he sat down.

Exactly a week later LBJ was cast in another applause-getting role as the conquering hero returning home in triumph. Forty years after graduating from Johnson City High School as president of his class of six, Johnson was back to address the thirty graduates of 1964.

While thunder crashed outside the steamy hall, where neighbors and friends sat in shirtsleeves waving makeshift fans, his arrival was a signal for everyone to stand and cheer. The President, a white carnation in the lapel of his brown suit, seemed almost sheepish as an Air Force band struck up "Hail to the Chief!"

6

"One Foot Wrong"

"I don't expect to muffle criticism," said Lyndon Johnson early in the 1964 election year. "Every one of you say we invite free speech in our country and we want free speech and we want criticism—don't you? Every one of you do. But there is a limit to how much you want, and there is a ceiling on how much is good for you."

When Johnson made that statement, on April 27, he was smarting because of the first truly bad publicity he had received as President—the lively accounts of his devil-may-care driving on a Texas highway. He never denied the reports, for the simple reason that they were essentially accurate. Instead he chose to regard them as criticism rather than straightforward reporting.

To LBJ, the speeding stories were prime examples of what he had in mind when, in his brooding session with Eugene Patterson, he had said, "You just wait and see what happens when I put one foot wrong." He had made his errant step, and he was blaming us for it, as if it had been our foot on the accelerator.

A thicker-skinned politician would have known his world had not ended on that Easter holiday in Texas, as the election returns were to prove, but Lyndon Johnson's skin was thin and sensitive so he sometimes acted as if he thought it had.

Ironically, the new President already had weathered unwelcomed publicity about the Bobby Baker case that had a potential for being far more damaging to him than any lark on the highway. Johnson did no carping in connection with Baker, however; it was a subject he preferred to ignore whenever possible.

Robert G. Baker, whose name appears nowhere in Johnson's memoirs, had been LBJ's "strong right arm, the last man I see at night, the first one I see in the morning"—in other words, an early Jack Valenti who was not burdened with Valenti's scruples.

Baker's wheeling and dealing as Johnson's personally anointed secretary to the Senate's Democratic majority had ended with Baker's resignation while under investigation by the Senate Rules Committee. Johnson then was Vice-President and many of us had wondered if the inquiry might ultimately prompt John Kennedy to dump LBJ from the 1964 ticket. While Kennedy lived, however, there was absolutely no testimony to connect his Vice-President with Baker's questionable maneuverings.

On the day of Kennedy's death, Rules Committee investigators obtained at least a whisper along such lines from a Washington insurance man, Don B. Reynolds, who was not told of the assassination and thus did not know he was giving testimony about the new President.

Reynolds contended that after he wrote a $100,000 life insurance policy on Johnson's life in 1957, Walter Jenkins had phoned and made arrangements for Reynolds to buy $1,208 of advertising time from the Johnson family's KTBC-TV in Austin. The insurance man called it a kickback. Reynolds also testified that at Bobby Baker's suggestion he had provided a $585.75 stereo music set for installation in LBJ's home.

On January 23, 1964 Johnson appeared in the White House Fish Room, so named because FDR had kept tropical fish there, and read a statement on troubled relations with Panama. It was not a press conference but the UPI's Merriman Smith, apparently at the prompting of a presidential aide, asked if Johnson would entertain "a question or so," such as, "How do you think things are going up on the Hill?" The President responded with a brief discussion of the status of administration legislation, then volunteered his first and only substantive statement about the Baker case:

"You are also writing some other stories, I think about an in-

surance policy that was written on my life some seven years ago
and I am still here. The company in which Mrs. Johnson and my
daughters have a majority interest, along with some other stockholders, were somewhat concerned when I had a heart attack in
1955 and in 1957 they purchased insurance on my life made
payable to the company. And the insurance premiums were never
included as a business expense, but they thought that was good
business practice in case something happened to me so Mrs. Johnson and the children wouldn't have to sell their stock on the open
market and lose control of the company. That insurance was
purchased here in Washington and on a portion of the premiums
paid Mr. Don Reynolds got a small commission. Mr. George
Sampson, the general agent for the Manhattan Insurance Company, handled it and we have paid some $78,000 in premiums up
to date and there is another $11,800 due next month which the
company will probably pay to take care of that insurance.

"There is a question which also has been raised about a gift of a
stereo set that an employee of mine made to me and Mrs. Johnson. That happened some two years later, some five years ago.
The Baker family gave us a stereo set. We used it for a period and
we had exchanged gifts before. He was an employee of the public
and had no business pending before me and was asking for nothing and so far as I know expected nothing in return any more than
I did when I had presented him with gifts.

"I think that that is about all I know that is going on on the
Hill, but I hope that covers it rather fully. That is all I have to say
about it and all I know about it."

Johnson's statement fell far short of covering rather fully the
questions that had been raised by Reynolds. The President told us
almost more than we wanted to know about the insurance policy
without mentioning the alleged kickback. He said nothing to remotely suggest there was any link between his stereo set and Don
Reynolds.

The President turned and left the room before any of us could
ask questions going to the heart of the matter. He never publicly
discussed the kickback allegation at any time. Neither was he ever
interrogated about the leaking of derogatory information about
Reynolds from Pentagon personnel files that were supposed to be

secret. When Clark Mollenhoff of the Des Moines *Register* and *Tribune* asked at a press conference, nine days after the Fish Room scene, if LBJ thought Walter Jenkins should testify under oath, the President replied:

"The general question was raised with me at my last meeting. I spoke with candor and frankness on that subject and about all I knew about it. I said then that I did not plan to make more statements on it, and I did not."

Although reporters made several subsequent efforts to question Johnson about the Baker investigation, he was not responsive. Baker eventually went to prison and Johnson went about his business. The President's transparently slick bit of business in the Fish Room worked as he intended, aided no doubt by a general reluctance to bear down hard on a man who had come so recently to the highest office because of a jarring national tragedy.

In this instance, LBJ was in no position to complain about the conduct of the press corps. The Baker investigation, in fact, was the only major news story involving Johnson's sensitivities about which he did not complain. Where Bobby Baker was concerned, silence was LBJ's golden rule.

As springtime approached and the "kickback" headlines faded, the President's spirits soared, to the point where I reported he appeared to "have spring fever—rarely has he displayed such high good humor." More than the weather was involved, of course. He won his battle with the rail negotiators and he was winning on Capitol Hill. There was a hint of roses in the air.

When William Thatcher, president of the Farmers' Union Grain Terminal Association of St. Paul, dropped around for a chat, Johnson puffed up with pride as Thatcher told him in our presence: "We were started on a depression. You have saved our whole Northwest area from a depression."

Smiling and noting our poised pencils, Johnson prompted, "Go ahead."

"Boy," exclaimed the farm leader, "what a victory you are going to have this fall!"

When officials of the American League handed the President a season baseball pass, he playfully boasted: "I've got a good arm. I'm an old first baseman."

"Left-handed?" asked a photographer.

"No, right," grinned LBJ. "I wouldn't want to do anything imprudent."

A week later, with the weather warming, Johnson acknowledged that "on beautiful days like this, the President and schoolboys have a hard time staying indoors." He scheduled as many ceremonies as possible for the Rose Garden.

Brighter skies in Washington meant even balmier weather in the hill country where, as the President enthused at one point, "the cows are fat, the grass is green, the river's full, and the fish are floppin'." A few days before Easter he and the family headed west to heed a friend's admonition that LBJ liked to recall: "The best way to fertilize your land is with the owner's own tracks."

Once ensconced at the ranch, Johnson seemed bent on continuing to extend to the press corps the bountiful hospitality we had enjoyed at Christmas. There were visits to Cousin Oreole, lectures on animal husbandry and discourses on the cultivation of bluebonnets, the Texas state flower and one of the springtime glories of the hill country.

Bluebonnets thrive, the President explained, in a chalky white soil of the type found near the LBJ Ranch. The soil's color, he related, accounted for the name given neighboring Blanco County, which has Johnson City as its county seat.

"Down here it's called 'weak' country," he said, explaining that it produced a weak strain of grass. "You'll hear cattlemen say, 'I've got strong country.' That means the soil is darker and produces a strong grass."

A heifer raised in Blanco County, when ready for shipment, might weigh about 450 pounds, he reported, whereas a similar animal raised in a neighboring county with "strong" soil might hit the scales at 500 pounds.

Driving up to Cousin Oreole's door, he honked and she emerged in a yellow coat. The President was effusive in complimenting her on the garment. Winking at photographers, Ms. Bailey countered, "You know who gave it to me."

It was a time to survey the family's extensive properties, to grab the microphone from the dashboard of his Lincoln and call Mrs. Johnson with messages like, "Bird, tell your foreman he's got a water leak up here." Time to enjoy the country meals he savored

1. LBJ holds a walking press conference, August 20, 1964. (Abbie Rowe, courtesy National Capital Parks)

2. The President and Mrs. Johnson enjoying a swim at the LBJ Ranch.
(Y. R. Okamoto, courtesy the Lyndon Baines Johnson Library)

3. With LBJ in the "clean room" at Cape Kennedy, inspecting a Mars-bound Mariner spacecraft on September 11, 1964. (O. J. Rapp, courtesy the Lyndon Baines Johnson Library)

4. LBJ with his newborn grandson, Patrick Lyndon Nugent, 1967. (Y. R. Okamoto, courtesy the Lyndon Baines Johnson Library)

5. I'm asking the President a question at a press conference in the East Room, 1966. (Abbie Rowe, courtesy National Capital Parks)

6. Patrick Lyndon Nugent fooling around with the telephone and the safety of all Americans while Grandpa's back is turned, October 1968. (Y. R. Okamoto, courtesy the Lyndon Baines Johnson Library)

—ranch-style beans and deer sausage so peppery his wife could not abide it.

"Bird's an East Texan," the President once told Phil Potter. "All she likes is pork chops and candied yams."

She also enjoyed sitting by a roaring log fire, while he would hurry to open the door.

It was a comfortable marriage, however, with each partner having qualities that complemented the other's. After twenty-nine years together, the Johnsons still liked to drive into the hills and watch sunsets, sometimes holding hands like young lovers.

"I outmarried myself," he often boasted.

Also much a part of ranch life were the two daughters and a succession of beaux.

"Lynda Bird is so smart that she'll be able to make a living for herself," said Johnson. "And Luci Baines is so appealing and feminine that there will always be some man around waiting to make a living for her."

Contented was the word for Lyndon Johnson on that Easter weekend. He often stated, and believed, that he drew strength from his native soil, that a few days at the ranch offered the best of all tonics. Little realizing what was in store for him, Johnson invited the entire press contingent inside the guarded gates after Easter services for conversation, draft beer and, it turned out, a bit of driving.

"When you read a bad editorial," he told the assemblage, "you want to come back here where the deer and the antelope play."

Everyone was in a holiday mood and the President was at his most expansive. Piling a group of reporters into his Lincoln, he invited the rest to tag along in other ranch vehicles for an area tour. One newsman, an antique car buff, got the keys to an ancient fire engine that was kept on the place. He quickly discovered he could not keep pace.

One of the reporters who went off with LBJ gave a graphic account of the adventure to attentive colleagues in the tap room of the Headliners Club after returning to Austin that evening. As a consequence, a newsman who had missed the fun wrote a "speeding story" that, although mild enough compared to some that followed, was enough to move the episode out of the off-the-record category and send others scurrying after more vivid facts.

George Reedy, the recently installed press secretary, was asked about the initial account, which had become the talk of the press corps. Reedy's response was classic:

"Your question is assuming some conclusions based upon some facts of which I am unaware. As a casual newspaper reader, I have some awareness of the stories to which you have alluded. As I can gather from these stories, I know of no particular occasion that could be identified from them on which I was present. Consequently, I cannot draw conclusions on a series of facts which are not known to me."

At a news conference the following Saturday, Johnson was asked about published reports "that you hit speeds of perhaps up to ninety miles an hour in a zone with a speed limit of seventy miles an hour." The questioner said the reports were causing "concern that you are putting yourself in danger."

"I am unaware that I have ever driven past seventy," the President bristled. Only his listeners smiled.

If the affair had ended there, Johnson would have fared quite well. Two days later, however, *Time* reached newsstands with a detailed account that began:

A cream-colored Lincoln Continental driven by the President of the U.S. flashed up a long Texas hill, swung into the left lane to pass two cars poking along under 85 m.p.h., and thundered on over the crest of the hill—squarely into the path of an oncoming car. The President charged on, his paper cup of Pearl beer within easy sipping distance. The other motorist veered off the paved surface to safety on the road's shoulder. Groaned a passenger in the President's car when the ride was over: "That's the closest John McCormack has come to the White House yet." [As House Speaker, McCormack was next in line for the presidency in the absence of a Vice-President.]

Time reported that Hearst's Marianne Means, "her baby-blue eyes fastened on Johnson, cooed: 'Mr. President, you're fun.'" The magazine went on to recount that LBJ ran out of beer "and took off at speeds up to 90 m.p.h. to get some more." It said that when a passenger complained about the speed the President "took one hand from the wheel, removed his five-gallon hat and flopped it on the dashboard to cover the speedometer."

Johnson, who was trying to create for himself an image of prudence and caution, especially because it seemed likely that the "reckless" Barry Goldwater would be his November opponent, strove mightily to make light of the horrible publicity by masking his fury with humor.

As guest of honor at the annual dinner of the Gridiron Club of Washington and its membership of press corps bureau chiefs and reporters, he mused, "I don't know whether a fellow is safer being a guest of the newspaper people or whether he is worse off having them as his guests."

To the Chamber of Commerce convention: "Everybody is going to walk, at the LBJ, from now on, and I am going to do what Lady Bird tells me, and we are going to make everybody drink nothing but pure rain water and Pepsi-Cola."

Toasting Mayor Willy Brandt of West Berlin: "Mayor Brandt, when Bismarck said, 'We Germans fear God but nothing else in the world,' I can only conclude that there were no magazines in Germany in those days."

The plain truth is that Johnson was a very careless driver, mostly because his zest for conversation distracted him from his duties behind the wheel. He would crane his neck to address back-seat passengers and let the car wander into the left-hand lane.

Karl Bauman of the AP was with the President and Mrs. Johnson on a bumpy, twisting drive around one of their outlying ranches months after the Easter incident when LBJ, who had been trying to spot deer and wild turkeys in the brush, announced, "Bird has more confidence in my driving now."

"Lyndon," she said, "I have confidence in your driving when you're not conducting a scenic tour."

I was seated behind Johnson in his Lincoln convertible one afternoon when the hazards of riding with him became manifest. John Connally was in the front with the President and Alvin Spivak of UPI was beside me. LBJ had recently installed eight-foot-high wire chain fences around some of his ranch fields, to keep selected deer and other wild life separated, and we were making an inspection tour.

Johnson repeatedly looked back at Al and me as he talked until, suddenly, a sixth sense prompted me to retract the elbow I had draped over the door. With a crunch, the car veered into one of the fences, raking its side from front to rear. The President turned the wheel and drove on, continuing to talk without interruption as though nothing had happened. None of the rest of us said a word to suggest that we'd even noticed he had had an accident. The "emperor" was fully clothed.

On public highways Johnson always tried to drive under seventy after his unpleasant Easter experience, and speeding on ranch roads was next to impossible. Occasionally, however, a speed-related story would get into print, open old wounds, and sometimes produce amusing aftereffects.

An AP photographer, positioned outside the ranch gate to follow LBJ to church on a Sunday, got up to eighty-five miles an hour in a vain effort to catch up with Johnson—a fact we reported. The White House Press Office duly noted that we had not accused the President of driving that fast (although privately we assumed he had been speeding) and asked the Secret Service to do a time-and-distance calculation. I confess most of us were a bit skeptical when an agent subsequently reported that Johnson's average speed had been forty-two miles an hour!

A New York reporter, who had been recuperating in his hotel room since falling down the press plane ramp upon our arrival in Texas, was called by one of his editors who demanded to know why he had not filed a speeding story like ours.

"Hell, the story isn't true," the newsman replied.

"How do you know it isn't true?"

"Because I was in the back seat!"

Additional unwanted publicity, albeit on a matter far less cosmic than the President's driving habits, had LBJ fuming afresh less than a month after his Easter outing.

Posing in the Rose Garden with members of a task force that hoped to promote increased foreign investment in American-issued common stocks, Johnson began romping with Luci's beagle puppies, Him and Her. Seducing them with sugar-coated vitamin pills, he rolled them over on the grass, scratched their stomachs, then hoisted each in turn by the ears. While they yelped, LBJ joked:

"You see what a dog will do when he gets in a crowd of bankers?"

"Why did you do that?" asked a reporter.

"To make Him bark," said Johnson. "It's good for him. And, if you've ever followed dogs, you like to hear them yelp."

Doug Cornell of the AP, who had begun covering the White House during Franklin D. Roosevelt's first term, wrote an account of the episode that was widely published and inspired protests against the President's behavior from some humane societies.

An aggrieved Johnson complained the following day that he'd only done it at the request of an Associated Press photographer, adding that Cornell then "wrote a story about my being inhumane." Neither statement was correct. Johnson pulled the dogs' ears without prompting and Cornell's article had been a job of straight reporting, not an accusation.

Although Johnson took the affair very seriously, nationally the dog caper aroused more mirth than outrage. The New York *Daily News* editorialized that LBJ "didn't really intend any cruelty to dumb animals. . . . He thought they were a couple of senators." Mrs. Dorothy Lutz presented Johnson with a life membership in the Vanderburgh County (Indiana) Humane Society and declared: "I've seen men pinch their wives, and I think the women enjoy it. If the dogs get used to a few tugs, chances are they like it too." Beagles were held up for the President's admiration wherever he went and "Beagles for Johnson" clubs were established. Then someone cited Proverbs 26:17: "He that passeth by, and meddleth with strife belonging not to him, is like one that taketh a dog by the ears."

We tried to persuade George Reedy to tell us how the White House mail was running on the subject, but he declined.

"You are robbing yourself of one of the great weapons of political bunkum," a newsman suggested.

"I am happy to forgo that weapon," replied the erudite press secretary, "along with the crossbow and the arbalest."

As long as Johnson remained in office, he harked back with regularity to the great beagle flap and invariably mentioned Cornell, the AP or both. Within a month he had discovered a method of lifting the beagles by the ears without producing a yelp. After demonstrating his technique with Him, he told us:

"He doesn't yelp unless an AP photographer gets too close to him."

At the LBJ Ranch, Johnson once demanded that Cornell pose for a photo while hoisting one of the beagles by the ears. Doug managed it gently and without prompting a yelp.

I doubt that Lyndon Johnson ever forgot an article or broadcast that disturbed him, or the identity of the newsman responsible. Since virtually every White House reporter did something sooner or later that displeased the President, as I had predicted, we learned from experience that he had the memory of an elephant.

One of the women reporters who had been with LBJ on his ill-fated drive was at Andrews Air Force Base to cover his departure on the day Richard Nixon became President. Johnson had always suspected her of tattling on him at the Headliners Club so, as he made his farewells to the assembled reporters and photographers, he kissed her on the cheek and said, with a trace of steel in his voice, "Come down to the ranch sometime and I'll take you for a drive."

Mrs. Johnson knew what she was about when she selected her husband's 1964 Christmas gift. It was a framed quotation of Lincoln's that began:

"If I were to return, much less answer, all the attacks made on me, this shop might as well be closed for any other business."

7

"The Best of All"

Lyndon Johnson sometimes would make statements that most of us considered a bit ridiculous, yet he obviously expected us to accept them at face value. Discussing the 1964 Democratic National Convention, for example, he seemed bent on casting himself as a disinterested bystander, promising to "let the delegates at the convention make their choice freely," then decide upon his own course in the light of their collective decision.

I did not believe, any more than I ever had [Johnson wrote in his memoirs], that the nation would unite indefinitely behind any Southerner. One reason the country could not rally behind a Southern President, I was convinced, was that the metropolitan press of the Eastern seaboard would never permit it. My experience in office had confirmed this reaction.

So he would tell us that he had not made up his mind whether to seek an elected term, then turn around and respond to noisy welcomers at Detroit Metropolitan Airport by declaring, "This welcome moves me to recall an old song, 'Will You Love Me in November as You Do in May?'"

I doubt there was a single reporter in Washington who had the slightest doubt about Johnson's imminent candidacy, and even the President found occasional humor in his performance as Hamlet. In early May, shortly before flying to Atlantic City for a speech in

Convention Hall, where the Democrats would gather in August, he was asked if he saw anything wrong about an article that his questioner planned to write, to the effect that LBJ's appearance would be a sort of dress rehearsal for his acceptance speech.

"Well," said the President, "I would be the last man in the world to show my sensitivity by criticizing a story that had not been written."

Soon after the month of mourning for John Kennedy ended, I began getting queries from newspaper editors about LBJ's likely choice for the vice-presidential nomination. It was a guessing game that would not end until the convention itself.

At Max Freedman's dinner party, before Johnson's mood turned to one of brooding, he had discussed the field of potential running mates before a rapt audience that included Hubert Humphrey. The President mentioned Senators Eugene McCarthy and Thomas Dodd, among others, but said not a word about Humphrey. It was a teasingly cruel performance. One guest has been quoted as saying that LBJ "played Hubert on a pole like a bait with trout."

As weeks passed and no definitive clues were forthcoming, Johnson did nothing to discourage speculation that he was favorably disposed toward Peace Corps Director Sargent Shriver, Governor Edmund G. Brown of California, Mayor Robert F. Wagner of New York, Ambassador Adlai E. Stevenson, Secretary of Defense McNamara, Mike Mansfield, Humphrey, Dodd and McCarthy. Even Attorney General Robert F. Kennedy got an occasional smiling nod.

"Just look what's happened," exclaimed the ambitious Humphrey. "The President sent Bobby Kennedy to the Far East. He sent Sargent Shriver to deliver a message to the Pope. Adlai Stevenson got to escort Mrs. Johnson to a theater in New York. So I asked the President, 'Who's going to enroll Lynda Bird in George Washington University? I'll volunteer!'"

In the eyes of many voters, Robert Kennedy had the strongest emotional claim on the nomination, although few reporters thought he had a chance of getting it unless LBJ found himself backed into a corner. The President's relationship with the younger Kennedy had been strained since 1960 and we could not ignore Johnson's burning desire to outshine the murdered Kennedy, an ambition that could be thwarted were it to appear that he needed the brother at his side if he were to survive politically.

Johnson customarily invoked John Kennedy's memory with reverence, but in private conversation he would aim an occasional jibe at the shade of his predecessor and onetime rival. When discussing his efforts to win enactment of Kennedy's legislative program, for example, LBJ would emphasize that his aim was to write a record in the lawbooks, adding, "I'm not going to build any libraries for myself." Since a fund drive for the Kennedy Library was getting under way, no one could mistake the reference.

LBJ also liked to portray himself as more experienced and knowledgeable about foreign affairs than Kennedy, particularly after reading any critical mention of his own conduct of foreign policy. Johnson would cite his long tenure on the House Armed Services Committee and his collaboration with Eisenhower on decisions involving Lebanon and Korea. He would talk scornfully about Kennedy's reputation for seeking information "from a fifth desk officer" at the State Department instead of going to the top, to Secretary Rusk. Then would come LBJ's clincher: "I appointed Kennedy to the Foreign Relations Committee and he only attended a few meetings."

One of Johnson's White House aides suggested to me that Shriver would make a logical choice for Vice-President because he had a Kennedy connection, as an in-law, without bearing the name. At first blush, it seemed plausible that Shriver might serve as a substitute for Robert Kennedy, and it was known that the President had become friendly with Shriver through Bill Moyers, who technically was "on loan" to Johnson from the Peace Corps. With this in mind, a group of us asked Johnson about Shriver during a relaxed moment aboard Air Force One. Hunching forward in his seat, the President half rose, then grabbed his buttocks and exclaimed:

"Sarge Shriver! Sarge Shriver couldn't find his ass with both hands!"

That was more than enough to convince me that a Kennedy connection was worthless in LBJ's eyes, although I realized he was indulging in Johnsonian hyperbole. I had heard him insist that men as eminent and capable as Shriver were unable to "pour piss from a boot with the instructions written on the heel."

Actually, public opinion polls indicated that Johnson had made himself so pre-eminent on the political scene that any running mate was likely to detract from his strength. He was thus in the enviable position of being able to stand aside from partisan wrangling while ambitious Republicans clawed at each other in the primaries.

"I am a fellow that likes small parties," the President told an impromptu news conference, "and the Republican Party is about the size I like." To the Friendly Sons of St. Patrick he suggested the Democrats were so peaceful that "the Irish may move to the Republican Party where the feuding is really going on." Johnson particularly relished the primary joustings of Barry Goldwater and Nelson Rockefeller, telling a Democratic dinner crowd in Chicago:

"I see by the papers that Barry and Rocky have decided to cut down on their appearances in California. That reminded me of the fellow down in Texas who said to his friend, 'Earl, I am thinking of running for sheriff against Uncle Jim Wilson. What do you think?'

" 'Well,' said his friend, 'it depends on which one of you will see the most people.'

" 'That is what I figure,' said his friend.

" 'If you see the most, Uncle Jim will win. If he sees the most, you will win.' "

With barely restrained glee the President would note that many Republicans had not decided who they wanted as their nominee, adding: "One old man was asked how he was going to vote in the California primary. He said, 'Well, I haven't decided yet, but I will tell you this—when I do make up my mind, I am going to be awfully bitter.' "

Not so amusing to Johnson were the strivings of Governor George C. Wallace of Alabama in the Democratic primaries, although LBJ managed to discount the segregationist Governor's respectable showing in Wisconsin by observing, "Governor Wallace got twenty-five per cent of the votes and seventy-five per cent voted against him."

Just a month before the Democratic Convention, Johnson still was referring to his party's candidate in the third person and talking about campaigning for "the ticket," as though he would do what he could for whatever stranger happened to be favored by the delegates. At another news conference six days later, however, he finally paid obeisance to political realities by setting forth the qualifications he thought were needed by the Democratic vice-presidential candidate:

". . . I think that we want the person that is equipped to handle the duties of the vice-presidency, and the presidency, if that awesome responsibility should ever fall upon him. I think he should be a man that is well received in all the states of the Union among all of our people. I would like to see a man that is experienced in foreign relations and domestic affairs. I would like for him to be a man of the people who felt a compassionate concern for their welfare and who enjoyed public service and was dedicated to it.

"I would like for him to be attractive, prudent and progressive. I would like for him to be one who would work co-operatively with the Congress and the Cabinet and with the President. . . ."

Most of us felt that Hubert Humphrey came closer than any of his potential rivals to meeting Johnson's tests, although his acceptability to the South was open to question. A colleague who presumably had Humphrey in mind rose to ask a question that caused Johnson's hackles to rise:

Q.: Mr. President, I don't mean for this question to be facetious, but in your prescription for a vice-presidential running mate, were you thinking of an ideal, or did you have some living person in mind?

A.: No, I don't have any prescription. I was attempting to be helpful and courteous to one of the questioners. . . . I had prepared no brief on the subject. I tried to be open and frank about it. . . .

The news conference was held in the Oval Office during the noon hour but the real news of the day came shortly after 6 P.M. when the President called the press corps into the Fish Room and read a statement that eliminated from consideration for second place on the Democratic ticket all cabinet members as well as all those who regularly sat with the Cabinet. It was, of course, a transparent maneuver to eliminate Robert Kennedy from contention without seeming to single him out.

"I could have helped you a lot," Kennedy had told Johnson a day earlier when he had gotten the word. Actually, Kennedy's po-

tential value as a running mate had been greatly reduced by the
nomination of Goldwater as the Republican nominee. As Jack
Bell pointed out in *The Johnson Treatment,* the President was
weakest politically in the industrial East when he took office, and
Kennedy was strongest there, but the choice of Goldwater upset
that equation by making Johnson weakest in the South and West
where Kennedy could be of little help.

In *The Vantage Point,* Johnson candidly acknowledged that
other factors also were involved. "John Kennedy and I had
achieved real friendship," he wrote. "I doubt that his brother and
I would have arrived at genuine friendship if we had worked together for a lifetime." And in another passage: "Perhaps his political ambitions were part of the problem. Maybe it was just a matter of chemistry."

The "Bobby problem" had been solved, however crudely, but
LBJ faced yet another dilemma that could not be disposed of readily. In March the *Wall Street Journal* had published a two-part
series detailing what everyone knew, that the Johnsons were a
very wealthy family. No total figure was given for their holdings
but in June the Washington *Star* came up with an educated guess
of nine million dollars. Then, just a week before the Democratic
Convention, *Life* published an estimate of fourteen million dollars. Deeply disturbed, Johnson fumed to a group of us:

"I was swimmin' in the White House pool with those fellows
from *Life* a few weeks ago and we weren't wearin' any suits. But
how in the hell could they claim that my pecker is fourteen inches
long if they didn't actually measure it!"

The President's response was to provide, through George Reedy,
a precise measurement of the family fortune. We were handed
an audit report by Haskins and Sells that showed net assets of
$3,484,098 for LBJ and members of his immediate family. This
remarkably low figure was arrived at by valuing their properties at their original cost, ignoring subsequent large increases in
market value. Republican National Chairman Dean Burch scoffed
that this was "like listing the value of Manhattan Island at twenty-
four dollars."

Meanwhile the charade about LBJ's true intentions—would he
run and who would run with him?—not only continued but
soared to new summits of ridiculousness.

On August 18, six days before the opening gavel of the convention, Johnson told us that he expected to go to Atlantic City on the evening of August 27, his fifty-sixth birthday, "if I go at all." A startled reporter cut in:

Q.: Mr. President, did I understand that you might not go to Atlantic City at all?
A.: No.
Q.: I misunderstood.
A.: Evidently. I didn't say I would, or I wouldn't.
Q.: Will you go, if you are asked?
A.: We will announce that when we know definitely what we are going to do.

In his memoirs Johnson insisted that he was still debating whether to accept the presidential nomination as late as the afternoon of August 25, the second day of the convention. Mrs. Johnson echoed this claim in her published diary. However serious the debate, Johnson was sufficiently resolute by the evening of August 25 to send word secretly to Humphrey, in Atlantic City, that the Minnesotan would be his running mate. Of course, Humphrey could tell no one except his wife.

We were in the President's office the following day when he invited us to join him for another walkathon in the midday sun. The temperature was eighty-nine degrees and the humidity was at least as high. Having traversed all foreseeable rubicons, Johnson was in an exceptionally buoyant mood.

Asked about Barry Goldwater's latest charges against the Administration, LBJ declined to pass judgment on the GOP nominee's probity but allowed, "As a matter of fact, he's conducting himself to suit me right now."

Johnson also reported that the Democratic Convention suited him, although we later learned that he considered it a boring piece of television theater. The President said his Italian-American barber, Steve Martini, had agreed that the keynote address by Rhode Island's Italian-American Senator, John Pastore, was great; "it made him proud to be an American." LBJ was equally impressed, he said, by the decisiveness of Speaker McCormack in dealing, as convention chairman, with a dispute over seating of the Mississippi delegation. He mimicked the Speaker's ma-

chine-gun delivery: "All-those-in-favor-say-aye-all-those-opposed-
no-the-motion-is-carried!"

Disclosing that he had been examined by a panel of physicians
immediately after another recent hike, the President fumbled
around in a jacket pocket and pulled out a much-thumbed piece
of paper.

"Whoops, that's a poll," he announced, adding that he might as
well read it to us anyway. After hearing the tidings recorded on
the paper, some of us wondered if he hadn't pulled out precisely
the document he had been looking for. It reported that Lyndon
Johnson was favored by sixty-six per cent of the women, seventy
per cent of all voters between the ages of twenty-one and thirty-
four, seventy-three per cent of the Catholics, eighty-six per cent of
the blacks, and ninety-seven per cent of the Jews.

As we negotiated lap after lap, our ranks thinned considerably.
A reporter for the Chicago *Sun-Times* dragged himself into the
press room and phoned a half-frantic, half-admiring message to
his bureau chief in Atlantic City:

"He's going around again. Twelfth time. We're dropping like
flies. It's a death march!"

Johnson finally located the medical report, which he no doubt
had ordered with the aim of pre-empting the high ground in an
area where his qualifications might be challenged, because of his
severe heart attack, and read it:

"President Lyndon B. Johnson has no symptoms [*sic*]. His exercise
tolerance continues to be superb. Physical examination, including the
examination of the eyes, lungs, heart, abdomen, lower intestinal tract,
and reflexes, is normal. His blood pressure is normal. . . . There is no
health reason why he should not continue an active vigorous life."

As we neared the end of a record-setting fifteen-lap ordeal—
more than four miles—those of us with deadlines were anxious to
get to the press room and file the real news that LBJ had dropped
toward the end of his loping stroll, that Senators Humphrey and
Dodd were flying down from Atlantic City to exchange ideas, suggestions "and maybe recommendations."

When Johnson had been asked straight out to reveal his vice-
presidential pick, he snapped, "How can I tell you something I
haven't made up my mind about?" A reporter who suggested the

Humphrey visit seemed to point toward the Minnesotan was told, "I wouldn't recommend that you write that unless you want to get way out on a limb." Well, I decided to climb out on the limb with an "urgent" lead that, ignoring Dodd, began:

WASHINGTON, Aug. 26 (AP)—President Johnson, evidently tipping his hand on his choice for a running mate, summoned Hubert Humphrey to the White House this afternoon to exchange views on the vice presidency.

My office called me, in some alarm, an hour later to relay word from Atlantic City that official convention painters had been seen in the basement of Convention Hall lettering "Dodd for Vice President" placards. I recommended that we stick with what I had already reported, and we did, but neither Johnson nor Humphrey did a thing to make the decision easier. Neither was a bit communicative about who, if anyone, had been chosen. Dodd was equally reticent.

About 7 P.M. we were called to the Oval Office where LBJ announced he was inviting us to the second-floor living quarters for drinks and canapés to celebrate his approaching birthday. But we'd have to hurry because—surprise!—he would be flying to Atlantic City in about an hour to personally anoint a running mate.

We did not know it at the time but Johnson had sought advice from Pierre Salinger, who then was serving as an appointed Senator from California, on how to breathe more life into what LBJ thought was a dull Democratic Convention. When Salinger suggested that the President go to Atlantic City a day ahead of schedule and personally end the suspense about the vice-presidential nominee, Johnson agreed with enthusiasm and groused to George Reedy, "Why don't you ever come up with some ideas like that?"

Before we went partying upstairs, there was an Oval Office exchange with the President that sheds light on how his secretive nature inevitably produced credibility problems:

Q.: Privately, before you make any announcement in Atlantic City, will you advise the person whom you will recommend to be your running mate?

A.: I have not gone into that. I have not thought of it. . . . I don't know whether I can reach him.

Q.: You don't know?

Incomprehensibly, in light of Johnson's rather extreme efforts to preserve his secret, he abandoned the game prematurely and impulsively before he ever got to Atlantic City. Before boarding Air Force One at Andrews Air Force Base he walked Humphrey over to a group of reporters who were covering the departure and said, quite casually, "I want you to meet the next Vice-President, Senator Humphrey."

An enlarged press pool already was aboard the plane at the time and we did not learn until we reached Atlantic City that the year's biggest political secret had become public knowledge in a puzzling fashion that never was explained. Along with a lot of delegates who were attending to convention business rather than watching television or listening to the radio, we were among the last to be informed.

As we flew north, however, Johnson invited all of us to crowd into his cabin and join him and Humphrey in watching a flickering television screen as John Connally nominated his long-time Texas friend and mentor for President. A half-hour demonstration and seven seconding speeches ensued, but we were spared most of this as the big jet landed while the festivities were in progress. And still we had not been told about LBJ's choice of Humphrey.

Johnson was escorted to an antechamber in Convention Hall, where he remained while the delegates made him their nominee by acclamation—something even FDR never managed to achieve. Then, in a din of cheers and shouts and hoopla music, the President mounted the rostrum and, doing his best to squeeze every remaining bit of suspense from his announcement, declared that for a running mate he was turning to "the man best qualified to assume the office of President of the United States . . . my close . . . my long-time . . . my trusted colleague [he paused so long at this point that the delegates hooted with laughter] . . . Senator Hubert H. Humphrey [pronounced 'Umphrey'] of Minnesota!"

Weeks earlier, with an eye on Bobby Kennedy, LBJ had rearranged the convention schedule to have the presidential and vice-presidential nominations on the same night and delay until the final day a memorial salute to John F. Kennedy. That his precaution may have been well advised seemed apparent the next evening when Robert Kennedy, tears shining in his eyes, quoted a moving passage from Shakespeare in introducing a film tribute to his brother. Young Kennedy touched off sixteen minutes of sustained applause, a remarkable display of emotion in the absence of bands or organ music to keep the demonstration alive.

The President was not in the hall for the Kennedy program, explaining that he did not want to intrude on a moment that belonged to the Kennedy family. He appeared almost immediately afterward, however, to listen to Humphrey's acceptance address and to deliver his own.

As Johnson left the podium, he was intercepted by Harry Reasoner, then with CBS, who inquired whether LBJ was concerned about the likely election day reaction of some whites to his firm espousal of civil rights legislation, a reaction that had been given the label, "white blacklash."

"Yes," the President responded, "we have concern about what you newspapermen have built up as a backlash by constant repetition." After pausing to frown in the direction of the Convention Hall organ, he declared that polls indicated ten to fifteen per cent of the country's Democratic voters would desert their party because "they may not like the way we spell our names, they may not like some of the programs we pass like taxes or civil rights or nuclear test ban treaty or defense bills."

But, he argued, this was nothing compared to the number of Republicans who would abandon Goldwater—a phenomenon Johnson referred to as "frontlash." Lecturing Reasoner, and a nationwide television audience, he declared:

"So if you're really concerned with lashes, now that you've fairly explored the backlash, let's get into this frontlash and you'll find about one out of every three Republicans have stated that they are part of the frontlash. . . ."

Frontlash was not a figment of Johnson's fertile political mind but a reality among Republicans who had come to fear, during the long season of GOP primaries, that Barry Goldwater might do violence to the Social Security system, dismantle the Tennessee Valley Authority or lob a nuclear bomb into the men's room at the Kremlin.

While Goldwater was being tagged as "trigger happy" by his Republican rivals, Rockefeller and Governor William Scranton of Pennsylvania, Johnson had been building for himself a reputation for prudence and caution. When Castro cut off the water supply to the U.S. base at Guantánamo, LBJ rejected military retaliation in favor of a successful strategy of making the outpost independent of Cuban-supplied water. As he delighted in telling audiences: "We have dealt with the latest challenge and provocation from Havana without sending the Marines to turn on a water faucet. We believed it far wiser to send an admiral to cut the water off. . . ." Many an American wondered what Goldwater would have done in similar circumstances.

More serious, however, was the first major Vietnam-related crisis of Johnson's administration. Barely two weeks before the Democratic Convention, North Vietnamese torpedo boats attacked the destroyer *Maddox* in the Gulf of Tonkin. Again, LBJ's response was a measured one: he dispatched a protest coupled with a warning of retaliation if it happened again.

Privately, the President sometimes seemed even more cautious than in his public actions. To a group of us he expressed off-the-record doubts about the attack itself, declaring, "How can I be sure there were torpedo boats out there? Maybe those radar operators were lookin' at big waves!"

Another attack came two days later, this time on the *Maddox* and the *C. Turner Joy*. Johnson had little choice but to retaliate, on a onetime, tit-for-tat basis. He could not afford to show weakness in the face of those who had dared open fire on Americans in uniform; politically, such a course would have been as disastrous as courting a trigger-happy image for himself.

The President and his men also had been thinking for several weeks about the wisdom of seeking some form of Congressional authorization for American military involvement in Southeast Asia. The Tonkin Gulf attacks provided a tailor-made occasion for Johnson to request, and receive, a broadly phrased resolution "to give convincing evidence to the aggressive Communist nations, and to the world as a whole, that our policy in Southeast Asia will be carried forward—and that the peace and security of the area will be preserved." There were only two "nay" votes in the Senate, none in the House.

The President certainly gave no indication that his decision to seek a resolution involved any agonizing on his part. So far as we could determine at the time, he simply followed his natural inclination to preserve flexibility and protect his options by demanding from Congress sufficient authority to deal with any foreseeable situation.

Of course, Johnson was not thinking about these events on the evening of August 27. Leaving Harry Reasoner, he moved on to his birthday party, a gathering of four thousand in an enormous ballroom. There he found cheers and affection in great measure.

Afterward there were fireworks on the famed boardwalk. Watching from a balcony, LBJ saw three tons of gunpowder ignited to produce his portrait, six hundred feet square, in red, white and blue.

"I've been going to conventions since 1928," the President announced, "and this one is the best of all."

A band struck up "Hello Lyndon," his theme song for the forthcoming campaign. Another tune might have been more appropriate: "I Did It My Way."

8

"One Great Democratic Tent"

Lyndon Johnson was up early the morning after the Atlantic City birthday bash. With Hubert Humphrey in tow, he encountered Katharine Graham, publisher of the Washington *Post* and widow of one of the President's good friends, and impulsively invited her to join them aboard Air Force One. Pleased at what she took to be an offer of a ride home, Mrs. Graham went along. Only after the big jet was airborne did she learn they were bound for Texas, not Washington.

Making do with the wrong clothes for ranch living, Mrs. Graham got a rich taste of life with LBJ: a mammoth birthday barbecue in Stonewall, non-stop chatter by her host, tours of the alien countryside, and a look at Humphrey trying to smile for photographers while perched gingerly atop a Tennessee walking horse.

While five thousand neighbors were consuming six thousand pounds of beef, Johnson strode into Stonewall's rodeo ring to deliver his first speech of the 1964 campaign, a rambling oration in which he endorsed peace and declared that, as a candidate, "we will not indulge in any fear or any smear." Actually, appeals to the many voters who were fearful of what a President Goldwater might do were to lie at the very heart of his electioneering.

"Men worry about heart attacks," he would tell us, clutching his chest. "Women worry about cancer of the tit." A forefinger would be extended to jab at the breast of his nearest listener. "But everybody worries about war and peace. Everything else is chicken shit."

Traditionally, Democratic presidential candidates have launched their campaigns in Detroit on Labor Day. But when LBJ followed past practice, his press secretary declared with a straight face, "I'm not labeling this a campaign trip." The President, it was argued, was bound for a holiday civic meeting sponsored by his good friends in organized labor. So Johnson appeared before massed thousands to deliver a "non-partisan" address in which he emphasized Goldwater's call for loosening controls over the use of nuclear weapons, saying: ". . . I am not the first President to speak here in Cadillac Square, and I do not intend to be the last. Make no mistake, there is no such thing as a conventional nuclear weapon."

Three days later fear again was his keynote at a Democratic dinner in Harrisburg, Pennsylvania:

"There are abroad in this responsible land reckless factions, contemptuous toward the will of majorities; callous toward the plight of minorities; arrogant toward allies; belligerent toward adversaries; careless toward peace. . . .

"They demand that you choose a doctrine that is alien to America—that would lead to a tragic convulsion in our foreign relations; a doctrine that flaunts the unity of our society and searches for scapegoats among our people. It is a doctrine that invites extremism to take over our land."

The President was invoking memories of the best-remembered passage in Goldwater's acceptance speech: "Let me remind you that moderation in the pursuit of justice is no virtue, and I would remind you that extremism in the defense of liberty is no vice."

The Harrisburg speech was something of an autumn phenomenon because it was a campaign text that Johnson actually read in full. More often he spoke extemporaneously, customarily making passionate references to a magic button that could be used by a President to unleash nuclear war. The button was mythical but it dramatized a point that invariably drew a receptive response from Johnson's audiences:

". . . You will decide which thumb you expect to be in the vicinity of that button. You will decide which voice [sic] you want to pick up that 'hot line' if Moscow calls."

Responsibility in the conduct of government was the winning issue for LBJ, but he did not want reporters putting the words into his mouth. A newsman noted at an August press conference that Johnson had "mentioned responsibility in government a great deal" and asked if that would be a campaign issue. "No," Johnson replied, "I had not felt that I was overstressing any particular thing, and I had not intended to indicate that." Of course not. But by September he was telling a crowd in Hartford:

". . . I want to talk today about what I know is on your minds and what I believe is in your hearts—and that is responsibility.

"Say what they will, change their stands all they wish, no partisans can conceal the issue before America this year because that issue is responsibility."

As he traveled the country Johnson operated without the help of an appointed campaign manager. He never got around to naming one because he did not have to; the campaign manager was the candidate himself. LBJ was mindful not only of large issues but of the nuts and bolts of politics, as he demonstrated with lines like this: "I want to conclude by reminding you that you still have three more days to register."

Johnson also took pains not to neglect the memory of John F. Kennedy, usually coupling talk about "the button" with a recollection of Kennedy's conduct during the war-threatening Cuban missile crisis of two years earlier: "I saw the generals with all their stars, and the admirals with all their braid, and the Secretary of State with a long record of diplomatic performance behind him . . . and the Secretary of Defense, the former manager of the Ford Motor Company, at a salary of more than half a million dollars a year that he gave up to serve his country. But the coolest man in that room was at the head of the table, John Fitzgerald Kennedy.

"I never left my wife and daughters in the morning knowing whether I would see them that night, because those missiles were about to become operational. But I saw those two men [Kennedy and Khrushchev] . . . eyeball to eyeball, with their knife right on each other's ribs and never quivering and never moving until Mr. Khrushchev picked up his missiles and put them on his ships and took them back home.

"We have much to remember, much to be thankful for, and all of our lives will be better because he [Kennedy, of course] passed our way."

In the months before he died, Kennedy had deepened American involvement in Southeast Asia, increasing the corps of U.S. advisers in South Vietnam and inching them closer to a combat role, although near the very end he sometimes seemed to be having some second thoughts. Vietnam was not a significant campaign issue because, if anything, the Republican nominee favored even greater military help for the Saigon government. Vietnam was of concern to the voters, however, and Johnson addressed the subject in his speech at the Stonewall barbecue:

". . . I have had advice to load our planes with bombs and to drop them on certain areas that I think would enlarge the war and escalate the war, and result in our committing a good many American boys to fighting a war that I think ought to be fought by the boys of Asia to help protect their own land.

"And for that reason, I haven't chosen to enlarge the war. Nor have I chosen to retreat and turn it over to the Communists. Those are two alternatives that we have to face up to.

"The third alternative is neutralization in Vietnam. . . . But there is no country that is willing to do that, that we know of, so neutralization is not very practical at this stage of the game. . . .

"The fourth alternative is to do what we are doing, to furnish advice, give counsel, express good judgment, give them trained counselors, and help them with equipment to help themselves. We are doing that. . . ."

Periodically Johnson would express anew his apparent conviction that Americans should not assume a combat role in Vietnam. Privately, he would cite advice he said he had heard from General Douglas MacArthur: "Son, don't you ever get tied down in a land war in Asia." But then he would go out and make a speech that could be interpreted differently, as in Manchester, New Hampshire:

"In my country we are very proud of what we call the Texas Rangers. Sometimes when we have a little row or misunderstanding in our country, they call out a Ranger.

"One of our old cowpuncher friends took some cattle up to Kansas City to sell, and one of the fellows out in the stockyards said to him, while they were waiting for the bidders to come in,

'Please tell me what is really the difference between a sheriff and a Texas Ranger?' The old man . . . ran his hand through his hair and deliberated, and he said, 'Well, a Ranger is one that when you plug him, when you hit him, he just keeps coming.'

"And we must let the rest of the world know that we . . . have the will and the determination, and if they ever hit us it is not going to stop us—we are just going to keep coming."

One thing Johnson tried not to do during the campaign was make any direct reference to his opponent. In fact he sought to avoid applying harsh words to Goldwater, even when he did not mention him by name. Sometimes LBJ slipped up, however, as was the case after the GOP candidate proclaimed the Administration to be "soft on Communism." Johnson told a news conference: "I see in the papers—that is the only information that I have—that the new and frightening voice of the Republican Party is merely trying out this charge at the moment to see if it works. On that basis, my own advice would be to drop it." Then he caught himself and, although using words that actually sharpened his thrust, pretended to absolve Goldwater of responsibility by suggesting the accusation "was the product of some third-string speech writer and accidentally got into the public print without prudent or careful screening."

The President's desire to avoid direct attacks on Goldwater was dramatized for me when he addressed the September convention of the United Steelworkers. Encouraged no doubt by an enthusiastic reception, Johnson made an impromptu change in one of his standard speech lines that usually went like this: "Any jackass can kick a barn down. It takes a carpenter to build one." On this occasion he said, "You know it takes a man who loves his country to build a house, instead of a raving, ranting demagogue who wants to tear one down."

I was in the motorcade pool that was supposed to follow LBJ to the small Atlantic City airport, where we would watch him board a helicopter for the flight to Washington. When we got there, however, Jack Valenti and others began waving for us to leave our cars, which were going to take us back to the press room at Convention Hall.

"The President wants you to ride back with him," Valenti announced. Once we were settled in the tiny but comfortable cabin, we learned why.

"You-all notice that in the speech back there I didn't say any-thing mean about Goldwater," the President began. "I talked about 'ravin', rantin' demagogues,' *plural*. I wasn't referrin' to any single individual. I just thought you-all might have misunder-stood."

We did not argue with him. Instead, when we got back to the White House, we reported Johnson's claim to George Reedy, who went to the West Wing basement and listened to a tape recording of the speech. Reedy returned with a brief message: "He said 'demagogue.' "

It was during the long chopper ride from Atlantic City that I got my first and only stock tip from a President. Johnson had recently appointed a prestigious board of directors for the Com-munications Satellite Corporation and visions of space age com-munications had captured his imagination.

"Put every penny you can get your hands on into Com-munications Satellite stock, even if you have to borrow," he ad-vised. "It's gonna go up and up and up!"

I did not heed this wisdom but I did relay Johnson's tip to Bob Clark of ABC, who nearly doubled his money in a few weeks' time.

During most of September, Johnson emphasized speaking ap-pearances that he could claim were non-political, which presuma-bly is one reason he wanted to avoid direct assaults on his oppo-nent. The President planned a three-stage campaign for which he had a shorthand description: "Inform, convert, agitate." Septem-ber was the month for informing, by his lights, although to most of us it was high-powered campaigning no matter what he called it. This was to be followed by a nationwide search for converts and, finally, a period of agitation designed to bring voter interest to a peak and motivate the eligibles to get to the polls on election day.

Early in September, Johnson told a news conference: "We have a job to do here and we are going to try to do that first. When, as, and if we can we will make as many appearances as we think we can without neglecting the interests of the nation." So three days later he was in Cadillac Square exhorting the union faithful.

Some of LBJ's forays undeniably were non-political, at least to the extent that any campaigning incumbent can go anywhere and do anything in the guise of a non-partisan.

After Hurricane Dora hit coastal sections of Florida and Georgia, Johnson set out on less than an hour's notice to get a firsthand look. Because there was not time to charter an airliner for the press, we all got aboard Air Force One. For those seeking jet-speed thrills, it was an exciting trip. We seemed almost to skim the waves as we flew close offshore in the Jacksonville area. When we landed, Douglas Kiker, then with the *Herald Tribune,* heralded the achievement by shouting, "First stop is the laundry!"

Johnson also found a dam to dedicate, in Oklahoma, and visited with the folks at the Oklahoma State Fair while he was in the general neighborhood. At the Fair entrance, he startled reporters and bodyguards alike by vaulting into the saddle of a palomino quarter horse that galloped briskly around in front of several thousand spectators while the President kept one hand on the reins and, with the other, waved his Texas hat in the air triumphantly, Buffalo Bill-style.

One clearly non-political event in September was the Washington visit of Manlio Brosio, an Italian diplomat who recently had been named Secretary General of the North Atlantic Treaty Organization. But even in this instance LBJ was able to capitalize politically on the occasion. Wearing his presidential hat, Johnson whisked Brosio halfway across the country to visit the underground nerve center of the Strategic Air Command near Omaha, emphasizing in the process, perhaps with more subtlety than was his custom, the campaign issue of control over nuclear weapons.

Shortly before the Omaha trip, Johnson was disturbed and angered by the Very Reverend Francis B. Sayre, Jr., grandson of Woodrow Wilson and dean of the Washington [Episcopal] Cathedral. Discussing Johnson and Goldwater from his pulpit, Dean Sayre told his congregation and, through widely published news accounts, the nation:

"This summer we beheld a pair of gatherings at the summit of political power, each of which was completely dominated by one man; the one a man of dangerous ignorance and devastating uncertainty, the other a man whose public house is splendid in its every appearance but whose private lack of ethic must inevitably introduce termites at the very foundation.

"The electorate of this mighty nation is left homeless, then, by such a pair of nominees. It knows not where to turn, stares fascinated at the forces that have produced such a choice—frustration and a federation of hostilities in the one party; and, in the other, behind a goodly façade, only cynical manipulation of power. . . ."

Fuming, LBJ blamed the cleric's harsh attack on his brother, Sam Houston Johnson. During an Air Force One flight he told us that Dean Sayre was "my brother's confessor," and that Sam Houston must have "filled him full of nonsense about me." He suggested the brother had done so during an illness, which most of us interpreted as a reference to Sam Houston's recurrent battles with alcohol.

"My brother has the finest political mind in the family," said the President, but he added that sickness prevented him from using his talents to the fullest. Suggesting his brother was an ingrate, LBJ declared, "I've spent more than half a million dollars on that man for doctors and hospitals and other expenses, tryin' to take care of him."

The President apparently both enjoyed and feared alcohol. His father had been a drinking man and he also had the example of Sam Houston, who wrote in *My Brother Lyndon:*

Lyndon sometimes objected to certain aspects of my daddy's life style—drinking, for example. My daddy, being a state legislator, would frequently meet some of his political cronies at the saloon and spend a few hours there discussing the latest developments at the state capitol. Well, that was what Lyndon objected to: Old Demon Rum.

Lyndon Johnson, when he was drinking, had an impressive capacity for Cutty Sark scotch mixed with soda; it was his favorite highball. A big man at nearly six feet four and two hundred pounds, he could drink a great deal without seeming to be affected by it.

Throughout his years in the White House, Johnson intermittently would go for months at a time drinking nothing stronger than diet soft drinks. Then, for what seemed to me rather brief periods by comparison, he would revert to Cutty Sark, usually in moderation although not invariably.

LBJ appeared to me to be most inclined to drink when he was feeling good, when he thought he had the world by the tail. I thought his long periods of abstinence coincided rather closely with times of trial and trouble. The campaign of 1964 was, for him, a triumphal progress, however, and a tumbler of Cutty Sark often was close at hand. This was the case, for example, on the trip to Omaha with Manlio Brosio.

At SAC headquarters Johnson was the perfect host, escorting Brosio into subterranean chambers linked by radio and telephone to missile launchers and nuclear bomber fleets around the globe. General Thomas S. Power, the SAC commander, handed the President a red telephone and invited him to speak to all units of the command over the primary alerting network.

"This is the President," said Johnson. "Do you hear me?"

"That's a one-way conversation," Power interrupted. "We give commands and they follow orders. They're not interested in talking back."

Those of us within earshot got a chuckle out of the exchange. The flight home, however, was not as amusing. After returning with Brosio to Air Force One, LBJ apparently repaired to his cabin and lubricated his conversation with the Secretary General and Under Secretary of State George Ball with an ample quantity of scotch. To be fair, the quantity may not have mattered so much as the circumstances. The President had returned at 4:22 A.M. from an arduous, twenty-hour campaign swing and, after very little sleep, had worked in his office and hosted a White House luncheon for Brosio before flying to Nebraska. He must have been bone tired.

Midway in the flight home Johnson emerged from his cabin and joined us at the table assigned to the press pool. He urged that we go aft with him and talk to Brosio. I demurred, arguing that we already had more good copy than newspapers could find room to print. Actually, I thought the President was a bit in his cups and that mutual embarrassment might result if we adopted his suggesion.

"If I were a newsman on this plane," Johnson declared, "I'd interview everybody on board, from the lowliest steward to the President of the United States."

I did not remind him that we still were operating under ground rules ordained by Kennedy and Salinger, that everything we heard aboard the plane was off the record unless the person talking ruled otherwise. I also could have sugggested, but did not, that he would have been the first to explode in protest if we began quoting his aerial conversations without permission.

"The AP isn't paying you to sit here and drink beer!" Johnson exclaimed at me. "I'm offerin' you an opportunity to talk to the wisest, most experienced diplomat that Italy's got, one of the great statesmen of Europe. For your own self-respect, Frank, come visit with this great man!"

The President rose and we followed. As he opened his cabin door, I could see Brosio with his back to us, deep in conversation with George Ball. Almost without breaking stride, LBJ reached out and, grasping the unsuspecting NATO official's arm, hoisted him out of his seat and marched him back to the bedroom.

Standing between the beds, which were made up as sofas, Johnson introduced each member of the pool to Brosio in a most proper manner. I felt much relieved. But then, looking over his shoulder as he headed into the adjoining bathroom, the President said:

"Now you-all interview the hell out of him while I go take a leak!"

We exchanged pleasantries with the patrician Secretary General, who was most gracious and gave no outward evidence of being upset. When LBJ returned we thanked him for allowing us to chat with Brosio, then vanished with all deliberate speed.

During the campaign I sometimes wondered whether some of Johnson's lengthier speeches might not have been fueled by Cutty Sark. They seldom were brief in any case. A crowd in Pittsburgh laughed when he announced that he was "not going to take over an hour to so" to speak. But an hour later he was still talking.

Johnson was raised in the Southern and rural tradition of long-winded political oratory. Out in the hill country when he was a young man, "speakin's" offered prime opportunities for entertainment, conviviality and, perhaps, some measure of enlightenment. Some of the stories LBJ told from the stump in 1964 might well have served the orators of his youth.

One concerned a small boy who left the cotton patch one afternoon so he could listen to a political speech. Returning about dark, the youngster had this exchange with his boss:

"Where have you been all afternoon?"

"I have been listening to the United States Senator Joseph Weldon Bailey."

"Well, the Senator didn't speak all afternoon, did he?"

"Mighty near, mighty near."

"What did the Senator say?"

"Boss, I don't remember, I don't recollect precisely what the Senator said, but the general impression I got was the Senator was recommending himself most highly."

In late September, while still professing that most of his appearances were non-political, Johnson announced plans for a clearly partisan journey that was to signal the end of the "inform" phase of his campaign. At a news conference that began in his office and ended with a walkathon, he told us he would visit five of the six New England states in a single day, September 28, "if the good Lord's willin' and the creeks don't rise."

The Lord and the creeks co-operated and we headed north for what, to me, was the most memorable day of campaigning that I ever witnessed. Indian summer is a golden time in New England, with the hills cloaked in brilliant autumn colors, and this particular season was a golden time for LBJ, an auspicious time to launch the more active "convert" stage of his vote quest.

Johnson's first stop was at Providence, Rhode Island, where he was welcomed by a very large crowd gathered behind a low chain-link fence in front of the airport terminal. Many deep, the throng stretched for about the equivalent of a long city block. The President headed straight for the fence, grinning and making brief eye-and-hand contact with many hundreds of Rhode Islanders as he sidestepped slowly, purposefully down the entire length of the barrier. After finally turning away toward his waiting motorcade, Johnson spotted me and Marquis Childs of the St. Louis *Post-Dispatch*. Beckoning to us, he snapped:

"You-all say I've got no charisma—that crowds don't respond to me like they did to Kennedy. You fellows stay right here beside me and I'll show you that you're wrong!"

With that, LBJ grabbed each of us firmly by the arm, squeezing hard enough to let us know who was boss, and led us back to the fence. There he loosened his grip and, in a challenging tone, said, "Watch this!"

The President thrust his hands forward and a sea of palms reached out toward him. Women shrieked. Grown men leaped into the air. Small children were compressed against the restraining fence by those in the rear who struggled frantically forward for a quick touching of hands.

"Watch out for the kids!" Johnson bellowed.

"Thanks for coming, Mr. President," voices responded from the crowd. ". . . We love you, Mr. President! . . . You're doing a great job."

Pandemonium followed Johnson along the entire length of fencing that he had traversed moments before. Many people found themselves shaking his hand for a second time, but this did nothing to diminish their emotional displays of wild jubilation. Pleased beyond measure, both hands in constant motion, LBJ murmured:

"Thank you. . . . Nice to see you. . . . How are you today?"

The job done a second time, the President moved toward his limousine without saying a word to Mark or me. I don't know whether Childs had said or written anything about Johnson's charisma or lack of it. I know that I had not done so and, in fact, had been impressed by crowd reaction to Johnson in other cities visited earlier. It may be that the President's challenge to us was impersonal, that we simply were handy representatives of a press contingent that did include some who were quick to draw unflattering comparisons between Johnson and Kennedy. Whatever his motive, LBJ's performance was impressive and left us in no doubt about the warmth of the welcome given him in Kennedy's home region.

But the airport episode was only the beginning of a daylong outpouring of humanity throughout New England. In downtown Providence crowds were huge by any standard as the President's motorcade inched forward toward a speech site on the Brown University campus. LBJ repeatedly ordered his Secret Service driver to stop so he could hop out and press palms. At one point Johnson walked for half a mile, shaking hands and leading a growing procession of well-wishers like a modern pied piper. Some people were trampled and injured in the crush around him. Mrs. Johnson lost a shoe. It was bedlam.

By coincidence, the Warren Commission had made public the evening before its long-awaited report on the Kennedy assassination. Although its members had agreed that a President must travel and meet the people, they noted that Kennedy twice had mingled with curbside crowds in Dallas and wrote, "The Commission regards such impromptu stops as presenting an unnecessary danger. . . ."

Johnson obviously did not agree. Later in the day, in Hartford, he began an informal talk to a group of business executives, gathered in a courtyard beneath towering office buildings, by look-

ing toward a larger crowd, restrained behind police barricades on
the street, and shouting:

"I want to first of all say to that policeman up there, if I may
have your attention, that any of those nice people that are standing on the steps, I believe in them having a little freedom. . . . If
they want to, just let them pull up that rope and let them come on
down here and talk to us."

Down they came, like a stampeding herd, while Johnson
beamed. It was the sort of thing we were to see many times during
the campaign. "Let me near them folks!" LBJ would yell, and
uniformed local police would give way. As the Warren Commission observed, "The Secret Service's difficulty in meeting its pro-
tective responsibility varies with the activities and the nature of
the occupant of the Office of President and his willingness to con-
form to plans for his safety."

The street crowds in Hartford, where Johnson's visit coincided
with the lunch hour, were perhaps even larger than we had seen in
Providence. Uncounted thousands filled broad streets from building line to building line, pressing up against the motorcade from
both sides and forcing drivers to slow to a crawl.

A jubilant Johnson sent an aide to fetch Ralph Santos, a CBS
television cameraman. Motioning the startled Santos to enter the
presidential limousine, LBJ directed the photographer to lie face
up on the floor, at Mrs. Johnson's feet, and aim his camera at the
crowd through the vehicle's transparent "bubble." Santos was
happy to comply, getting some unique film footage of a campaigning President who wanted an enduring record of the massive welcome.

Even inside the car, with its thick, bullet-resistant windows
tightly shut, Santos discovered that he could distinguish individual
shouts from the crowd. The President, he learned, had ordered the
installation of tiny microphones on the outside of the limousine so
he could gauge the reaction of his greeters and, in most instances,
savor their response.

Everywhere Johnson went in New England—in Burlington,
Vermont, and Portland, Maine, and Manchester, New Hampshire
—he was met by some of the largest crowds ever to gather on a
single day to welcome any presidential candidate.

One of the more amusing episodes occurred in Portland, where
Johnson rode in the Secret Service convertible with Governor

John Reed. Later the President chortled as he recounted his exploitation of Reed:

"That little ol' Republican Governor never saw anything like those crowds. I'd stop the car and get up on the back seat and say a few words and the people would roar. Then I'd say, 'Folks, I got your Republican Governor with me here this evenin' and I'd like for him to say a few words to you-all.' The Governor would try to scrunch down in his seat but I just reached down and jerked him up on his feet. Then he'd see all those folks welcomin' the President and he was pretty near tongue-tied."

By the time LBJ got to Manchester, the last announced stop, he was three hours behind schedule. Then, after midnight, he decided to visit Senator Edward M. Kennedy, who was recuperating in a Boston hospital from back injuries suffered in an airplane crash. That delayed Johnson's return to Washington until after four o'clock in the morning and made him happy-tired by the time he got together with Manlio Brosio.

The New England trip was not an unrelieved success in Johnson's eyes, however. For one thing, many of us noted in print and in broadcasts that his behavior had ignored the Warren Commission's concern about impromptu stops. Within a few days Johnson convened a news conference at which he argued that he had not violated a single commission recommendation. After accusing the press corps of writing "off the top of the head," he produced a letter from Secret Service Chief Jim Rowley, who wrote that unscheduled motorcade stops were "one of the most important deterrents to risk," that large crowds helped shield the President, and that plainclothes officers could circulate freely in their midst. Rowley, although he did not refer directly to articles that had employed such adjectives, insisted that his agents did not become nervous, jittery or worried in such situations. Said Johnson of the Secret Service:

"They are pleased with the way we're handling ourselves and we're pleased with them."

The New England triumph also was marred for Johnson by a fire that broke out in a motorcade car during the drive through downtown Providence. As the procession began inching up a hill toward the Brown campus, flames leaped from under the hood of a convertible carrying Jack Valenti, a group of news photographers, and Rear Admiral George G. Burkley, the President's personal physician. As the passengers leaped to safety, word of the fire was broadcast over a Secret Service radio channel, prompting agent Youngblood to grab LBJ by the ankles and pull him down into his seat while yelling at the driver, "Get the hell outta here!" Youngblood, who did not know then that an over-heated engine had caused the fire, was taking no chances.

Johnson had no fault to find with Youngblood, nor did he raise objections about the abrupt end of what had been a triumphant motorcade. He was furious the next morning, however, when he saw the front page of the New York *Daily News* devoted to a photo of Valenti, Burkley and the photographers leaping over the doors of the flaming auto.

"I got the biggest crowds I ever saw but there aren't any pictures of them in the paper," he complained. "All I see is photographers jumpin' out of an automobile. If they get a thrill out of takin' pictures of each other, they should hold a family picnic!"

To Admiral Burkley, Johnson said in my presence: "Any dumb son of a bitch would know enough to turn off the ignition when the engine temperature gets to four hundred and fifty degrees!"

Valenti was derided as the captain of "Fire Wagon Number Three."

I suppose Johnson had to have something to complain about during what mostly was a season of contentment. The New England trip clearly established that he need not worry about the outcome of the election. Quite obviously he was succeeding in accomplishing an objective he had enunciated during a June speech in Minneapolis: "bringing our capital and our management and our labor and our farmers all under one great Democratic tent. . . ."

A man who could pose with Henry Ford II holding up one arm while Walter Reuther held up the other did not have to be too concerned about Barry Goldwater. But he was.

9

"I Wish I Could..."

Not prone to overconfidence, Lyndon Johnson set about the conversion of the electorate as if every vote were vital. "I wish I could look into every face and shake every hand," he declared, reflecting the politician's traditional philosophy that every hand shaken might well represent another vote in his pocket.

As he crisscrossed the nation by jet, an undertaking that cost the Democratic National Committee $149,019 in payments to the Air Force, Johnson certainly acted like a man bent on reaching out to everyone. In a Los Angeles crowd two detectives watched a thirty-year-old transient make a quick move toward the wallet lodged in another man's hip pocket, then get shoved forward by the surging multitude. Ignorant of what was happening, LBJ smiled and amiably pumped the pickpocket's hand.

Every crowd was one to be savored. On the platform in front of a state office building in Reno, Johnson heard Senator Howard Cannon announce that fifteen thousand persons were in attendance. After the President rose to speak, Valenti sent up a note that prompted LBJ to interrupt his discourse in mid-sentence:

"Flash! Flash! Flash! Correction! They just brought me a message and said the chief of police said *fifty* thousand—not fifteen thousand!"

Riding from Stapleton Airport to the Denver Coliseum after

dark, Johnson became a pitchman for his own rally, shouting through his limousine's built-in public address system: "Come down to the speakin'. It won't take long. . . . You'll be home in time to put the kids to bed."

Crowds along the route were startled to hear the President's disembodied voice addressing them from the darkness. Six nuns stared in amazement to hear the familiar drawl: "Hello, sisters, how are you?"

On seven occasions en route to the Coliseum, LBJ jumped out of the car and climbed on the trunk lid with announcements like: "I'm just here to appoint you-all to look after me. If you'll look after me in November, I'll look after you for the next four years."

To another curbside gathering in the Mile High City, the President cautioned: "Now don't get overconfident. A vote's not worth anything until it's in that ballot box, until that lever's pulled [he pronounced it lee-ver]."

"My wife certainly is not overconfident," Johnson told a late September news conference, "because she is exploring where to vote in absentia. Before a very important election her car was turned over and a reporter asked her, 'What was your first thought when you came to?' and she said, 'I wished I had voted absentee.'"

Every vote mattered to Johnson, and he never let his listeners forget it. If somebody simply had to vote against him, LBJ declared, "I won't question your patriotism, I won't question your Americanism, I won't question your ancestry. I may quietly in the sanctity of our bedroom whisper to Lady Bird my own personal opinion of your judgment!"

The President professed to be outraged when Barry Goldwater scheduled a campaign tour through Texas.

"In all my life in politics," Johnson told us, "I never went campaigning in my opponent's home state. That just isn't appropriate. Why, I wouldn't even consider campaigning in Arizona. I couldn't do something like that."

A few days later, on an October Sunday, Air Force One set down at the airport in Phoenix, Goldwater's home town, en route from Austin to Long Beach, California. Anticipating our amusement at his change of policy, Johnson explained with a perfectly straight face:

"We had to go to church somewhere and Lady Bird heard

they've got a mighty fine preacher at the First Presbyterian Church here. We thought we ought to stop by and hear him. That's all we're gonna do. I'm not here to make any campaign speeches. This is not a day for politics. This is a day for God."

Before leaving the airport to drive to church, LBJ naturally could not resist climbing on the trunk of his car and surveying a large crowd studded with political placards. Then, of course, he had to do his welcomers the courtesy of saying a few words.

Arizona was growing twice as fast as the rest of the country, the President reminded them, "but you have one problem, and it is a mighty big problem." The crowd laughed appreciatively and Johnson, grinning broadly, held up his hands for quiet. "No, no, no," he protested. "I told you this wasn't going to be a political day, and it is not. You got the wrong impression. [More laughter.] Now wait a minute! You have one big problem, and that problem is [pause] water."

Driving away from the airport with Roy Elson, the Democratic Senate candidate, Johnson spied a girl with a sign that read, "Goldwater My." Beneath this was a drawing of an ass. "I see your sign," LBJ said through a bullhorn. "It's a nice sign and a very pretty girl." Stopping, he hopped out and autographed the placard.

The First Presbyterian Church happened to number Elson among its communicants and the pastor, the Reverend Charles R. Ehrhardt, was ready for LBJ and the campaign press corps with a five-page mimeographed sermon text, "On Being Satisfied With Ourselves."

Johnson had ample reason for satisfaction. The crowds that marked his progress through Phoenix, on a beautiful day that found Goldwater secluded at his nearby Camelback Mountain home, were large and friendly. Even as Air Force One taxied toward the runway on departure, a steward came to our table, where LBJ had joined us, and announced, "Mr. President, we've gotten word that there's a huge crowd even at the far end of the runway." The President peered out the window beside him toward a junkyard where scores of autos had been smashed flat and stacked one atop the other.

"My Gawd," he exclaimed, "there's a hell of a lot of people out there!"

Dick McGowan of the New York *Daily News* looked straight

across the table at Johnson and cracked, "Magoo for President!" Johnson, whose vision was limited without glasses, which were in his pocket, stared silently at McGowan.

In those early weeks of the "convert" stage of the Johnson campaign, the President periodically would gather the press pool around him on Air Force One and go over detailed compilations of state polls by Gallup, Harris, local Democratic organizations and others. Running his finger down the tabulation, he would offer a personal assessment of his chances in each state. Only rarely did he come upon a state that he was willing to predict he would carry. In fact he seemed bent on giving the impression that he was fighting for his political life against a surging Republican opponent.

It was such patent nonsense that, after witnessing the exercise on several occasions, I exploded: "Hell, Mr. President, I'll bet you five dollars you take forty-eight of the fifty states!" It was a foolish offer at even money but it reflected my irritation at what I regarded as an insult to our intelligence. Johnson looked up quickly and took the bet:

"I'll bet you a one-hundred-dollar Texas hat against your five dollars that I don't," he snapped, "and if you win, I'll sign an affidavit that it didn't cost more than five dollars and it was covered by the Paul Douglas rule!"

I lost the bet, of course, and weeks later sent a five-dollar bill to the President. Shortly thereafter I was walking in front of him along the East Wing corridor when he boomed out, "Frank! Frank!" I turned and went up to him. "That five dollars you sent me," he said, "I thought you'd like to know I put it in the collection plate at church on Sunday!"

My bet was lost in the South, which came as no surprise. It was in that region that candidate Johnson received his heaviest heckling during the campaign. The worst incident was recorded in front of the new white marble Municipal Building in Augusta, Georgia, in late October. Drowned out three times by chants of "We want Barry!" Johnson finally pointed straight at his tormentors and said in a voice so soft that he had everyone straining to hear:

"I think it is better to use the head and the heart than to use the tongue and the voice. I know when you see people, as you have

seen them at some [Republican] conventions when they don't
want other people to talk, when the Governor of a great state [Nel-
son Rockefeller] is not even permitted to speak to his own convention because others would interfere, or when the President of
your own country would be stopped and interrupted while he was
trying to talk to you in your own land—can you imagine what
kind of leadership that would be for the world if that were prac-
ticed?

". . . I was always taught as a little boy when people didn't
know any better, and when they made mistakes, and when they
were rude, and when they didn't show good manners, to turn your
other cheek and say, 'Dear Lord, please forgive them, for they
know not what they do.' And I think that is the way that the people of the fifty states are feeling. We don't feel hurt, and we don't
feel angry. We just feel sorry. And I think that on November
third, they are going to feel sorry, too. [Cheers.]

"I was in an election campaign four years ago and I returned to
my home state in the last days of the campaign. We went to the
hotel [in Dallas] to wash up before we went to a luncheon meeting, but the entrance was blocked and the hecklers were there,
and they harassed us and they hounded us and they knocked my
wife's hat off, and they spit on us, and they called us traitors and
they called us treason artists, and they had ugly signs and they
dealt not in a single issue that we were debating. They had only
to talk about personalities and little petty things because they were
little petty people. . . . It took us more than an hour to walk
across the block because of the chants and the saliva [*sic*] that
was running out of their mouths and, really, some of them were
diseased. . . ."

Johnson at that point returned to his standard campaign message and, for the next twenty minutes, spoke only to cheers.

One way or another, LBJ usually found a way to silence campaign heckling, sometimes through ridicule, often through humor.
When a group of young men shouted boos and catcalls at him in
Jacksonville, Florida, Johnson turned to them and said: "I want
to greet some of these people over here with another philosophy.
Nearly every meetin' we have, they send some of their children
over. . . ." The din subsided. On another occasion he declared
that he did not mind name-callers and mudslingers because "they

may enjoy it and get their own blood pressure up and feel a pecul-
iar sensation, but if they can just keep on talkin' maybe we won't
have to keep on travelin' so much."

When supporters of the President responded to hecklers at a
Los Angeles rally with chants of "We want Johnson," he shushed
them, saying they should be courteous to neighbors who had
dropped by because they liked to "associate with good people
every once in a while."

Taking note of opposition demonstrators in a Baltimore ar-
mory, Johnson said: "I will bet you that some of those people that
came in here unexpected and kind of delayed us for a moment
. . . are going to join with us and elect that good Democrat Royce
Hanson [to the House]. I believe some of them have already
dropped their original signs that they brought in and now they
have Royce Hanson signs over here!"

LBJ would often tell a story when confronted by noisy Goldwater partisans: "Once Al Smith was making a speech in this city
and a heckler yelled, 'Tell 'em all you know, Al. It won't take
long.' And Al, without hesitation, answered, 'I'll tell 'em all we
both know—and it won't take any longer!' "

The South produced the most memorable moment of high
drama in the Johnson campaign, after the President strode into a
New Orleans hotel ballroom and began addressing a gathering of
more than two thousand Democrats and, via live television, state-
wide audiences in Louisiana and Mississippi.

Johnson first paid tribute to the memory of Huey Long, who in
fact had been one of his early political heroes because of Long's
populist interest in doing something for the disadvantaged. To
praise the Kingfish in Louisiana nearly twenty years after his assassination did not require political courage on LBJ's part, but the
section of his speech that followed was as gutsy as any campaign
speech I ever heard.

"There is not any combination in this country that can take on
Russell Long, Allen Ellender, Lyndon Johnson and a few others if
we are together," the President asserted. "But if they divide us,
they can make some hay. And all these years they have kept their
foot on our necks by appealing to our animosities, and dividing
us."

After proceeding to defend the 1964 Civil Rights Act, Johnson continued, "I am not going to let them build up the hate and try to buy my people by appealing to their prejudice."

Then he told of young Sam Rayburn visiting an old Southern Senator, years back, who told Rayburn that the South could have a great future if only it could develop its economic potential.

"Sammy," Johnson quoted the Senator, "I wish I felt a little better. . . . I would like to go back down there and make one more Democratic speech. I just feel like I've got one in me. Poor old state, they haven't heard a real Democratic speech in thirty years. All they ever hear at election time is 'nigger, nigger, nigger!'"

This took the breath away from most of us. The crowded ballroom became strangely silent, then was rocked by a thunderous cheer. I am not certain that all who joined in the applause approved of what LBJ had said, but they surely had to admire his courage in saying it. The campaign produced no moment of greater drama—and the President lost Louisiana and Mississippi.

The Johnson campaign had a good many positive aspects, despite the focus on fears generated by Goldwater's sometimes careless rhetoric. Civil rights, Medicare, education, help for the poverty-stricken—these and other Great Society topics received at least as much attention from the President as the ubiquitous question of whose hand should be poised beside the nuclear button. The latter remained the most potent issue for LBJ, however, and his own oratory on the subject was not always moderate. As he told a Nevada audience:

"We know how the West was won. It wasn't won by men on horses who tried to settle every argument with a quick draw and a shot from the hip. We here in the West aren't about to turn in our sterling-silver American heritage for a plastic credit card that reads, 'Shoot now, pay later.'"

To a California crowd, he mused: "I am one President who had rather reason and talk than fight. Fight I will, if fight I must . . . but I just won't do it as a Sunday afternoon exercise just to entertain somebody."

Goldwater reacted to the incessant pummeling with a speech that he hoped would prove to be a master stroke. He declared that if he were elected he would invite the nation's favorite father figure, Dwight Eisenhower, to go to Vietnam and advise him on the proper course to take in the struggle there. Some observers likened this to Ike's own 1952 campaign pledge that he would "go to Korea" and see what could be done to end an increasingly unpopular war there.

LBJ was ready for Goldwater's pronouncement. Indeed, he usually seemed to be at least a step ahead of his opponent. With relish, he let us in on a secret.

"I knew all about Senator Goldwater's speech before he even delivered it," the President confided, without saying how he came by the knowledge; quite possibly his political intelligence agents obtained an advance text distributed to the Goldwater press corps.

"So I called up General Eisenhower at Gettysburg and I told him, 'You don't have to wait for Senator Goldwater to get elected in order to go to Vietnam. I've got a Boeing 707 all warmed up and waiting at Andrews Air Force Base and I'll send a helicopter after you any time you care to go.' General Eisenhower didn't know what I was talkin' about, and he didn't have any plans to go to Vietnam. Senator Goldwater delivered that speech without ever checkin' with the General."

The LBJ campaign continued to roar ahead in high gear until the evening of October 14. We were at the Waldorf Astoria Hotel in New York City that night, with Johnson waiting to address the annual Al Smith dinner, when our offices in Washington began calling with reports that Abe Fortas and Clark Clifford were trying to hush up a scandal involving the President's oldest and closest assistant, Walter Jenkins. As the dinner began, the story broke. Jenkins, a member of LBJ's staff for twenty-five years, had been arrested a week earlier on a charge of committing "disorderly conduct" with a Soldier's Home inmate in a men's room at the YMCA, two blocks from the White House.

It was a bombshell. No one could gauge the impact on the electorate. Angry and fearful, the President had Jenkins' resignation within the hour and ordered an FBI investigation to determine if the national security had been compromised.

As we were flying to Rochester, New York, the next morning, Johnson told a group of us, "I couldn't have been more surprised if Lady Bird had run off with Bill Douglas!" He apparently was too concerned about the effect on his campaign to express any compassion for Jenkins.

Adding to the impression that the President's world had been abruptly turned upside down were other developments of far more enduring significance. In a single eighteen-hour period the Jenkins arrest surfaced, Nikita Khrushchev was ousted as top man in the Soviet hierarchy, Britain rejected its Conservative Prime Minister and elected a Labor government, and China successfully exploded its first atomic bomb.

After these developments the President needed a tonic, and the people of Brooklyn provided one. Campaigning there with Robert Kennedy, who was running for a Senate seat, Johnson was greeted by a crowd estimated to total one million. A turnout of such magnitude may seem improbable but I saw no reason to question it at the time. The size and enthusiasm of the vast throng along the motorcade route were truly impressive.

Johnson was jubilant. He sent word to Bill Eaton, then of UPI, and me to come forward to the tanklike Secret Service convertible in which he was standing with Kennedy. We called the car the *"Queen Mary."* The vehicle was packed but LBJ urged us to get aboard anyway. Bill and I could find no room except atop the trunk, where we clung rather precariously for several blocks.

The Ringling brothers could not have jammed more people into an automobile. Hardly believing my eyes, I counted twenty-seven individuals either inside or hanging to the outside of the big Cadillac. Surely it was a sight never duplicated in any other presidential campaign.

From my rather unique vantage point, I had to feel concern for the safety of the Brooklynites who surged against the motorcade from both sides, the cars brushing them as they passed. At one intersection I saw a rather large group of black-clad men, women and children whom I took to be members of a conservative, evidently Jewish sect. As the *"Queen Mary"* drew near with Johnson and Kennedy, the soberly garbed spectators were seized by a strange frenzy and fell to the pavement in a writhing mass, arms and legs twitching perilously close to the wheels of the limousine. Ethel Kennedy, perched on the back of the seat ahead of me, showed genuine fright at this awesome sight.

Back in Manhattan that evening for an appearance in Madison Square Garden, the President was joined by Mrs. Johnson, who, we suspected, had flown up from Washington to urge him to express concern about the plight of Walter Jenkins and his stricken family. Mrs. Johnson already had issued a statement of her own but LBJ had kept silent.

After we boarded a prop plane that served as Air Force One for a middle-of-the-night return to the capital, Johnson finally handed us a statement that paid tribute to the "personal dedication, devotion, and tireless labor" of his long-time associate. It concluded: "For myself and Mrs. Johnson, I want to say that our hearts go out with deepest compassion for him and for his wife and six children—and they have our love and prayers. . . ."

The President appeared to be still smarting, however, over what he must have perceived as an incalculable blow to his candidacy. At least that is how I interpreted his behavior when we were served steak sandwiches during the flight. I was sitting with LBJ on one side of the cabin while Mrs. Johnson and Mary McGrory of the Washington *Star* faced each other at a table across the aisle. A bowl of potato chips was set out between the two women.

LBJ chewed away at his sandwich and encountered an unmanageable piece of gristle. Putting a hand to his mouth, he extracted the gristle and flung it across the cabin, straight into the bowl of potato chips.

Once he was back in Washington, the President suspended his campaign for a few days, not because of the Jenkins arrest but in order to study and assess international developments. By the time he returned to the stump the FBI had stated it found no evidence that Jenkins, who had been sent flowers by J. Edgar Hoover, had "compromised the security or interests of the United States in any manner." Equally important, quick soundings indicated no significant shift in voter sentiments, and Goldwater had made no major effort to capitalize on the misfortune that had overtaken Jenkins and his erstwhile boss, except to make veiled references to LBJ and his "curious crew."

Even the rather mild jab by the Republican candidate got under Johnson's skin, however, causing him to blunder. Stopping in San Diego, he told local television-radio reporters that Eisenhower "had the same type of problem" with an appointee, adding: "We Democrats didn't capitalize on a man's misfortunes." The American people, he suggested, would not think much of a candidate who talked about such an incident.

It did not take long for the press corps to learn that Johnson's potshot was ill founded and unfair; that he had been guilty of shooting from the hip. Eisenhower had considered giving a White House job to the son of a prominent Republican Senator but the young man never was hired because an FBI check had shown him to be a homosexual. LBJ's remark served therefore as a reminder that most of his top associates had never been investigated by the FBI.

Johnson told us, incidentally, that Cartha (Deke) De Loach, assistant director of the FBI, was one of Walter Jenkins' closest friends; that they were members of the same parish and were weekend golfing buddies. "Deke De Loach is going to succeed J. Edgar Hoover when the appropriate time comes," LBJ related.

The President's loss of political composure because of the Jenkins case was only momentary. He soon realized he was going to win big, and he found the realization intoxicating. Noting the President's euphoria, Robert Goralski of NBC News approached Johnson at a crowded speech site one night and playfully thrust a ball point pen in front of Johnson's mouth, as if it were a microphone. LBJ obligingly talked directly to the pen as Goralski proceeded to interview him.

"I know I'm gonna beat Goldwater," the President announced to four of us aboard Air Force One. "What I'm tryin' to do with all this travelin' is to help elect as many deserving Democrats as I can. And there are certain Republicans that I'd like to see get unelected."

Then he made us a proposition that seemed rather astounding at the time, and still does.

"You-all know a good bit about the Republicans in Congress," he declared, "and there must be at least a few of them that *you* think deserve to be defeated. Give me some names and either Hubert or I will try to get into their districts in the next few days and talk against 'em."

Our stunned silence finally was broken by a political reporter who said he couldn't think of anyone he'd rather see defeated than Representative (later Senator) Bob Dole of Kansas.

Johnson looked across the cabin at W. Marvin Watson, a conservative Texas Democrat who had been borrowed from the Lone

Star Steel Company to serve as LBJ's personal campaign co-or-
dinator during the final three weeks before the election.

"Marvin," said the President, "get ahold of Hubert and find out
if he can get into Dole's district. If he can't, I will."

I was riding on the chartered press plane a day or so later when
Malcolm Kilduff, the assistant press secretary, approached me
with a puzzled expression and reported that he had just gotten
word by radio that LBJ would stop at Wichita for an airport rally
the next day. I told Kilduff about Bob Dole, and he was as surprised as I was that Johnson meant to keep his seemingly impromptu promise.

The flight to Wichita taught me something about the marvels of
automated jet age aviation. By invitation, I went to the cockpit of
Air Force One to witness the landing. Strapped into a seat behind
the pilot, I donned earphones so I could monitor instructions from
the Wichita control tower.

In the far distance we could see two airports, one straight ahead
and the other off to the left. The presidential pilot announced that
we were headed for the one directly ahead. The co-pilot disa-
greed, arguing that we would land at the second field. A chart was
consulted rather quickly but the issue was not resolved. As instructions came in from the ground, the two men turned dials and
knobs until, almost inch by inch, the big jet banked toward the
airport favored by the co-pilot. It became apparent that the President's personal pilot can be fallible.

I told a competitor about the experience and he vowed that he
also would witness a touchdown at the earliest opportunity. A few
mornings later, feeling somewhat the worse for the night before,
he was in the President's cabin, enjoying conversation and bloody
marys, when he sensed the plane was beginning its descent, this
time into Los Angeles. Rising from his seat, he intoned rather
gravely, "Excuse me, Mr. President, I must go forward and land
the plane!" Johnson appeared to ignore the departure but, once
the would-be pilot was out of earshot, he leaned close to Karl
Bauman and gave him an exclusive bulletin story.

At Wichita, at least ten thousand turned out for LBJ and he
tarried for an hour, urging the election of Dole's Democratic opponent and all other members of the Democratic ticket. I'm still
somewhat puzzled about Johnson's appearance there, however,

because I learned on the ground in Wichita that Humphrey had scheduled a stop there that evening, then canceled it after the President's rally was announced. Perhaps Marvin Watson was more than zealous in carrying out Johnson's instructions. In any event, Bob Dole was re-elected.

Even when LBJ did not have a specific purge target in mind, and I know he would have recoiled from that term, he invariably studded his speeches with plugs for local Democrats. Hardly a speech was delivered in which he did not recite Sam Rayburn's advice on the selection of U. S. Representatives: "Pick them young, pick them honest, send them there and keep them there!"

Johnson's sense of the ridiculous often added spice to his endorsements. At a campaign breakfast in Florida, he delighted listeners with a pitch for Senator Spessard Holland:

"Spessard is very serious about spending money at any time. He is a great man for economy. He does loosen up a little when it comes to spending money in Florida. He came to see me the other day, and he got another eighteen and a half million dollars for Florida. And then he went out and made a speech on economy right out there in front of the White House! Spessard Holland is a great Senator and a great friend of mine."

The same sense of humor moved Johnson to recall an appearance in Indiana in behalf of another Senate friend in 1958:

". . . Just as I went to the podium a very young, attractive man said to me, 'Don't forget that I'm a candidate for Congress from this district and mention my name, Joe Barr.' So I talked about the glories of the Democratic Party and the necessity of their sending a Democratic Senator to the Senate.

"Then I recalled what this young, attractive fellow had said to me . . . and I said, 'And I have one other favor to ask of you. There is a young, progressive, attractive, well-educated fellow who is running for Congress,' and I couldn't think of his name.

"'I want to tell you people that he is one of the finest candidates I have ever observed,' and I still couldn't think of his name.

"'And I believe if you send him to Congress he will make one of the ablest Congressmen any district ever had,' and I still couldn't think of his name.

"About that time I heard a fellow whisper, 'Barr, Joe Barr.' And I looked around and it was the candidate himself!"

Joe Barr never became a household name but his signature went out on a lot of dollar bills as Johnson's third Secretary of the Treasury.

A far more familiar name, that of the President's old mentor, Sam Rayburn, was invoked by LBJ not only to urge the election of Democrats but also in discussions of the proper attitude of national leaders in a nuclear age.

"We must constantly be deliberate, prudent and restrained," Johnson would declare. "Before we shoot from the hip, as Mr. Rayburn, that great political leader, used to say, the three most important words in the English language for everyone are, 'Just a minute.' "

Two days before the election Vietcong explosives rocked the U.S. air base at Bienhoa, killing five Americans, wounding seventy-six, and destroying six B-57 bombers. Ambassador Maxwell Taylor recommended a retaliatory air strike against North Vietnam. Johnson refused. The President favored agitation in the final hours of the campaign, but of a sort more in keeping with the bandwagon psychology he was striving to bring to fruition. After saying "Just a minute" to Taylor, he had this message for the voters:

"Your mamas and your papas and your grandpas, some of them are going to forget this. But I am depending on you young folks who are going to have to fight our wars, and who are going to have to defend this country, and who are going to get blown up if we have a nuclear holocaust—I am depending on you to have enough interest in your future . . . to get up and prod mama and papa and make them get up early and go vote."

Election day brought Johnson sixty-one per cent of the total vote, a record that bested Franklin D. Roosevelt's landslide high of 1936 and the one-sided victories of Dwight D. Eisenhower. Weary but very pleased and proud, the President addressed the nation from Austin's Municipal Auditorium at 1:40 A.M. on November 4:

"I doubt that there has ever been so many people seeing so many things alike on 'decision' day. And with the help of all of them, we will be on our way to try to achieve peace in our time. . . ."

10

"I Am the King!"

Soon after the balloting Lyndon Johnson took a group of reporters on one of his periodic tours of the LBJ Ranch, stopping along the way at the family graveyard. Indicating the spot where he would be buried, the President declared, "If Goldwater had won that election, there's where I'd be right now!" With that, he unzipped his trousers and urinated on his grave-to-be.

Most of Johnson's startled guests did not know what to make of the performance. However, a few accepted it as a manifestation of crosscurrents besetting the President's extraordinary ego, which was at once terribly fragile yet enormously robust, which alternately produced moods of moroseness and near-manic euphoria. In the quiet of the graveyard LBJ seemed to lay bare in vivid fashion contradictions deep within himself, as if he feared humiliation yet was disdainful of death itself.

In the autumn of 1964 few ego bruises were in evidence. With his administration now bearing a seal of unmistakable public approval, Johnson was savoring a triumph that must have exceeded his fondest pre-presidential dreams, in those days when vaulting ambition had been checked by a keen sense of political realities. In the weeks just prior to the election, however, he sensed the historic victory that would be his and looked beyond to fresh dreams of a glory transcending national boundaries.

Four of us in the press pool were chatting with him and drinking highballs when LBJ, seated in the high-backed chair in his airborne sitting room that we sometimes referred to as the "throne chair," abruptly became reflective.

"Look around the world," he mused aloud. "Khrushchev's gone. Macmillan's gone. Adenauer's gone. Segni's gone. Nehru's gone." He paused. "Who's left—De Gaulle?" His voice took on a sneering tone as he mentioned the French leader.

Leaning back, the President thumped his chest with both hands and declared, "I am the king!"

When the flight ended and we got aboard a helicopter, Press Secretary George Reedy addressed us in an unusually firm tone: "Gentlemen, you did not see the President of the United States tonight."

It has been a long time since Thomas Jefferson walked to his own inaugural from an undistinguished rooming house. The deference paid to a President these days, and the perquisites that are his, might be cause enough for any incumbent to begin harboring kingly thoughts. Johnson surely embraced without embarrassment all the trappings of the "imperial presidency," even as he retained a common touch that was, even for a politician, uncommon. The fact is that he knew he was uncommon, that his talents transcended ordinary bounds. Indeed, a certain measure of imperiousness must have come naturally to him.

Earl Mazo told me of an election night that he spent at the LBJ Ranch when he was chief political reporter of the old *Herald Tribune*. As the returns began coming in after dinner, Senator Johnson led his aging mother, his wife and Mazo into the living room. They were followed by Willie Day Taylor, family friend and employee, who wheeled a multi-instrument telephone console to a place beside Johnson's chair. While the others watched, the Senator began juggling two or three telephones at a time, snapping out questions to Democratic leaders throughout Texas and absorbing their replies.

A dog barked outside, breaking LBJ's concentration. Slamming down all the phones, Johnson shouted, "Kill that goddamn dawg!"

His old mother hopped out of her chair and led Lady Bird, Mrs. Taylor and Mazo into the yard. The latter, after peering into the darkness in search of the offending animal, suddenly thought to himself, What am I doing out here—ready to kill a dog simply because Johnson ordered it? Mazo returned to the house and the three women soon followed. Their brief excursion, although futile, had dramatized LBJ's ability to mesmerize those around him, to inspire reasonable people to contemplate an unreasonable act simply because he demanded it in a moment of unthinking anger.

Perhaps there was something regal about his behavior. Certainly he did not always act, or react, in the pattern of most mortals. My friend Karl Bauman dumped a full tumbler of Bourbon and water onto Johnson's shirt and trousers by accident and, naturally, offered profuse apologies. LBJ ignored Bauman's expressions of regret and continued talking as though nothing untoward had happened. However, as Karl related it, "I never knew so many men with towels could materialize so quickly!"

I once was startled aboard the presidential plane when Sergeant Paul Glynn of the Air Force, one of two airmen who served as LBJ's valets, approached the President, who was sitting with legs crossed, and, kneeling before him without saying a word, quickly removed one of Johnson's shoes and socks, bathed the naked foot, then put on a fresh sock and replaced the shoe.

Talking all the while, Johnson paid no heed except to cross his legs in the opposite direction when it was time for Glynn to attend to the other foot. After seeing that, I was not surprised to be told that the sergeant also clipped the President's toenails.

In his Secret Service memoir, Rufus Youngblood wrote that in Glynn's absence agent Jerry Kivett once was called upon to dress Vice-President Johnson for a formal dinner. When LBJ complained that Kivett was doing an inferior job, the bodyguard replied, "Well, sir, you have to consider that this is the first time in my life I ever dressed another full-grown man!"

Johnson expected unquestioning service from employees, and his demands often enough were imperious. I was told by an aide to C. Douglas Dillon that one reason Dillon, a very cool and proper multimillionaire, resigned as Secretary of the Treasury was because LBJ was not bashful about inviting him to bathroom conferences while attending to bodily functions. The President's secretaries sometimes were asked to take dictation under similar circumstances.

While touring the Lewis Ranch near Johnson City, 831 acres he purchased in 1962 for $53,171, Johnson led Garnett Horner of the Washington *Star* into a one-hole outhouse to conduct a bit of private business. Emerging, LBJ announced, "That's where the powerful medicine is made."

Newly assigned Secret Service agents posted on guard duty outside the President's ranch house had to be warned: "If you hear a rustling in the bushes near the Old Man's bedroom door during the night, don't shoot. It's probably him taking a leak." Johnson sometimes found it more convenient to pop out the door than walk to the bathroom. In short, he always did pretty much as he pleased.

Long before he became President, Johnson and his wife enjoyed such trappings of wealth as private planes and twin white Lincolns with two-way radios. The presidency brought other luxuries, even cowboy boots decorated with the presidential seal. When news of the boots got into print and drew an adverse reaction, LBJ insisted he had not ordered them and he never was seen wearing them again.

At the time of John Kennedy's death, Air Force One had just over forty seats in a fuselage that could have accommodated four or five times that number. And Johnson wanted more, so he could fly with the entire New York Congressional delegation if he chose. The number of seats was doubled, and in a fashion that did nothing to diminish LBJ's semi-imperial status. All seats in the main passenger cabin were reversed, so they faced the rear—toward Johnson. Between this cabin and Johnson's sitting room-office, a clear plastic divider was put in place, so the President could watch his guests and vice versa. When he wanted privacy the transparent panels could be covered.

Because LBJ often invited fellow passengers into his private compartment, where seating space was limited, the Air Force pleased him by ripping out the wall of his bedroom and replacing it with one that could be pushed to one side, like the top of a roll-top desk. In that way, extra seating was provided.

I suspect, however, that Johnson thought of himself more as a big daddy than an imperial President. Expansive by nature, he could have adopted as his trade mark his typical invitation "Y'all come." He took a proprietary interest in everything and everyone.

He would not think twice, for instance, about saying, in a state dinner receiving line, "Mr. Prime Minister, I want you to meet a member of *my* Supreme Court." He even talked in one speech about the "State of *My* Union Address," which we recorded as a Freudian slip.

Old hero FDR had displayed much the same expansiveness in telling a friend about his Atlantic Charter meeting with Winston Churchill: "I had thirteen warships at that meeting, but Winston had only two or three. One of his broke down, and I had to lend him a destroyer!"

A few months after the 1964 election I wrote a widely printed article about Johnson's Tenth District Congressman, James Jarrell (Jake) Pickle from Big Springs:

> Pickle, a political professional to the quick, goes out of his way to dispel any notion that he is Johnson's man in the House.
> "I don't think of myself as the President's Congressman," he says. "I prefer to think of him as my constituent."

I received from Pickle a thank-you note of sorts a few weeks later that read in part: "Undoubtedly, you did a mighty fine job and while I appreciate your fine work, I must confess that this has created a few problems also!" When I next saw him, Pickle confided that LBJ had let him know who was whose constituent.

Had it been within his power, Johnson doubtless would have had all of us working for him as "my press corps." As it was, he exercised an oversight function where we were concerned. It was shortly after the election that he had the AP and UPI news tickers moved into the Oval Office, where they were housed near his desk in a massive cabinet that also contained three console-size TV screens hidden behind sliding doors. This enabled the President to sharpen his talent for "instant analysis."

News photographers who were admitted to LBJ's inner sanctum to take exclusive pictures worked under tighter reins than we reporters did, however. Johnson had no power to censor our articles before they were published and could only complain after the fact. But whenever he gave permission for exclusive pictures he insisted on exercising prior restraint.

Harvey Georges, an AP photographer, started to walk out of the Oval Office after an exclusive picture-taking session in late

1964 but Johnson grabbed him and demanded that none of the photos be published without his personal approval. Georges replied that he was not certain his office would accept the idea of advance censorship. "Well, telephone them and tell them what I said," ordered LBJ. Georges agreed and headed for the door. "Use the phone on my desk," snapped the President. Following orders, the photographer dialed his boss and, at first, could not convince him that he was calling from the Oval Office. But the AP ultimately felt compelled to go along with the restrictions imposed by Johnson because the pictures could not have been taken without his special permission. In the end, the President approved ten out of a dozen photos submitted.

The late Moe Levy, a Dallas-based NBC News cameraman, had a more unsettling experience when his producer balked at doing as Johnson had directed while they were trying to do some special filming at the Texas ranch. Levy had known the President for years and was on such friendly terms with him that LBJ had given him a goat that the cameraman had admired during a ranch tour. Not long after that episode Levy was given permission to make a film of the President inside the ranch house. Arriving with producer and crew on a weekend afternoon, Levy was told by LBJ: "Lady Bird and I are going out for a drive, and you-all can set up your gear while we're gone—but don't touch any of the furniture." While the Johnsons were absent Levy's producer insisted that a few living-room chairs would have to be moved to produce the type of setting that he wanted. Levy's protests were ignored.

When the President returned he immediately detected the rearrangement and exploded: "Moe, get your goddamn equipment out of here right now—and bring back the goddam goat!"

By comparison with valets, Secret Service agents and others looked upon by Johnson as employees, we in the press corps were coddled. To work for the man was to do his bidding quickly and without questioning his orders. As he often told us, "I don't get ulcers, I give 'em!" He even claimed that some of his employees during Senate days had kept bottles of "sweet milk" on their desks so they could soothe their troubled innards.

One of Johnson's aides told me about the plight of a helicopter crew that had the misfortune to set the President down on Judge Moursund's ranch in a field of freshly cut hay that clogged the jet engine intakes. LBJ was picking up Moursund to fly to Lake Lyndon B. Johnson for a boating excursion but, because of the hay, the pilot could not get the craft off the ground.

"The Judge and I are going into the house and play a game of dominoes," Johnson announced, "and when we come out, it *will* fly!"

It did.

Cruising on the Potomac aboard the presidential yacht, LBJ was distressed when a breeze came up and began rippling a movie screen set up on deck. Insisting that the screen be kept steady so he could watch a film, he was told that the skipper could do nothing about it because the breeze was coming from straight aft.

"Use your head, man!" snapped Johnson. "Turn the damn boat around and back it up the river!"

The big yacht cruised in reverse for all of the several miles from the Woodrow Wilson Bridge in Alexandria, Virginia, to its berth at the Washington Navy Yard.

Raised in semi-arid country that he helped sprinkle with federally-financed artificial lakes, Johnson took great pleasure in boating. He and the family corporations kept an eighteen-foot inboard speedboat and a twenty-eight-foot cabin cruiser on Lake LBJ, and a smaller boat on the Pedernales. In Johnson's case, *speed*boat was an apt label. From a variety of sources we learned that his lake outings rivaled his highway excursions for thrills and near misses. Although both AP and UPI kept photographers and rented outboards busy each time he visited the lake, we had little success in keeping track of his fun. After being repeatedly frustrated by Secret Service agents who used their own boats to keep us away, we rented boats faster than theirs one weekend. The triumph was short-lived. Next weekend the presidential bodyguards were equipped with jet-powered boats that were more than a match for ours.

The one time Austin photographer Ted Powers got close enough to snap a long-lens picture of the big-bellied man sunning himself topside on the cabin cruiser, LBJ was vehement in denying that he had a paunch to match the one in the photo. Close study of the negative suggested otherwise.

The President also acquired an Amphicar, a red convertible that could operate on either land or water. "Come take a ride in

my new car," he invited Cousin Oreole, then playfully drove
straight into the Pedernales while she screamed with alarm.

Returning to his alma mater in San Marcos about two weeks
after the 1964 election, LBJ was in a reminiscent mood.

"We have come a long way since those days when I lived in the
school garage here on campus," he said. "Incidentally, I lived
there three years before the business manager knew about it. And
I don't think he ever would have if the coach hadn't told him I
was bathing in the gymnasium."

Johnson certainly had come a long way, and he relished his
lofty position. Although he complained about being "locked up
behind that big iron fence," and sometimes referred to the White
House as "Lonely Acres," in more realistic moments he would respond to expressions of commiseration for his awesome burdens
with "Don't feel sorry for me—you should feel sorry for yourselves." Then he would recite the advantages of high pay, ample
household help, a private air fleet, a personal physician and medical staff, freedom from commuter worries and, most important,
the satisfaction of dealing with the challenges of a never ending
job.

The LBJ Ranch afforded Johnson the same perquisites and
comforts, and had the added advantage of being the place that he
called home. After the blitzing of Goldwater he spent long weeks
there, restoring his energy, planning for the 1965 Congressional
session and, as befitted his dreams and his ego, supervising the
building of monuments to himself and his rural ways in the surrounding hill country.

The inherent immodesty of his projects sometimes amused us
but time proved that he planned well. Despite their rather remote
location, the Johnson historic sites now rank among the most popular tourist meccas associated with any American President.

Johnson's first major project, launched in 1964, involved the
restoration of the small frame house, a block off U. S. Highway
290 in Johnson City, where he had spent much of his boyhood.
Built in 1886, it had an old well in the front yard and a water tank
and a windmill in the rear. LBJ had delivered his first speech as a
House candidate from the front porch.

At the President's direction, the back porch was glassed in to
serve as a museum for such family memorabilia as a grade school

report card that showed him meriting C-plus in deportment. Most of all, the porch exhibits memorialized his relationship with his mother, Rebekah Baines, who had taught him at her knee that, "In every noble enterprise, the shadow of a noble woman lies."

LBJ had only a surname during the first three months of his life because his parents could not agree on a given name. His father wanted to name him for a friend, W. C. Linden, and Rebekah finally accepted a compromise. She wrote, "Lin*den* isn't so euphonious as Lyn*don* would be."

When discussing his parents, Johnson would salute his father's political abilities and praise the elder Johnson's early legislative stand against the Ku Klux Klan, a position of principle that could have gotten Sam Ealy Johnson tarred and feathered, as the son liked to recall. However, real warmth was most evident when the President talked about his poetry-writing mother. Under glass at the boyhood home is a letter that he wrote her from college:

My Dear Mother, The end of another busy day brought me a letter from you. Your letters always give me more strength, renewed courage and that bulldog tenacity so essential to the success of any man. There is no force that exerts the power over me that your letters do. I have learned to look forward to them so long and now when one is delayed a spell of sadness and disappointment is cast over me.

I have been thinking of you all afternoon. As I passed through town on my way home to supper I could see the mothers doing their Xmas shopping. It made me wish for my mother so much. . . . I love you so much, Your son . . .

After he was elected to Congress, Johnson, who had chosen to recite at an elementary school ceremony a poem entitled, "I'd Rather Be Mamma's Boy," received from Rebekah a letter that also rests in the display case on the porch:

. . . How happy it would have made my precious noble father to know that the firstborn of his firstborn would achieve the position he desired. It makes me happy to have you carry on the ideals and principles so cherished by that great and good man. I gave you his name. I commend you to his example. You have always justified my expectations, my hopes, my dreams. How dear to me you are you cannot know my darling boy, my devoted son, my strength and comfort. . . .

Nine years before he became President, Johnson received from his mother at Christmas a collection of family sketches and biographies, clippings, photos and genealogical notes that he called "Mother's Album." After reaching the highest office, he gave the rights to publish it to the non-profit Johnson City Foundation that he and his family had established, and the collection was published in a hard-cover edition in 1965, a further tribute to the relationship between mother and son.

During the restoration of the Johnson City house we often followed the President there after Sunday services. Because it was not yet open to the public, we always remained outside until, on a Sunday weeks before the official opening, LBJ beckoned us to enter.

"Bird will fuss a little about it," he muttered, "but come on in and look at it."

After showing us the small rooms with their period furnishings, and the White House telephone hidden in a closet that housed the hot water heater, the President plopped down in a rocker and talked for an hour, off the record. Unfortunately, I kept no notes, for he usually was uncommonly entertaining when talking about the hills of home and his kinfolk.

"My grandfather moved away, fifty years before I discovered America, from the prairies of Texas to the hills in order that he could enjoy more freedom," Johnson once recalled. "He wanted to get away from the trains that passed through every night and disturbed him. He went out into a new, uncharted wilderness, and he chose well, because he settled in Johnson City almost one hundred years ago—and there hasn't a train come through there since."

On election day the President had taken us to a group of limestone buildings surrounded by weeds and reached by a rude dirt road, a few blocks away from the boyhood home. We saw a fort, barn and house built by the President's grandfather in 1853, with slits in the ground-floor walls for defense against marauding Comanches. LBJ recounted a family legend that his grandmother, Eliza Bunton Johnson, had been home alone with the children during a raid and hid in a fruit cellar where she stuffed a diaper in her baby's mouth to muffle its cries.

"Every time Grandma got pregnant," he reported, "they took her to the plains so the Indians couldn't attack her."

The frontier was close to reality for Johnson and he wanted to preserve its relics. In 1965 the Johnson City Foundation bought the old stone buildings, from which Granddaddy Johnson had driven cattle to the railhead in Kansas City, and twenty surrounding acres to be restored as yet another monument to the President's heritage.

A final Johnson shrine was created the following year at the site of what he claimed was his birthplace, close to the LBJ Ranch, although some relatives disputed the location. A four-room building of frame and stone, long unoccupied or used occasionally by migrant farm families, was rebuilt from the ground up as a birthplace replica.

Dozens of neighborhood women conducted tours at the boyhood home and birthplace, for which Johnson showed gratitude by entertaining them at ranch parties.

My colleague Karl Bauman wrote one Sunday that LBJ would be returning to Washington after conducting a tour of the birthplace for the press corps. Seeing this item on his AP ticker at the ranch, Johnson was outraged at the implicit suggestion that he planned to upstage the official volunteer tour guides. When we gathered for the tour LBJ refused to even step inside the house. He rocked on the porch while Mrs. Jessie Hunter, chief guide, showed us around.

Work on the various restorations was paralleled by expansion of the President's properties. When he ran for Vice-President, his holdings had consisted of the ranch house near Stonewall and just over four hundred acres. By 1966 his ranch lands encompassed fifteen thousand acres. It was a lot of property to take care of with just four full-time employees: foreman Dale Malechek, assistant foreman Dale Meeks, who also piloted the family's corporate airplane, and Mary Davis, the cook, and her husband, James.

Farm chores were complicated by an LBJ decision to turn part of his property into a zoo; he thought the animals would please the children who would be visiting the ranch after he left office. Dr. Christiaan Barnard, the South African heart surgeon, reported after a visit that Johnson "has as many wild animals on his ranch as we have in Kruger National Park."

The post-election months also saw an expansion of the facilities available to the President in Texas. The government built him a spacious $700,000 office in Austin's high-rise Federal Building.

And it spent $34,000 to insulate the ranch hangar and transform it into a room "to accommodate news conferences, television broadcasts and the entertainment of foreign dignitaries."

In this comfortable environment the President continued to entertain us quite regularly. Ranch tours were as colorful as ever, as Bauman wrote at the time:

> At one point [LBJ] climbed into his pig pen and tried, with limited success, to shoo the animals into one corner for close inspection. He also chased steers, running across the fields, flapping his arms and whooshing his hat in the air. And when he came to a bull purchased from Senator Wayne Morse, he perched his hat on the animal's head.

Johnson took great pride in his bulls. Showing off a prize specimen to a press contingent that included women reporters, he turned to me and said, "Frank, how would you like to be hung like that?"

When two cabinet members paid a post-election visit, the President piled them into a golf cart and, with horn blaring, made a beeline for CBS cameraman Ralph Santos, who was kneeling in the driveway to reload his camera. After LBJ had made one pass at Santos, Mrs. Johnson yelled, "Honey, don't!" But the exuberant LBJ came around again, missing by an inch.

Johnson then spied Doug Cornell of beagle fame and, feeling more charitable than on some past occasions, joked, "You may not get a Pulitzer Prize, but you got me a lot of votes."

After-church expeditions in Texas took on the trappings of hegiras and ranged far beyond the LBJ Ranch itself. "I'm going to see some pretty country," Johnson would announce. "You-all can come along if you want to." A favorite destination was the Lewis Ranch, where the President hoped daughter Luci would live someday.

We would form a twenty- or thirty-car caravan, driving over rutted, rocky back-country trails so dusty you could hardly see the auto ahead. Near the crest of one hill I watched fascinated as a low-hanging tree limb snapped off the aerials of about ten cars in succession. The trail was too narrow to permit evasive maneuvers.

Finding a newborn lamb beside a ranch road, Johnson stopped and, after looking around, announced that it had been abandoned by its mother. He instructed a bemused Secret Service agent to care for the animal, then drove off.

The President contended the Lewis property "wouldn't produce enough to pay the taxes," but then he would spot deer in a field and declare that the sight made the investment worth while.

When he was feeling particularly expansive, Johnson would show off the wine cellar at the small frame house on the Lewis place and pass some around to everybody. But his mood changed abruptly the day he found a light burning outside the building. Turning it off, he grumbled: "This is the kind of waste I want to stop. Why in the devil would you want a light on out here?"

For all the camaraderie, the ranch stays that followed the election produced their share of conflict between the President and the press corps. Some incidents were picayune, others more substantive.

In early December the Press Office volunteered a series of written questions and answers that supposedly reflected the observations of presidential physician George Burkley on LBJ's health and habits. A sample:

Q.: Does he like a highball and if so, what does he like?
A.: Yes—Bourbon and branch water.
Q.: And how often?
A.: Before dinner.

We knew perfectly well that LBJ drank Bourbon only if the scotch ran out, and we were equally certain that the President himself had ordered the "Bourbon and branch water" response because it sounded more down to earth, more American. But we wondered why he felt compelled to undermine his own credibility in such a transparent and needless fashion.

At about the same time USIA photographer Yoichi Okamoto returned from his Johnson-imposed exile, although Press Secretary Reedy insisted, no doubt because LBJ told him so, that Okamoto "is not here on a full-time basis." The fact is that Okamoto worked more than a forty-hour week and remained at the White House until Johnson left office. We wondered why we could not be told the simple truth.

Other examples involved the President more directly:

—He told us that he had no intention of naming Marvin Watson to the White House staff, even as he was doing his best to overcome Watson's objections to moving to Washington. Watson was on the payroll a few weeks later.

—He said on background, not for attribution to him, that it would be impossible to again keep the federal budget under $100 billion. Yet he managed to do it.

—He confided that he did not plan to deliver a detailed State of the Union Address in 1965 but instead would make a generalized philosophical statement. The address proved to be long on details, short on philosophy.

One of the strangest episodes occurred two days after Christmas and provided fresh insights into LBJ's style of maneuvering and manipulating. To a small group of newsmen at the ranch after Sunday services, Johnson declared that he planned to make major changes in his sub-cabinet line-up. The only men who need not worry about being replaced, he said, were Deputy Secretary of Defense Cyrus Vance and Under Secretary of State Ball.

The reporters were told they could print the story on two conditions: it had to carry a Washington dateline and Johnson could not be revealed as the source. The President said this was necessary because "some wives won't sleep tonight."

Karl Bauman got around the attribution problem by quoting "a source in a position to know President Johnson's mind." Bauman wrote that this source said LBJ would accept the pro forma resignations of "a good number" of under secretaries and assistant secretaries.

Most members of the press corps were unaware of Johnson's revelation until their editors called to demand similar accounts. Those who had not bothered to trail Johnson to church asked for a news conference. When they got one, LBJ baldly denied having any knowledge of the reported shake-up.

In fact there never was any sub-cabinet upheaval. Johnson apparently spread the report because he wanted the resignation of just one man, Under Secretary of Labor John Henning, but AFL-CIO President George Meany intervened to block the planned firing.

Jack Valenti, in his memoir of LBJ, *A Very Human President,* has written that most Chief Executives "are not long in the White House before it is patently clear that the press gives them a royal pain in the ass." If we had complaints about Johnson, he had his share about us. Not long after the election, for instance, he took to complaining privately that we were getting too demanding. He also argued that many of us were sniping at him to put on a show of independence because so many newspapers had endorsed him over Goldwater.

I found myself making one of my periodic trips to LBJ's doghouse during this period, for reasons that continue to elude me. As often happened, it took awhile for me to realize that I was being given the freeze. The first inkling came shortly before Christmas when a White House car pulled up to the house and an Army sergeant in chauffeur's uniform—all White House vehicles are driven by Army men in civilian clothes—came to the door with a small gift-wrapped package and a letter.

Opening the letter first, I found it was signed by the President and Mrs. Johnson and expressed holiday good wishes as well as pleasure at the fact that I had been with them during the campaign.

Then I opened the box, a gift from the Johnsons. It contained nothing but cotton batting.

When I went to the White House, I learned from colleagues that virtually every reporter and photographer who had spent so much as a single day covering the President's campaign had received a gold-filled tie clip as a memento. Since I had covered more of the campaign than any other member of the press corps, missing only a one-day trip to St. Louis, I went to George Reedy and reported that my gift box had been empty. I supposed a mistake had been made, until Reedy told me, "Sorry, Frank, we don't have any more."

Reedy's quick response, without even pretending to make a check, convinced me the oversight was deliberate. Further evidence along that line was supplied later by Edward T. Folliard of the Washington *Post*. Johnson handed Folliard a tie clip days after the supply supposedly was exhausted. When the reporter expressed his gratitude, the President immodestly suggested, "Your grandson will appreciate it even more, Eddie."

I searched my memory for something I might have said or written that could have offended LBJ. I could think of two possibilities. He had asked me, following a well-attended campaign appearance, if I had ever seen a crowd like that while covering Jack Kennedy. I told him that I had, "many times." The second occasion also involved a Kennedy and often was cited by Horace

Busby as proof that you could argue with the President and cause him to change his mind.

"The trouble with Bobby Kennedy is that he has no heart," Johnson told me one evening in Busby's presence.

"I don't agree with that, Mr. President," I replied. "Just a few months ago Bill Eaton was walking with Bobby Kennedy from the White House to the Justice Department. When they got down by the Willard Hotel, Bobby noticed a poster of a crippled child in a window. He told Bill about the kid's illness and the family's circumstances. He really was very upset, and he walked the rest of the way with his head down, looking at his shoes."

"Well," said Johnson, "maybe he does have a heart—where children are concerned!"

Some weeks after receiving the empty box I met a friend of Johnson's, Everett Collier of the Houston *Chronicle,* and told him about the missing tie clip. Collier expressed confidence that it had been an honest mistake and said he would speak to the President about it.

Shortly thereafter Valenti approached me and said, "Frank, I understand you didn't get an LBJ tie clip. That's a terrible mistake." With that, he removed the souvenir clip from his own tie and handed it to me.

11

"*Mollie and the Babies*"

In his approach to domestic problems Lyndon Johnson was nothing if not bold. Convinced that the men of government were wise enough to devise solutions for any problem, he had scant patience with those who argued that progress would be too costly, too dangerous, or even futile.

"That reminds me," he said, "of the old fellow at Fredericksburg when we started the train up there. He preached against it. He discouraged it. He wouldn't subscribe to it. He wouldn't even be on the committee promoting it. But when the train finally came and we had the queen . . . cut the ribbon, he was in the back yakkin' that we will never get the train started. And when she pulled out, and the steam was over his head . . . he said, 'Well, they will never get her stopped!'"

In his own way LBJ was an evangelist in arguing for social justice and, because of long exposure to old-time religion, he talked like one. Making his case for salvation on earth, he told a group of newspaper editors:

"Believe me, God is not mocked. We reap as we sow. Our God is still a jealous God, jealous of His righteousness, jealous for the last of the little ones who went unfed while the rich sat down to eat and rose up to play. And unless my administration profits the present and provides the foundation for a better life for all humanity, not just now but for generations to come, I shall have failed."

The President often recalled the parting advice offered by his politician-father when LBJ boarded the train to travel to Washington as a freshman House member: "Son, measure each vote you cast by this standard: Is this vote in the benefit of people? What does this do for human beings?"

He liked to cite the fact that he was one of only three House members from the South who voted for Franklin D. Roosevelt's first minimum wage law, setting a standard of twenty-five cents an hour. Of the three, he was the only one to survive the next round of Democratic primaries.

In the days when he was a Congressional secretary, Johnson would remember, he left standing orders with the pages' office that he be called each time Huey Long took the floor. LBJ said he wanted to be there because he never heard a Long speech "that I didn't think was calculated to do some good for some people who needed some speeches made for them and couldn't make them for themselves."

For LBJ, the New Deal drive to allay the mass poverty of the 1930s never ended. It simply was being extended and expanded in 1965, part of a continuum of progress. And thirty years after the Great Depression, images of terrible want were fresh in Johnson's mind:

"I personally, in 1935, saw little Mexican children go into the garbage cans in San Antonio, Texas, in back of the cafeterias, and take grapefruit rinds that had been discarded from the tables at breakfast that morning, and take those grapefruit rinds out and hull them with their teeth to get something to eat. The poor were everywhere. That is what they talk about as 'the good old days.'"

Johnson would tell of a social worker visiting a poor family at mealtime and, after asking one child why he was not eating, being told, "It is not my day to eat." Or of a housewife lamenting, "I have forgotten how to cook, for I have nothing to cook."

The President often recited a vivid account of suffering witnessed during his travels as Vice-President:

". . . I stood in a mud hut in Africa, in Senegal, and I saw an African mother with a baby on her breast, one in her stomach, one on her back, and eight on the floor, that she was trying to feed on eight dollars per month.

"As I looked into her determined eyes, I saw the same expression that I saw in my mother's eyes when she, the wife of a tenant farmer [*sic*], looked down upon me and my little sisters and brothers, determined that I should have my chance and my opportunity, believing that, where there was a will, there was a way."

Johnson's father was not a tenant farmer, and the family was one of the few in the Johnson City area able to afford a Model T Ford before World War I. However, the family finances never rested on a very firm foundation, as they fluctuated sharply with the success or failure of Sam Ealy Johnson's various projects. The President could say with honesty:

"I know what poverty means to people, I have been unemployed. I have stayed waiting in an employment office, waiting for an assignment and a placement. I have shined shoes as a boy. I have worked on a highway crew from daylight until dark for a dollar a day, working with my hands and sweating with my brow. This has taught me the meaning of poverty. . . ."

With a grin and a chuckle LBJ once quoted Luci as asking, "Daddy, as an outsider, how do you feel about the human race?" More seriously, he added, "The truth is that in this land of wealth and abundance and plenty too many of us are outsiders to the suffering, the want and the hopes of other human beings."

As President, Johnson never gave evidence of wavering in his concern for people. Throughout the 1964 campaign he promised to translate concern into action, to "do something for Mollie and the babies." His own landslide victory was paralleled by Democratic gains in the Senate and House. The votes were there to move ahead toward the Great Society.

First, of course, there was a triumph to savor: the inauguration ceremony that found Johnson standing without hat or overcoat in the frigid winter air; the festive balls where comely ladies, notably Barbara Howar, waited to dance with the hero of the hour. As the festivities ended, long after midnight, the happy President was filled with enthusiasm:

"I hope you have had as much fun as we've had today. Tomorrow it's back to work. We're on our way to the Great Society!"

Three days later, at 2:26 A.M., an ambulance deposited LBJ at the Bethesda, Maryland, Naval Hospital. Awakened by my office, I drove there with haste and learned that Johnson, worn down by the celebration, had been brought low by a heavy cold.

Within hours, dozens of reporters and photographers were making their headquarters in the hospital's spacious auditorium-theater, which prompted a small boy to wail, "Daddy, why can't

we see *Mary Poppins?*" The father replied, "You should have
voted for Goldwater."

Around midday four of us were summoned to the President's
sickroom. Propped up in bed on pillows, a vaporizer steaming beside him, LBJ wanted the world to know that his ailment was not
serious.

"I wouldn't hesitate right now to put on my britches and go
back to the office if there was something that needed to be done,"
he told us.

A white handkerchief poked out of the pocket of Johnson's
bright red pajamas and he looked almost jaunty, until a dry, rasp-
ing cough seized him. "I think colds bother me more than most
people," he remarked, adding that he'd had pneumonia six or
eight times. This startled us because his published medical histo-
ries had made no mention of respiratory problems. We had noted,
however, that he carried a vapor inhaler in his pocket and used it
often.

Luci, then seventeen, perched beside the President, caressing
him and, when he coughed, patting him gently on the back. She
was the only member of the family who was available to console
him. Mrs. Johnson and Lynda also were patients at the hospital
and LBJ told us that he thought they had given him the cold.

What was he taking for the cough? Brown's Mixture, a venerable patent cough syrup.

The next morning Sir Winston Churchill died at the age of
ninety. Holding a second bedside news conference, Johnson announced that he wanted "very, very much" to attend the funeral,
adding, "A lot depends on how I feel in the next day or two."

Johnson did not cough and his voice no longer was hoarse. He
insisted he just had a sore throat, "but they call it by a fancy
name." He did not even require hospitalization, he contended, but
declared that he could not object "if they wanted me to come out
here where there are a lot of nice, pretty girls to wait on you."

We asked if he might have gotten sick because he had not worn
an overcoat at the inaugural ceremony. That had nothing to do
with it, he said, because he had worn "electric underwear"—his
term for thermal long johns. Unwilling to concede that he might
have shown poor judgment, he snapped, "As a matter of fact, I
was too hot."

Johnson spent four days in the hospital with what came to be called "executive flu," because he had a lot of fellow sufferers in the top ranks of government.

One hundred hotel rooms had been reserved in London for the White House press corps and others who would accompany LBJ if he went to the Churchill funeral. We awaited the answer. There was a published report that the decision would follow a medical checkup, but George Reedy told us he did not expect a single "Dr. Kildaire-style" examination, "at the end of which someone emerges with a dramatic announcement." Reedy was wrong.

A medical team examined Johnson late in the afternoon of January 27, after which seven of us were escorted to the presidential bedroom in the White House. As I wrote: "The newsmen who saw the President agreed he looked sicker than they had expected. Hair disheveled, he lay in a four-poster canopied bed speaking softly, coughing lightly from time to time and blowing his nose."

"I don't have the bouncy feeling that I usually have," he acknowledged, then announced that, on medical advice, he would not go to London. Instead he was naming Chief Justice Earl Warren and Dean Rusk to represent the United States. This was another surprise.

"Is there any special reason why you didn't name Vice-President Humphrey?" he was asked.

"No," he replied.

As we filed out of the room Johnson assumed his man-in-charge air, picking up his bedside telephone and saying, "Get me Secretary Rusk."

At home and abroad LBJ drew criticism for not sending Humphrey to the Churchill rites. His decision even prompted reports that, just a week after Humphrey's oath-taking, the new Vice-President had been downgraded already. Stung and angry, Johnson responded with unseemly sarcasm at a February 4 news conference:

"I am glad to have the press reaction and the reactions abroad on the protocol involved in connection with funerals. I had served as Vice-President for three years and it had never occurred to me, and I had never had it brought to my attention so vividly, that it was the duty and the function of the Vice-President to be present at all official funerals. . . .

"In light of your interest and other interests, I may have made a mistake by asking the Chief Justice to go and not the Vice-

President. I will bear in mind in connection with any future funerals your very strong feelings in the matter and try to act in ac-
cordance with our national interest."

Privately, Johnson contended the furore was caused by a single
reporter who, he said, had wanted to go to London with
Humphrey. Even seven months later LBJ introduced Humphrey
to the President's Council on Aging with the crack, "If he is not
out of the country attending some funeral, he will be here working
for you."

At that point it would have taken much more than mishandling
of a funeral delegation to shake Johnson's massive political base.
There were critics, to be sure, but the Great Society was abuilding.

Nearly a year earlier the President had told a Chicago audience,
"We have been called upon—are you listening?—to build a great
society of the highest order. . . ." Alas, the phrase fell upon deaf
ears, even after LBJ repeated it in more than a dozen subsequent
speeches and statements. The Great Society label only caught hold
after Reedy's office distributed an advance text of Johnson's 1964
University of Michigan commencement address in which the term
was capitalized.

Richard Goodwin, a Kennedy aide given new status by Johnson, was primarily responsible for the Michigan speech and several of the President's other more memorable addresses. In one
rambling, off-the-record discourse Johnson told us:

"I use Dick Goodwin for pathos. I like people who can cry with
me. Dick and I can see an old woman on the street and cry.
Valenti cries too—and Humphrey cries with us."

Sometimes it appeared that Johnson was prepared to cry over
every domestic problem, but he did not see it that way. In fact he
argued that he was being restrained in proposing Great Society
legislation. "I don't want to go charging hell with a bucket of
water!" he told a small group of us during a back-yard hike. He
reported that cabinet members kept coming to him with new ideas
for legislation but were given mixed-metaphor advice: "Put them
on the back burner, let them settle in the stomach and digest for a
while." LBJ said he kept telling his people to go to Congress and
"find out what they'll go for up there." He said he would be
satisfied to get affirmative action on just five programs in 1965:
aid to education, Medicare, voting rights, assistance for depressed
areas, and aid for Appalachia.

Noting that most of his social welfare programs were keyed to help those with annual family incomes of two thousand dollars or less, he predicted that in future years the floor would be raised to three thousand dollars and then four thousand. To him, fighting poverty was more than a humanitarian endeavor; it made sense economically.

"If we can raise the annual earnings of ten million among the poor by only one thousand dollars," he would say, "we will have added fourteen billion dollars a year to our economy." I got his point, although I did not follow his arithmetic. In any event he saw his proposals as a way to make people "taxpayers instead of tax-eaters."

In mid-February, Johnson drove to a Washington hotel and told the National Industrial Conference Board, "The Great Society is not a welfare state—nor is it a spending state." Bill Eaton and I were present and we both distinctly heard a businessman in the middle of the large audience react by shouting, "Ha!" Since it was rather unusual for the President to receive any sort of heckling from an audience of businessmen, Eaton and I both reported the reaction. Bill was fortunate in that his account did not appear on the UPI ticker behind LBJ's desk, whereas mine did.

George Reedy was summoned at once to the Oval Office and directed to go to the basement office of the White House Communications Agency, which is staffed by the Army's Signal Corps, and listen to the speech as recorded on tape by WHCA. Johnson never said a word to me about it, but he told colleagues:

"Cormier must be goin' deaf. George Reedy listened to that tape and there was no 'ha!' on it. And you know those Signal Corps microphones are so sensitive they could pick up a fart in the back row!"

Actually the microphone had been aimed directly at LBJ's mouth as he spoke. It would have been miraculous had the exclamation been recorded.

I might add that the President's esteem for me was not advanced when the New York *Daily News* published my offending paragraph as a "Guest Editorial."

A few weeks later it was Senator Harry Flood Byrd's turn to do a slow burn. Firm in his opposition to Medicare legislation, Byrd was neatly mousetrapped by the President. Actually Johnson had considerable affection for the aging Virginia conservative and once publicly kissed the Senator's hand following funeral services for a member of Byrd's family. LBJ also liked to tease Byrd by reminding him that they had both come to Washington in the same year and thus were "about the only two original New Dealers that are still around." Affection played no part, however, in the push toward the Great Society.

Johnson needed early hearings on the Medicare bill by Byrd's Senate Finance Committee, so he invited him to a bipartisan meeting to review the status of the legislation. Unbeknownst to Byrd, LBJ also directed that television cameras be set up in the Cabinet Room. When the Oval Office meeting ended, Johnson innocently, or so it seemed, invited the Congressional delegation to accompany him to the Cabinet Room, where he urged each one in turn to say a few words about the bill for the cameras. Calling on Byrd last, he bore down on the trapped Senator:

"Senator Byrd, I know you will take an interest in the orderly scheduling of this matter and in giving it a thorough hearing. Would you care to make an observation?"

"There is no observation that I can make now, because the bill hasn't come before the Senate. Naturally, I am not familiar with it. All I can say is . . . that I will see that adequate and thorough hearings are held on the bill."

"And you have nothing that you know of that would prevent that coming about in a reasonable time? There is nothing ahead of it in the committee?"

"Nothing in the committee *now* [emphasis added]."

"So, when the House acts and it is referred to the Senate Finance Committee, you will arrange for prompt hearings and thorough hearings?"

"Yes," Byrd agreed.

Carl Albert, then the House Democratic leader, commented afterward, "That's the best example of the 'Treatment' in public that anyone ever got."

Medicare became law far sooner than many had expected. Even though Byrd voted against it, the Senator honored his public commitment to give the measure prompt consideration. And Johnson flew off to Independence, Missouri, to sign it in the presence of Harry Truman, who had first backed the idea years before. Said LBJ:

"The people of the United States love and voted for Harry

Truman, not because he gave them hell—but because he gave them hope."

The advance text of LBJ's speech at the Truman Library contained the word "podiatrist" but it was passed over in delivery. Asked why he had omitted the word, the President acknowledged, "I didn't know how to pronounce it."

Health and education ranked at the top of Johnson's agenda. And he had a homey way of expressing his concern about both subjects: "Forty-nine per cent—one out of every two boys we draft has to be sent home because he is physically or mentally unqualified. That is the kind of folks you are raising. If I had to do that with my calves, I would go broke every year."

Johnson was convinced that federal investments in health and education would pay big dividends. As he told supporters of the 1965 education bill at a White House reception:

". . . I hope the people of America can realize that we now spend about $1,800 a year to keep a delinquent youth in the detention home; we spend $2,500 for a family on relief; we spend $3,000 for a criminal in a state prison . . . but we only spend $450 a year per child in our public schools."

Johnson's own education was hard-won, and was followed by an experience that remained forever fresh in his memory—the teaching of Mexican-American children at a poor border school in Cotulla, Texas, when he was but twenty years old. His reminiscences with us often seemed to involve Cotulla as much as Johnson City.

Believing that "education is the guardian genius of democracy," Johnson was jubilant when Congress passed his education bill, and he offered an amusing account of how it came about. The recital began with a recollection of his attendance at a B'nai B'rith dinner at which he was honored for his espousal of civil rights legislation:

". . . I made, I thought, the greatest speech of my life. And they stood and applauded me and took my picture and gave me the award. And I came back home and worked hard the next morning —and picked up the afternoon paper that night and I saw, 'B'nai B'rith Denounces Johnson's Education Bill.' And I was rather distressed.

"And then the next thing I heard, some of the Catholics were upset because they couldn't get the books [for parochial schools]

. . . and because of provisions in the bill that were obnoxious to them. And so we talked to a few cardinals and we worked very hard on the matter, and we worked out an arrangement where everybody could get a peep at the book a little bit and we got them adjusted. And I thought, 'Now if this line just holds for a few hours, maybe I can get a roll call.'

"And lo and behold, a friend of mine down in Texas—a very prominent doctor who is a leader of the Baptist faith—heard about what had happened . . . the Catholics were going to get some of these things. He called me up, called up one of my assistants, and said, 'What in the world has happened? Has the Pope taken the President over?' My assistant said, 'No one had taken him over. The President is out swimming.'

" 'What's my President doing swimming in the middle of the day with all the work he's got to do?'

" 'Well,' said my assistant, 'he's out there with Dr. Graham.'

"He said, 'Is that *our* Billy?'

"Well, it was 'our Billy,' one of the greatest religious leaders of this country.

"So before the sun went down that night, we had the cardinals and we had the rabbis and we had 'our Billy.' And they were all aboard—and the greatest educational measure ever considered by any legislative body became the law of the land."

On April 11, 1965, Johnson sat at a vintage school desk on the lawn beside the one-room schoolhouse of his childhood and signed the billion-dollar education bill. With him was Mrs. Chester Loney of Rough and Ready, California, age seventy-two, who had been his first-grade teacher when she was known as Miss Kate Deadrich. Noting that she had taught "eight grades at one and the same time," Johnson said:

"Come over here, Miss Katie, and sit by me, will you? Let them see you. I started school when I was four years old, and they tell me, Miss Kate, that I recited my first lessons while sitting on your lap."

She nodded in agreement as he recalled this bit of family lore.

A ranch tour for Miss Kate followed the ceremony, with LBJ driving his Lincoln into a field of cattle where he sounded a special horn that sent them into a mating dance. Hopping out of the car, Johnson summoned photographer Okamoto and gave precise instructions about the picture he wanted. Okie dutifully stretched out on his belly in the field and took a ground-level shot of coupled animals with Miss Kate, seated in the Lincoln, in the background. That was *"our* Lyndon," particularly in the springtime. Two days later, back at the White House, I reported:

WASHINGTON, April 13 (AP)—President Johnson had his annual attack of spring fever today, soaking up sunshine on Harry Truman's White House balcony with three foreign ambassadors, newsmen and the husband of a European queen.

Johnson's high spirits in the noonday sun were reminiscent of his balcony scene last spring with poet Carl Sandburg and photographer Edward Steichen. On that occasion he held a shouted news conference with reporters gathered on the lawn below.

This time newsmen and photographers were invited to join the chief executive on the crimson-floored balcony, just off the first family's living quarters upstairs at the White House. They were summoned to record Johnson's formal meeting with Prince Bernhard of the Netherlands, husband of Queen Juliana.

Protocol quickly vanished. . . .

After the Prince was photographed, Johnson invited reporters to crowd around him and get their own pictures taken with the Washington Monument in the background. The newsmen were so numerous they had to pose in relays.

The Prince, meanwhile, stood to one side by himself, looking bemused at this display of presidential informality. He didn't seem shocked, though.

While all this was going on, Johnson wondered aloud what had happened to three ambassadors who had just left him after presenting diplomatic credentials.

A roar of police motorcycles from the driveway below signaled their imminent departure. A White House aide shouted down to halt the motorcade and get the envoys back upstairs so they, too, could have a moment in the sun with Johnson.

Up trooped Ambassadors Torben H. Renne of Denmark, Sir Patrick Dean of Great Britain, and Radomiro Tomic of Chile. More pictures followed, with Johnson ushering Bernhard back into camera range.

The whole while, Johnson engaged in running banter with reporters.

The temperature was near 60 and the sun beamed brightly from a sky studded with puffy white clouds. The President obviously relished these evidences of spring, which apparently served to reinforce a good humor evident since his weekend stay in Texas where blossoming fields of bluebonnets proclaimed the change of seasons.

There was only one discordant note during the 1965 balcony scene.

People kept soiling their hands on the white-painted wrought iron railing, which no one had thought to dust.

Johnson's easy informality also was much in evidence a few weeks later following a live radio broadcast of a radiotelephone conversation with two Gemini astronauts who were aboard a recovery carrier in the Pacific. LBJ talked to them from the Fish Room, then headed across the hall to his office. Sid Davis of Westinghouse was near the door, winding up his broadcast of the event, when a large hand grasped his shoulder. Thinking someone did not know he was on the air, Davis jerked his shoulder free of the grip.

"Sid, are you broadcastin' there?" came a familiar voice.

"We are on the air, sir," announced the startled reporter.

"Well, I declare," said Johnson. "I bet it's a good broadcast."

"It is," the normally modest Davis agreed.

"If it's as good a broadcast as you are a reporter—well, I'm really proud of you."

"Thank you very much, sir. [Pause.] That was the President talking, and he's in a very good mood. . . ."

LBJ had invited the astronauts to join him at his ranch. Always eager to get back to Texas, he complained one day that he had to stay in Washington to preside at the installation of Lawrence F. O'Brien as Postmaster General. But ABC's Bill Lawrence suggested that O'Brien take the cabinet oath at the fourth-class post office at Hye, Texas, near the ranch, where LBJ recalled mailing his first letter at the age of four. Johnson leaped at the idea and we were off.

The postmaster at Hye, Levi Deike, returned from a vacation in New Mexico to find communications men setting up a microphone and loudspeakers in front of his brightly painted general store and post office, an area landmark because of its white and green gingerbread façade.

"What's taking place here?" he asked.

Informed that a new Postmaster General would be installed at a front-porch ceremony, in less than two hours, Deike was incredulous: "In a two-by-four place like this!"

"It was about fifty-three years ago," Johnson recalled at the event, "that I mailed my first letter from this post office. And Larry O'Brien told me a few moments ago that he is going out to find that letter and deliver it."

The President then invited everyone into the store and out of the rain that was falling, promising them "hors doves." Taken by surprise, Mrs. Deike got out a loaf of processed Cheddar, opened a box of crackers and spread paper towels on a counter. Johnson sampled the cheese and crackers, then warmed himself at an oil stove.

The post office section was in a corner and LBJ next strolled there to inspect the lock boxes. Fumbling without result with the combination lock of Number 276, he announced, "This is mine."

The Post Office Department made an inviting target for Johnson's gibes, as he had demonstrated at the oath-taking of O'Brien's predecessor, John Gronouski, as Postmaster General.

"It was called to my attention recently that in 1961 a speed record was set in delivering the Inaugural Address of President Lincoln to the West Coast. Using pony express, copies of Lincoln's address were delivered from Washington to California in seven days and seventeen hours by seventy-five ponies, at a cost of five dollars per one half ounce. Today, for only five cents, we can send three ounces of presidential addresses across the country—at about the same rate of speed."

One 1965 cabinet change, occasioned by the resignation of Secretary of the Treasury C. Douglas Dillon, was especially pleasing to LBJ. The President was not overly fond of Dillon, who struck him as something of a stuffed shirt. As successor, Johnson chose Henry Fowler, a Washington lawyer who had once served as Dillon's Under Secretary.

"Doug Dillon would put on a white tie and go to a tea party," the President complained privately, "while Fowler would be writing what Dillon was going to say the next morning."

A powerful House Democrat circulated a report that Dillon's post would go to David Kennedy, a Chicago banker who eventually became Richard Nixon's first Secretary of the Treasury.

"I don't even know the man," Johnson insisted, deploring erroneous "leaks" that he argued could do serious damage to the individual involved: "He goes home and his wife asks, 'Why didn't you get the job?'" We suspected LBJ had caused Kennedy's name to be whispered to the Congressman—so the House member's trustworthiness could be tested.

Johnson drafted Fowler for the Treasury post, and he told about it with relish at Fowler's oath-taking ceremony:

"The day he was appointed I called him into this room about

one o'clock and I said, 'I have not come to ask but to tell, and I want you to do the same thing. Would you mind going home now for lunch and telling Trudye that you are going to be named Secretary of the Treasury.' And he said, 'We had planned to leave for Europe on Tuesday; what do I say about that?' I said, 'Don't bother me with details.' "

Jack Valenti once predicted that history would know Johnson as "The Great Persuader." Fowler surely could not disagree, nor could many members of Congress. According to a calculation by *Congressional Quarterly,* the Senate and House approved 68.4 per cent of the President's 1965 legislative proposals, the highest proportion since it began keeping such statistics in 1954. LBJ's success ratio a year earlier had been an impressive 57.6 per cent, compared with Kennedy's 1963 low of 27.2 per cent. Said Johnson upon receiving the 1965 award of the American Platform Association:

"I only wish my college teacher could be here to see what is happening now. Because in my first term in college, when I made the debating team as a freshman—which was slightly unusual—when I got my grade cards my teacher gave me the lowest grade I ever received in college. . . . He gave me a "D" in argumentation!"

The savvy Johnson did not claim all credit for his legislative achievements, however. There was credit to spare for the Congressional leaders of both parties. Said Johnson of Senator Everett Dirksen: "We sat across the aisle and sliced each other up—but when it counts, he always comes to the top, like a cork." And Speaker John McCormack was sadly underrated in LBJ's estimation because McCormack had lived in Sam Rayburn's shadow for twenty-five years. Of McCormack he said:

"He isn't modernized. He doesn't have the TV image. He doesn't use Stacomb and he goes home to his wife every night at seven-thirty. But he's the man you pass the ball to when you need another yard. He always carries it through."

Recurrent reports of presidential phone calls to cajole Congress members were a source of irritation for Johnson. When Marquis Childs wrote that LBJ telephoned Dirksen on an average of three times a day, the President told us: "I had my staff check my diary and they found only twelve calls to Dirksen in one hundred days, and ten of those concerned Republican appointments."

Of course, he added, when a big bill was being voted on, he wanted someone to "man the dike—if there's a leak in it, I want to get somebody to fix it." The fixer, using the term in no pejorative sense, often was Johnson himself.

Legislatively, almost everything got fixed to his satisfaction during the first year of his elected term. Inevitably some bills were amended, but LBJ tried to be philosophical about the changes.

"Most of you like to have your stories printed just as you write them," he told us. "But we don't have that kind of system in government. I can't resign, as you can if your editor changes your story too much and inserts different facts."

Bills reached the President's desk in such numbers that he worried about the cost of the ceremonial pens he used to sign them, pens that he handed out by the gross. In signing five bills one week, he gave away 587 pens. At $1.11 apiece, the cost came to $651.57. Johnson found a new model that could be purchased in quantity for seventeen cents apiece.

It should be noted that Johnson did not actually use all the gift pens, although each souvenir came boxed with a slip of paper asserting that he had indeed used it to sign a specified bill. To foster the illusion, each pen was dipped in ink before being boxed.

The final bill to clear Congress in 1965 was Mrs. Johnson's own —the Highway Beautification Act. Her husband's exertions on its behalf became as legendary as her own. When the measure was in the drafting stage Johnson called a cabinet member at 7 A.M. and demanded, "What are you doing about getting rid of auto junkyards along the highways?" A Senator was told, "For God's sake, I've got to get Lady Bird off my back!" To another the President reported: "Lady Bird keeps running in here saying, 'Lyndon, you get all your bills passed. Why can't you get mine through?'"

Ironically, the final vote on Mrs. Johnson's bill coincided with a "Salute to Congress" the President had scheduled to express his gratitude for all that had been achieved. With the House still in session to act on the beautification bill, Johnson told the sparse assemblage of partygoers:

"I regret very much that all the members of Congress could not be with us, because they saw their duty, and I hope they are doing it. . . ."

12

"We Shall Overcome"

Lyndon Johnson's first legislative request to Congress, voiced at the joint session five days after Kennedy's murder, was for quick action on civil rights:

". . . no memorial oration or eulogy could more eloquently honor President Kennedy's memory than the earliest possible passage of the civil rights bill for which he fought so long. We have talked long enough in this country about equal rights. We have talked for one hundred years or more. It is time now to write the next chapter, and to write it in the books of law."

Dick Gregory's reaction, shared by many, was one of pleased surprise. "Twenty million of us unpacked our bags," he cracked. The vision of a Southern-born President, which is the way LBJ described himself, becoming a dedicated champion of the civil rights cause was, perhaps, surprising. For many years in Congress, Johnson had "voted his district" and gone along with segregationist attitudes.

"I have always opposed the poll tax," the President told a news conference in 1965. Actually he had voted repeatedly to perpetuate the tax that was, of course, designed to disenfranchise poor blacks. His opposition to anti-poll tax bills was recorded in 1942, 1943, 1945, 1947 and 1950. He voted against an anti-lynching bill within days of his election to the House in 1937. He opposed the establishment of a Fair Employment Practices Commission, a Truman goal, in 1946 and 1950. In one Senate debate he declared, "We cannot legislate love."

As recently as 1957, when Congress was considering a major civil rights bill, Senate Democratic Leader Johnson had sent inquiring constituents a form letter:

I do not know where you could have gotten the idea that I am supporting "the so-called bill for civil rights legislation now before Congress." Certainly I have made no statement to that effect nor have I intimated to anyone that I plan such support.

The bill that has been introduced is one to which I am very much opposed, as I do not believe it would advance any legitimate cause.

Nevertheless Johnson within months was maneuvering the bill toward passage, albeit after promoting compromises that had weakened some of its most important provisions. It was the first civil rights bill to claim his support, and the first to be enacted since 1875. Many colleagues conceded it would not have passed without LBJ's efforts, and he often pointed with pride to the achievement.

I have never heard or read of Johnson evidencing racial prejudice in his personal behavior, even in the years when his voting record on the subject was dismal. Indeed, soon after his election to the Senate in 1949 he said in a speech:

"Perhaps no prejudice is so contagious or so dangerous as the unreasoning prejudice against men because of their birth, the color of their skin, or their ancestral background. Racial prejudice is dangerous because it is a disease of the majority endangering minority groups. . . . For those who would keep any group in bondage, I have no sympathy or tolerance. . . . My faith in my fellow man is too great to permit me to waste away my lifetime burning with hatred for any group."

Johnson was one of only three Senators from the Old Confederacy who refused to sign the 1956 "Southern Manifesto" opposing the Supreme Court's landmark school desegregation decision. I assume that he followed his conscience, although he surely was aware that a substantial minority of his Texas constituents were brown or black, and that his Senate leadership role was national and not regional in scope. Harry McPherson, a long-time aide, wrote in *A Political Education* that LBJ's refusal to sign was possible, from a political standpoint, "because he was sound on oil and gas."

By 1963, certainly, there could be no question where Johnson's heart lay. On Memorial Day, at the Gettysburg battlefield, the Vice-President delivered one of his most memorable addresses, one that put him squarely in the pro-civil rights camp:

"Until justice is blind to color, until education is unaware of race, until opportunity is unconcerned with the color of men's skins, emancipation will be a proclamation but not a fact. To the extent that the Proclamation of Emancipation is not fulfilled in fact, to that extent we shall have fallen short of assuring freedom to the free.

"The Negro today asks justice.

"We do not answer him—we do not answer those who lie beneath this soil—when we reply to the Negro by asking 'patience.'"

A few months later, as President, Johnson recruited Gerri Whittington as the first black to serve as a presidential secretary. On New Year's Eve he took her by the arm and escorted her into Austin's "whites only" Forty Acres Club, near the University of Texas campus. The club has been desegregated ever since.

Early in his administration, LBJ wanted to name a black newsman, Carl Rowan, to head the United States Information Agency. First, however, he prepared a test for Rowan. USIA had recently produced a documentary film about the civil rights March on Washington that was climaxed by Martin Luther King's speech, "I Have a Dream." Segregationists in Congress and elsewhere were demanding that the film be withheld from distribution, arguing that it glorified King and his cause. Johnson invited Rowan to join him in the White House theater for a screening of the movie and, when the lights came on afterward, asked if the black man would permit its distribution. Rowan replied that he certainly would do so. LBJ gave him the job.

As a young man teaching in Cotulla, Johnson was devoted to his Mexican-American students, members of a minority that was not universally loved in Texas. In his chats with us, and in public speeches the President cited his Cotulla experiences as having marked the beginning of his interest in civil rights.

One tale he often told concerned his efforts to organize supervised play activity during recesses, demanding that other teachers help him instead of disappearing into the rest rooms to smoke: "And I said, 'You take the north corner, and you take the south one, and you take the west one, and let's have volleyball.' And I took my own first pay check and bought a volleyball for them [the pupils] and bought a playground softball for them." But he said six teachers went on strike rather than have him tell them what to do. By his account, a motion to fire him was put before the Board of Trustees, only to be tabled after an influential woman member countered with a suggestion that the six be fired instead. In the end everyone stayed.

"I have never understood it," Johnson said, "but the Mexican people have been voting for me ever since. . . . They have a grapevine and the word gets around."

Visiting the American Embassy in Mexico City as President, he added another recollection with a tragicomic ending:

"I have been coming across this border all my life. I have been working with the people of Mexico ever since I was a child. My first playmate was a little Mexican boy. We raced our horses together when we were both just learning to ride.

"I remember he told me he didn't want to run a race with me because his horse wasn't as fat as mine and therefore couldn't run as fast. I said, 'Well, I will just solve that problem. We will make him fat.'

"So we got out a bucket and got in the oat bin and we fed that horse nearly all afternoon. Then we filled him full of water and then we took him out and ran the race. Then the horse died."

After World War II, Johnson intervened when the authorities in Three Rivers, Texas, refused to permit the burial there of a Mexican-American serviceman who had been killed in the Philippines. LBJ arranged for his burial in Arlington. In recalling the episode, Johnson said that because of it he never joined in criticism of Major General Harry Vaughan, who was Truman's controversial military aide.

"Harry Vaughan stood in the icy sleet at attention with a red wreath he brought to place on the grave of the Mexican boy," the President related. "He stood there for an hour, because he wanted to do it. I have never said anything about him—and I never will."

Another of his recollections concerned the desegregation of

Johnson City when he was a young man. A local contractor, Melvin Winter, submitted the low bid to build a big road into town, where no blacks had ever been tolerated. LBJ said Winter insisted on bringing in his black foremen, who camped by the river, and continued:

"Winter went to the barbershop and was having his head washed when the town bully, a big two-hundred-pounder, came in and gave him until sundown to get 'his niggers' out of town. Winter didn't accept that suggestion so they commenced to scuffle in the barbershop, then went out into the street. They had a terrible fight up and down the middle of the street, and the townspeople were lined up on either side of the block, taking sides and cheering. Winter finally got the upper hand and began to pound the bully's head on the pavement, yelling, 'Are my niggers gonna stay? Are they gonna stay?' That's the way Johnson City was integrated, and it's been that way ever since."

Johnson also remembered an incident that followed a speech he made in Dime Box, Texas, as a young Congressman. All the whites lined up to shake his hand, he related, but a large number of blacks hung back and looked on.

"I motioned for them to come over," he said, "and I shook hands with them all—just like I always did. But after I left town I got word there'd been an argument about it and a white fellow, who took my part, was beat over the head with a bottle and got a concussion. He didn't die, but I've never forgotten that."

In a 1964 speech aimed at persuading businessmen to give blacks greater opportunities, Johnson cited the experiences of the family's housekeeper-cook, Zephyr Wright, to personalize the evils of segregation:

". . . She finds that, when she comes from Texas to Washington, she can't go to the bathroom without taking three or four hours out of a drive to go try to locate one in certain sections of the town, or getting out on the highways and dodging the cars at night. She finds out that she never knows when she goes into a cafe whether she can get a cup of coffee or not—not because of lack of dignity, because she is possessed of more of it than the President; not because of lack of money . . . ; not because of lack of ability. . . . But it was all because of color and because of tradition and because of custom.

"Now you would not want that to happen to your mother, or your wife, or your daughter. But you can passively, nonchalantly . . . let that happen in your plant. . . .

"I possess no unusual powers of any kind, least of all persuasion, but I would like to be remembered more for my concern for my fellow man than for any other thing."

Johnson sometimes told a story about a hotly contested football game between two black high schools in Texas, when "separate but equal" was the rule in public education there. One team had a big, powerful and very talented running back named Leroy, who took a terrific pounding all afternoon. With time about to expire in the second half, Leroy's team had first down with goal to go and a chance to win the game. "Give the ball to Leroy!" the coach shouted from the sidelines. But somebody else carried it and was racked up for no gain. Twice more this happened. On fourth down, with a yard to go for a touchdown, the frantic coach hollered again, "Give the ball to Leroy!" This time the quarterback turned toward the sideline and yelled back, "Leroy say he don't want the ball!"

On civil rights, LBJ wanted the ball. As voting approached on the 1964 bill he told us that John Nance Garner, a fellow Texan and a successful poker player, "told me once that there came a time in every game when a man had to put in all his stack. Well, I'm shoving in all my stack on the civil rights bill." There was no equivocation in his stand, as he emphasized in a no-nonsense appeal to a group of Southern Baptist leaders who visited the White House:

". . . no group of Christians has a greater responsibility in civil rights than Southern Baptists. Your people are part of the power structure in many communities of our land. The leaders of states and cities and towns are in your congregation and they sit there on your boards. Their attitudes are confirmed or changed by the sermons you preach and by the lessons you write and by the examples that you set.

". . . There are preachers and there are teachers of injustice and dissension and distrust at work in America this very hour. They are attempting to thwart the realization of our highest ideals. There are those who seek to turn back the rising tide of human hope by sowing half-truths and untruths. . . .

"Help us answer them with truth and with action. Help us to pass this civil rights bill and establish a foundation upon which we can build a house of freedom where all men can dwell. Help us, when this bill has been passed, to lead all of our people in this great land into a new fellowship."

Johnson got the new law he wanted, but he wanted more. He wanted the federal government to lead the way in offering opportunity to blacks. To a group of Treasury officials convened to discuss equal employment opportunities, the President recalled Alben Barkley's story about seeking the vote of an old friend and being told that the friend still was considering his choice:

"Well, John," said Barkley, "I can't understand it. I appointed your brother postmaster. I appointed your sister in my office. I sent your son to West Point. And all through these years we have been friends. Now here, in the twilight of my career, when I need you most, you tell me you are not sure. What could have happened?"

"Well, Senator, you haven't done anything for me lately."

Added Johnson: "So that is the way I feel about equal employment opportunity over in the Treasury. What I want to know is, 'What have you done for me lately?' "

For all his recently developed zeal, Lyndon Johnson hoped that the next round of civil rights legislation could be delayed for at least a couple of years to allow Americans, particularly in the South, to adjust to the 1964 act. Martin Luther King, however, set in motion forces that would speed up the President's timetable. The Nobel laureate called for a massive campaign in 1965 to ensure the voting rights of blacks, sixty per cent of whom in the South were not registered to vote. As his target for demonstrations and protest marches, King chose Selma, Alabama, where only three per cent of the small city's black majority were on the voting rolls.

On Sunday, March 7, a King-organized March for Freedom began in Selma, with more than six hundred Negroes planning to hike fifty-two miles to the state capital of Montgomery. The marchers were met at the edge of town, at a bridge over the Alabama River, by state troopers and a mounted sheriff's posse. Armed with clubs, bullwhips and tear gas grenades, the lawmen demanded that the demonstrators turn back. The marchers refused and the white officers and deputies charged into their ranks with rampaging violence and brutality. Women and children were not spared. Horses trampled the fallen.

The scene was recorded by television cameramen. Their films, when aired on the major network news programs, inspired a national response of shock and revulsion that deeply affected public sentiment and immeasurably strengthened King's drive for new voting rights legislation.

Displaying the caution of which he had boasted during the campaign against Goldwater, Johnson sought to exert a calming influence on both sides and to find a means of permitting the blacks to demonstrate safely and freely. Yet he believed that King and his followers were not taking the best approach, although he recognized that demonstrations were inevitable, and that a Selma–Montgomery march had to take place.

"This march won't do any good," he told us privately, arguing that King and other civil rights leaders would do better to apply their pressure in Washington, "with Congressmen and Senators, and even me."

Some of the more militant rights advocates were put off by Johnson's caution. Within a week after the aborted march twelve white and Negro teenagers entered the White House, posing as ordinary tourists, and staged a sit-in along an East Wing corridor. LBJ later gave us his version of how he dealt with the demonstration on his own doorstep.

"I wanted in the worst way to find a way to see them, to talk with them and hear their grievances," he related. "But I wanted to play it cool so I just went right ahead handling my mail, thinking all the while, 'What can I do without being hasty, without being injudicious?' I decided to send a group over to talk to them: Bill Moyers, because he's a preacher, Cliff Alexander [deputy special assistant at the time], because he's a Negro and they'd know he was sympathetic, and my counsel, Lee White, because he's a good lawyer.

"Moyers asked what they wanted and one boy shouted back, 'We want to see the President.' Moyers could have kissed him. But then a girl leader shushed him and said, 'That's the last thing we want—that would spoil everything.' So they sent word that they wanted federal troops sent to Alabama. I didn't get my wish."

The next problem was to get the demonstrators out of the White House, especially since a Congressional reception was scheduled for that evening. Johnson already was planning to go to Capitol Hill shortly before the party, to unveil a portrait of Representative Albert Thomas, a fellow Texan who was dying of cancer.

LBJ directed that the protesters be carried away during his absence, but specified a number of conditions. He told us he insisted that both white and black policemen be used, and that the blacks escort blacks; that policewomen take out the female demonstrators, "so we wouldn't be accused of rapin' those little girls"; and that five unmarked police cars be used to carry the prisoners to the station house. The operation went off without a flaw.

A federal judge in Alabama next enjoined the authorities there from interfering with a Selma–Montgomery march and set the date for March 21. Further, he ordered Alabama officials to provide protection for the marchers.

Governor George C. Wallace wired Johnson to request a meeting. The President not only agreed but spent more than three hours with the segregationist state executive. Johnson already had announced that he would hold an Oval Office press conference afterward, but without cameras or microphones. But when Wallace emerged to speak of a "frank, forthright and friendly conversation," and to promise that he would have more to say on television the following day, Johnson altered his plans and, on fifteen minutes' notice, met with us in the Rose Garden before live TV cameras. Said the President:

"The Governor's expressed interest in law and order met with a warm response. . . .

"I told the Governor that we believe in maintaining law and order in every county and in every precinct in this land. If state and local authorities are unable to function, the federal government will completely meet its responsibilities.

"I told the Governor that the brutality in Selma last Sunday just must not be repeated. He agreed that he abhorred brutality. . . ."

Johnson also reported that he suggested Wallace "publicly declare his support for universal suffrage in Alabama," that he assure the right of peaceful assembly, and that he convene a biracial meeting back home "to seek greater co-operation and to ask for greater unity among Americans of both races."

Characteristically, LBJ filled in further details for us later, off the record. He reported that he told Wallace that Southerners were making great strides in space exploration, education, medicine and poverty programs—that people like Wernher Von Braun at Huntsville were on the brink of a great new world. Citing efforts to promote progress by Alabama's two Senators, Lister Hill and John Sparkman, he advised the Governor:

"Get off this civil rights issue and put some emphasis on these other areas. Start thinking in 1965, not 1865."

The President also reported that he argued Wallace could help himself politically by exercising moderation on racial issues. Johnson argued that the effects of a new voting rights law would be felt quite soon in the South and that there would be a political transformation in the region by the 1968 election.

LBJ apparently had great faith in the ability of individuals, perhaps even so dedicated a segregationist as Wallace, to change their attitudes, because he coupled his private report on the meeting with a down-home story along those lines:

"We had a judge down in my country who let the position go to his head, with everybody hailing him as 'Judge,' kowtowing; hotel people running to help him with his bags. He left the bench to run for the Senate but he was defeated. And later he told me what it was like when he came back and the porters in the hotel just turned their backs on him. Only a little Mexican newsboy remembered him. So he told me that if he ever got the chance to be a judge again he'd be a compassionate one. First chance I got, I named that man to the bench, and he's the best damned judge in Texas."

Johnson told us he actually thought he had influenced Wallace because the Governor went home and extended the voter registration deadline, and began talking about what Alabama had done in education. Indeed, Wallace himself paid a measure of tribute to Johnson's powers of persuasion, saying, "If I hadn't left when I did, he'd have had me coming out for civil rights." The confrontation between the two men was yet to come, however.

Wallace precipitated it by contending that it would cost as much as $400,000 to protect the "so-called demonstrators," that Alabama could not afford such a sum for that activity, and that LBJ should provide "sufficient federal civil authorities" to police the march, which was three days away.

The President called us into his office and contended that he did not have at his command enough federal civilians to carry out the task, but he asserted, "Governor Wallace has at his disposal over ten thousand trained members of the Alabama National Guard which he could call into service." However, Johnson added, if Wallace was "unable or unwilling to call up the Guard and maintain law and order in Alabama, I will call up the Guard and give them all the support that may be required."

Privately, Johnson said Wallace had promised at their Oval Office meeting that he would call up the Guard but was reneging on the pledge.

The President also was critical of King and his associates, complaining that they had not done sufficient planning. He said they had not thought about providing toilets along the way, overnight camping spots, food, or transportation for those who would be unable to complete the march. "I suggested they use cattle vans," he said. "It wouldn't be too long a stand-up ride—only eleven miles from the first cutoff spot." He reported that he did not want to use federal vehicles except as a last resort.

Following the news conference at which he advised activating the Guard, Johnson flew to his ranch for the weekend only to receive another telegram from Wallace, this one demanding that the federal government finance active-duty pay for the troops. The President gathered the press corps on the lawn at his ranch home to read an icy response, and a sarcastic one:

"Responsibility for maintaining law and order in our federal system properly rests with the state and local governments. On the basis of your public statements and your discussions with me, I thought that you felt strongly about this and had indicated that you would take all the necessary action in this regard. I was surprised, therefore, when in your telegram of Thursday, you requested federal assistance in the performance of such fundamental state duties.

"Even more surprising was your telegram of yesterday stating that both you and the Alabama legislature, because of monetary consideration, believe that the state is unable to protect American citizens and to maintain peace and order without federal forces. . . . I am calling into federal service selected units of the Alabama National Guard, and also will have available police units from the Regular Army to help you meet your state responsibilities. These forces should be adequate to assure the rights of American citizens pursuant to a federal court order to walk peaceably and safely without injury or loss of life from Selma to Montgomery. . . ."

In one of his off-the-record talks Johnson said that, if he had agreed to pay the Guardsmen as Wallace had asked, the Governor would have retained control. "I have to command my troops," said LBJ. "If one of my generals kills somebody, it's going to reflect on me."

A Unitarian minister from Boston was murdered on a Selma street before the march began and, on the day of the demonstration, a Detroit housewife and mother of five, Viola Liuzzo, was shot to death while driving between the two cities. These casualties aroused national anger and a concerted FBI effort was launched to locate those responsible. Just four days after Mrs. Liuzzo's death, Johnson announced on television the arrest of four Alabama Ku Klux Klansmen in connection with her death:

"Mrs. Liuzzo went to Alabama to serve the struggle for justice. She was murdered by the enemies of justice who for decades have used the rope and the gun and the tar and the feathers to terrorize their neighbors. They struck by night, as they generally do, for their purpose cannot stand the light of day.

"My father fought them many long years ago in Texas and I have fought them all my life because I believe them to threaten the peace of every community where they exist. I shall continue to fight them because I know their loyalty is not to the United States of America but instead to a hooded society of bigots.

"Men and women have stood against the Klan at times and at places where to do so required a continuous act of courage. So if Klansmen hear my voice today, let it be both an appeal and a warning to get out of the Klan now and return to a decent society before it is too late."

Privately, Johnson told us the speedy arrests were "nothing short of phenomenal—fascinating, unbelievable." He said he hoped the public never would get the details because the methods used were "similar to operations being carried out in North Vietnam."

Amidst preparations for the Selma march, the President spurred the drafting of a voting rights bill, and worried over how best to present it.

"I was getting a lot of flak that I wasn't acting soon enough, but I didn't want to be stampeded," he later recalled. At a party on Saturday night, March 13, he said, he had given his views on voting rights to Speaker McCormack. He quoted McCormack as reacting, "If I just had one wish, it would be that you say what you did just now to a joint session of Congress and to the American people—and say it now."

Johnson called in a bipartisan group of Congressional leaders the following day. Everett Dirksen agreed that an appearance before a joint session would be advisable, and that view was echoed by "Little John"—LBJ's term for Carl Albert who, as House Democratic leader, was overshadowed by John McCormack.

The President told us the first draft of the proposed address was prepared at the Justice Department, "and it was putrid." He added, "The fellows there are great at writing legal briefs, but they don't know how to write a message." He did credit Justice with providing the "running gears."

Horace Busby took over the speech-writing assignment, LBJ related, and worked on it straight through the night: "He didn't go home." Then he said that Jack Valenti and Dick Goodwin were brought in to help, Goodwin "for pathos" and Valenti because he could "take a pound of Busby and make an ounce of it—and the ounce is better than the pound."

No President in nineteen years had addressed a joint session for the purpose of proposing domestic legislation. Johnson did so at 9 P.M., Monday, March 15. The nation watched on television as he began, "I speak tonight for the dignity of man and the destiny of democracy." Then came the most powerful passage, one that lifted many Americans straight out of their easy chairs:

". . . even if we pass this bill, the battle will not be over. What happened in Selma is part of a far larger movement which reaches into every section and state of America. It is the effort of American Negroes to secure for themselves the full blessings of American life.

"Their cause must be our cause, too. Because it is not just Negroes, but really it is all of us, who must overcome the crippling legacy of bigotry and injustice.

"And we . . . shall . . . overcome!"

When a friend complimented Johnson the next day and asked who had written this most eloquent and moving of all the addresses he was to deliver as President, LBJ opened a desk drawer and pulled out a photo that showed him with his students in Cotulla.

"They did," he said.

Less than five months later Johnson went to the Capitol rotunda and signed into law the Voting Rights Act of 1965, declaring:

"There are those who said this is an old injustice, and there is no need to hurry. But ninety-five years have passed since the Fifteenth Amendment gave all Negroes the right to vote.

"And the time for waiting is gone.

"There were those who said smaller and more gradual measures should be tried. But they had been tried. For years and years they had been tried, and tried, and tried, and they had failed, and failed, and failed.

"And the time for failure is gone."

The President said then that, because of the new law, every American would "live more splendid in expectation." For some, expectations were not met quickly enough and, within days, the Watts section of Los Angeles was in flames. Johnson was appalled by the destruction, and said so, but he preferred to look beyond momentary violence.

"It is our duty—and it is our desire—to open our hearts to humanity's cry for help," he said. "It is our obligation to seek to understand what could lie beneath the flames that scarred that great city. So let us equip the poor and the oppressed—let us equip them for the long march to dignity and well-being."

In 1969, three days before leaving the presidency, Johnson was asked to cite his greatest accomplishment and the one that had given him the greatest happiness. The Voting Rights Act pleased him as much as anything, he replied, adding:

"This is really going to make democracy real."

13

"I Want to Make a Touchdown"

As a grade school youngster Lyndon Johnson memorized and recited a declamation that he occasionally repeated as President to express his pride in the American flag and all that it represented: "I have seen the glory of art and architecture. I have seen the sunrise on Mount Blanc. But the most beautiful vision that these eyes have beheld was the flag of my country in a foreign land."

LBJ held to the simple, even stubborn patriotism of an age when Americans, bursting with confidence after taming a continent and subjugating its native inhabitants, believed that all things were possible in their best of all possible lands; when they had unquestioning faith that their country always would find itself on the side of God and righteousness. It was a chauvinistic patriotism that Johnson expressed often as President and Vice-President, even in speeches overseas:

"My plane has landed in many continents, touched down in more than thirty countries in the past few years. The wheels have never stopped and the door has never opened that I have not looked upon faces which would not have liked to have traded citizenship with me."

Campaigning for re-election to the House in 1940, Johnson had dramatized his devotion to country by promising that if the United States entered World War II he would resign his seat and put on a uniform. After the Japanese attack—just six days, in fact, after he voted for a declaration of war—Johnson became the first member of Congress to report for uniformed duty. He did not resign from the House but instead took a leave of absence to serve as a lieutenant commander in the Navy.

For five months Johnson had a desk job in San Francisco. Then, on May 6, 1942, President Roosevelt intervened and sent him to the Pacific Theater as his personal representative. The following month, on June 10, LBJ climbed aboard a Martin B-26 Marauder, nicknamed the *Heckling Hare,* for a bombing mission over Japanese-held New Guinea. A dispatch to the New York *Times,* dated the same day, reported that the plane developed mechanical trouble and was forced to return to Australia before reaching its target; no mention was made of hostile fire. Johnson told a more dramatic story, as did others involved in the mission. By these accounts, the stricken craft was set upon by eight Japanese Zeroes and hit repeatedly, although miraculously no one aboard was killed or even wounded.

General Douglas MacArthur, who always appreciated the value of having friends in Congress, promptly awarded Johnson the Silver Star, the third highest decoration for valor. LBJ was credited with "gallant action" on a mission that "enabled him to obtain and return with valuable information." No member of the bomber crew was decorated.

Almost simultaneously, Roosevelt ordered all members of Congress to return from active duty. When LBJ next appeared on the House floor, he was a certified war hero wearing in his lapel a metal bar symbolic of his decoration. It was significant, I thought, that he continued to wear the Silver Star emblem throughout his presidency, more than twenty years later—long after most men had put similar symbols in a dresser drawer. Like Richard Nixon's enameled American flag, I suppose it was intended to serve as the badge of a proud patriot.

Shortly after he became President, Johnson told a group of us during a discussion of troubled relations with Panama, "Nobody's gonna piss on my flag!" Despite this red-blooded attitude, LBJ carefully avoided hostilities, but I recalled the phrase often as he took the fateful steps that were to mire his presidency, and the nation, in Southeast Asia.

Johnson's optimism and confidence in approaching problems beyond the water's edge matched his determination. He seemed certain, at least during his first two years in office, that he could handle any foreign policy problem judiciously and successfully. Indeed, the Panama crisis *was* cooled down. Guantánamo's water supply did *not* become a matter of war or peace. The Senate's old master of conciliation and compromise was on the job, and his performance was widely applauded.

In late January 1964, however, Douglas Kiker wrote in the *Herald Tribune* of "mounting evidence" that the new President "has yet to develop an effective technique for the day-to-day conduct of foreign affairs." The article, following as it did the heralded ranch summit with Ludwig Erhard, and in the absence of any noteworthy foreign policy blunders, caused Johnson to explode: ". . . regardless of what you hear and regardless of what some of the bellyachers say, we are a much-loved people throughout the world. We are respected and we appreciate it."

The President sought to refute Kiker's thesis with statistics. Through his friend Phil Potter, Johnson let it be known that he already had taken part in 175 White House meetings on foreign affairs and had made 188 telephone calls involving overseas concerns. Furthermore, Dean Rusk had been to the White House fifty-one times for conferences and Robert McNamara had participated in more than eighty. In time we came to recognize this as a typical Johnson reaction. Measures of quantity were expected to be accepted as guides to quality.

In truth, however, there was little well-founded criticism of LBJ's conduct of foreign policy during his first year in office. There was some joking about his Texas ways, as when Canadian Prime Minister Lester Pearson visited the LBJ Ranch and, upon being made acquainted with the beagle Him, cracked, "I don't have to ride him, do I?" But mostly Americans thought about Barry Goldwater and decided the incumbent President was doing just fine.

Mrs. Johnson may have worried a bit about her husband's conduct, but only out of a desire to see him succeed. LBJ himself reported with a smile that when Prime Minister Wilson of Great

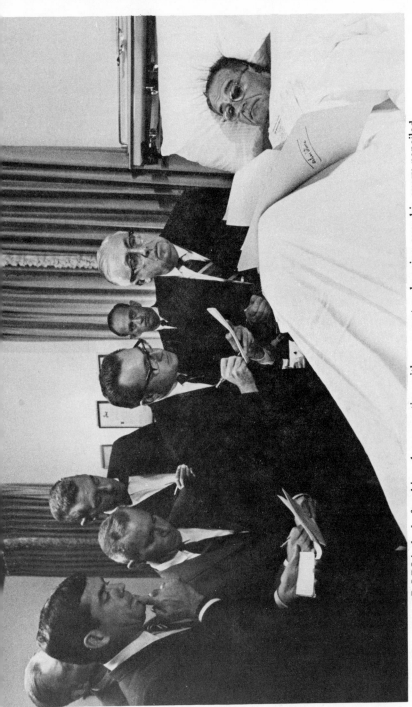

7. LBJ in bed after his polyp operation with us reporters hanging over his every penciled word, November 16, 1966. (Robert Knudsen, courtesy the Lyndon Baines Johnson Library)

8. LBJ and Lady Bird enjoying a moment of peace, September 1967.
(Y. R. Okamoto, courtesy Lyndon Baines Johnson Library)

9. LBJ presenting his bust to a bewildered Pope, December 23, 1967. (Y. R. Okamoto, courtesy the Lyndon Baines Johnson Library)

10. LBJ playing with Patrick Lyndon Nugent while I watch from the background, October 1968. (Y. R. Okamoto, courtesy the Lyndon Baines Johnson Library)

11. The President with a group of us during a visit to Mrs. Johnson's home town. I'm on the step below because he didn't want anyone to look taller than he. (Michael A. Geissinger, courtesy the Lyndon Baines Johnson Library)

12. LBJ and I converse aboard the presidential helicopter, July 4, 1967. (Michael A. Geissinger, courtesy the Lyndon Baines Johnson Library)

Britain was due at the White House she cautioned him, "Dear, this is judgment day and be sure you use plenty of it!"

There was a state dinner for Wilson that evening and among the guests were Chalmers Roberts, diplomatic correspondent of the Washington *Post,* and his wife, Lois. When Johnson approached as the couple were sipping after-dinner coffees in the Red Room, Roberts naturally asked how the meetings with Wilson had gone. The President replied that handling Wilson, who had been in office only a short time, was like approaching a girl the first time you dated her: first you cuddle up a bit and then commence feeling around to test her response. LBJ grabbed Mrs. Roberts and started to illustrate his technique. Other guests began to crowd around in wonderment and the President broke off the demonstration well short of seduction.

The meetings with Wilson in fact went well, as Johnson never doubted that they would. His confidence was such he even was convinced that success in thawing the aloof Charles De Gaulle only awaited an opportunity for him to apply the Johnson Treatment.

"My party in the Senate included both Harry Byrd and Wayne Morse," he would say. "If I could work with them I can certainly get along with De Gaulle."

Ho Chi Minh presented a different problem. Ho was even more remote than the French President so LBJ had to reason with him by indirection, if it could be said that Johnson attempted meaningful reasoning at all.

Upon becoming President, Johnson had embraced an ambiguous Vietnam policy inherited from John Kennedy. After meeting with Henry Cabot Lodge, the Ambassador to Saigon, two days after the assassination, LBJ accepted as his own Kennedy's pledge to "persevere to victory" over the Vietcong while at the same time promising to adhere to Kennedy's planned withdrawal of all U.S. troops from South Vietnam by the end of 1965. Two weeks after taking office the new President told State Department employees:

"We are heavily committed in South Vietnam, with eighteen thousand of our fellow American citizens there, and we should, all of us, not go to bed any night without asking whether we have done everything that we could do that day to win the struggle there and bring victory to our group."

As the press corps flew to Los Angeles with Johnson on February 21, 1964, Pierre Salinger distributed to us the advance text of an address that LBJ would deliver at a UCLA Charter Day Convocation, and alerted us to a key passage:

In South Vietnam, terror and violence, directed and supplied by outside enemies, press against the lives and the liberties of a people who seek only to be left in peace. For ten years our country has been committed to the support of their freedom, and that commitment we will continue to honor. The contest in which South Vietnam is now engaged is first and foremost a contest to be won by the government and the people of that country for themselves. But those engaged in external direction and supply would do well to be reminded and to remember that this type of aggression is a deeply dangerous game.

We were told that the "deeply dangerous game" reference could be interpreted as a warning that the war could be carried into North Vietnam or even to mainland China if the Vietcong's allies did not back off. Repercussions led to a denial by Dean Rusk of any intent to carry the war north of the demilitarized zone separating the two halves of Vietnam, and Johnson himself complained that he did not understand how the idea of an expanded war could have entered our minds. But LBJ did acknowledge that his words meant just what they said, whatever that was.

Throughout the election year the President kept telling us, "I'm not going north with Curtis LeMay [then the Air Force Chief of Staff], and I'm not going south with Wayne Morse." On November 28, after the balloting, LBJ recoiled when asked at a ranch news conference whether expansion of the war into North Vietnam or Laos was "a live possibility at this point." He responded:

". . . I don't want to give you any particular guideposts as to your conduct in the matter, but when you crawl out on a limb, you always have to find another to crawl back on.

"I have just been sitting here in this serene atmosphere of the Pedernales for the last few days reading about the wars that you have involved us in. . . . I would say, generally speaking, that some people are speculating and taking positions that I would think are somewhat premature."

Not terribly premature, it developed. On April 1, 1965, while hiking around the South Lawn with seven of us, the President volunteered that he indeed had ordered a major change in Vietnam policy, opening the way for regularized bombing of the north, following the Vietcong's pre-election strike against American airmen and planes at Bienhoa. In other words, carrying the war to North Vietnam had been a "live possibility" at the time of the ranch press conference.

Johnson did not launch his bombers immediately, of course. He waited for a series of provocations that had the effect of creating a sizable consensus in favor of air strikes. Even the Christmas Eve, 1964, bombing of a U.S. officers' billet in downtown Saigon, which killed or wounded dozens of Americans, did not produce direct retaliation.

A few weeks after the Saigon bombing a colleague asked Johnson for an assessment of the situation, in order to "cut down on the types of speculation that you have always advised us against regarding military matters." The President's reply, completely avoiding the thrust of the question, was sardonic:

"I would not ever entertain a hope of reducing your speculation. I'm an optimist and I want to look forward to the twenty-first century—but I can't go that far."

At 2 A.M., Saigon time, on Sunday, February 4, 1965, Vietcong guerrillas equipped with American-made mortars attacked sleeping U.S. servicemen at Pleiku. Eight Americans were killed and more than one hundred were wounded. Within hours, carrier-based Navy fighter-bombers struck at selected targets in North Vietnam. We were told that it was a reprisal raid and did not mark an escalation of the war, but we were misinformed. More raids followed and the whole character of the Vietnam conflict was altered.

For weeks the President insisted there had been no policy change. The obfuscation and transparent attempts at deceit reflected, I suppose, Johnson's instinctive caution as well as his penchant for secrecy. At that point I doubt that he knew precisely where he was headed but, perhaps equally important, he clung to a vain hope, which he revealed in private, that his display of resolve would produce a quick and relatively painless "victory."

During the early months of 1965, and in fact throughout the war, Johnson demanded greater restraint than was advocated by a number of his advisers and commanders. He placed strict limits on all raids north of the DMZ, and when the first 3,500 combat troops—two reinforced Marine battalions—were sent ashore, he restricted them to protecting American air bases. When a new Vietnam commander, General William C. Westmoreland, first began advocating search and destroy missions in March and April, LBJ opted for Maxwell Taylor's recommendation that U.S. forces be assigned only to preserve the security of American enclaves near the coast. Taylor had succeeded Lodge as the Ambassador in Saigon.

In boasting of his caution, Johnson liked to say: "I won't let those Air Force generals bomb the smallest outhouse north of the seventeenth parallel without checking with me. The generals know only two words—spend and bomb!"

A case can be made that the most reliable assessments of the situation in Vietnam at the time were being produced by American and foreign reporters there. But Johnson, with his great faith in McNamara and other advisers inherited from his predecessor, relied upon a steady flow of faulty statistics and errant assessments provided by official sources.

Most newsmen in Vietnam were "third stringers," the President told us, but he added that the caliber of the press corps was improving as it grew in size, along with the American commitment.

"Max Taylor keeps urging the newsmen out there to check out their stories before going with them," Johnson related, "but he tells me they won't do it, because they're afraid they'd find out they were off base."

The "third stringers" produced one account after another that informed the public and angered LBJ. One was an Associated Press report, perfectly accurate, that the United States had supplied the South Vietnamese with a non-lethal but temporarily disabling gas that could be used as a weapon.

"Gas is a dirty word, like dope," the President complained to me. "You might give your child Castoria, and there might be a little bit of dope in it, and someone would say you were doping your child. There's a lot of difference."

Johnson confided that the Saigon embassy people thought the AP's account "may have been an act of sabotage," and he hinted that the reporter who wrote it, Peter Arnett, would be investigated. More than ten years later a Congressional committee established that the newsman indeed was investigated, but to no avail, from LBJ's viewpoint. Arnett, termed "the best reporter of the war" by David Halberstam, remained in Vietnam and earned a Pulitizer Prize. He was there on the day that Saigon fell.

During our April 1 walk the President was asked whether any significance should be attached to a New York *Times* dispatch from Moscow quoting unaligned diplomats there as saying that North Vietnamese representatives were taking a softer line privately than in public. Yes, he replied, he hoped that as our firmness of purpose became manifest there would be more and more talk about negotiating rather than fighting.

"We're beginning to get defectors from the Vietcong," he told us, "and they're sending out feelers [not specified]. The situation out there has been most optimistic in the last three weeks. We're doing more and the Vietcong are doing less. The kill ratio has been increased in the past month from two to one to three to one."

For every setback, it seemed, Johnson was provided with an optimistic explanation. When the Saigon embassy itself was bombed, he assured us that this represented "a wild-swinging move of desperation" on the part of the enemy, otherwise known as the "other side."

The embassy bombing produced a typical LBJ reaction to a press account that threatened to breach the veil of secrecy he favored. The article that the President found offensive was a Washington *Star* report that he had ruled out a retaliatory strike against Hanoi.

"I ordered Dean Rusk to find out who gave out that story," he fumed. "I never made any such decision, and if I had, I wouldn't have announced it to the Washington *Star!*"

Later in the *same* conversation LBJ told me he had given orders that no air strikes be undertaken that could be construed as retaliatory, "because I don't want Hanoi to get the idea I'm a wild man."

Another and probably more persuasive reason for his restrained reaction to the embassy raid, I believe, was his hope for an early peaceful settlement.

"Hanoi has got to make more hard and rough decisions than we do in the next few weeks," he said. "They're out of food, they're out of planes, and they're hemmed in on two sides by enemies"— China and South Vietnam, not to mention the United States.

Hinting that he might be prepared to offer economic aid to North Vietnam in the event of a settlement, Johnson said he hoped to convince Hanoi's leaders that they had less to fear from the United States than from China.

"I think something may be moving in our direction," he declared. "You can kind of feel it a little bit; you can smell it a little bit. All I want is for you to give me a little running room. I want to make a touchdown for you if you'll let me."

In his quest for a quick touchdown, about which I am certain he was sincere, Johnson traveled to Baltimore and the Johns Hopkins University campus on April 7. There, by his lights, he held out an olive branch to North Vietnam in a major televised address that he titled "Peace Without Conquest." Asserting that "the infirmities of man are such that force must often precede reason, and the waste of war, the works of peace," he argued that once it became clear "we will not be defeated," it should also become clear "that the only path for reasonable men is the path to peaceful settlement." If Hanoi chose that path, he said, he would ask Congress to finance a billion-dollar development program for all of Indochina.

Privately, he enthused about the possible impact of his words on North Vietnam. But if the United States would not be defeated, neither would Hanoi. Nothing came of the initiative in which the President appeared to place much hope.

A month later Johnson, acting at the urging of McNamara and every important adviser except George Ball, authorized a massive 100,000-man increase in the U.S. troop commitment in South Vietnam. In addition, he finally gave Westmoreland the authority the general sought to conduct far-ranging combat missions.

I suspect that LBJ acted with reluctance, yet his decisions were consistent with his stated belief that Hanoi could be influenced by force.

Long before this most fateful of escalatory moves, however, Johnson had felt the lash of criticism, and it had hurt. On March 1 he had told a group of educators: "I don't know what will be written about my administration. Nothing really seems to go right from early in the morning till late at night."

But worse, much worse, was in store. The Dominican crisis that erupted abruptly in April, right after the Johns Hopkins speech, produced a situation in which LBJ was, in many respects, a captive of circumstance. Yet his own uncertainties led him to expound conflicting, often exaggerated explanations for his actions that undermined his credibility and inspired widespread doubts about the wisdom of his chosen course.

The civilian President of the Dominican Republic was the target of a revolt on April 24. Quickly, the situation in Santo Domingo became chaotic, with a "loyalist" military junta opposing a "rebel" grouping that also included military elements. The U. S. Embassy in Santo Domingo was fearful that a rebel victory would result in a Communist takeover, a prospect that Johnson had to regard as chilling.

On April 28 the U. S. Ambassador, W. Tapley Bennet, sent a cable to Washington that read in part: "The country team is unanimous that the time has come to land the Marines. American lives are in danger. . . ."

The President realized, of course, that the involvement of Marines would awaken Latin American memories of hated gunboat diplomacy, yet he felt that he could not risk being held responsible if failure to deploy troops led to the installation of another Castro in the Caribbean. The troops were sent.

"You can imagine what would have happened if I had not done so and there was an investigation and the press got hold of that cable," Johnson argued privately. But at that point he was justifying his action solely on the basis of safeguarding American lives, and he was exaggerating. Instead of quoting the Bennett cable accurately, he reported that the Ambassador had advised that "American blood will run in the streets."

Almost daily, it seemed, LBJ took groups of us out for South Lawn hikes during which he offered graphic—indeed, too graphic —explanations, some of which he later repeated in public:

"It has been necessary for a few Marines to go out and take an old lady and her little belongings, and with a crippled hip, carry her through the streets where the firing is taking place. . . .

"There has been almost constant firing on our American Embassy. As we talked with Ambassador Bennett, he said to apparently one of the girls who brought him a cable, 'Please get away from the window, that glass is going to cut your hand,' because the glass had been shattered, and we heard the bullets coming through the office where he was sitting while talking to us. . . .

"Some fifteen hundred innocent people were murdered, and their heads cut off, and . . . as we talked to our Ambassador to confirm the horror and the tragedy and the unbelievable fact that they were firing on Americans and the American Embassy, he was talking to us from under a desk while bullets were going through his windows. . . ."

Bennett later reported that he knew of no bullets being fired into his office, and that he never had cowered under a desk. Nor was it ever established that anyone was beheaded. And the only Americans harmed were two newsmen shot by Marines.

A few days after the troops were landed, Johnson made his second television address on the subject and, for the first time, suggested publicly that a Communist plot was involved. Simultaneously, the government made available a list of purported Communists who were supposed to be active in the rebel cause. The listing contained so many errors, however, that it did little for the Administration's credibility.

The TV appearance itself produced some disastrous moments, because of a mishap involving the prompting device that Johnson used in reading his speech—a device that projected his text onto two one-way mirrors at either side of the massive presidential rostrum that we referred to as "Mother," because it embraced LBJ like a womb.

Watching the scene in the White House theater, the site of the broadcast, I was stunned to hear Johnson repeat, word for word, a lengthy section of his address. Because he seemed to be oblivious to the fact, I actually wondered for a horrified moment if the President's mind had snapped under the strain of orchestrating simultaneous and controversial military interventions in the Dominican Republic and Vietnam.

I was reassured as I followed LBJ from the East Wing to his Oval Office afterward. He was hurling expletives at Jack Valenti;

he had known all along that he was repeating himself but had been held captive by the words flashed onto the mirrors. Valenti was not responsible for the misadventure and Johnson later summoned to his office an Army enlisted man he thought might have been at fault.

"Son," he said, "are you trying to gutfuck me?"

The foul-up probably was compounded by the blinding hot lights that were used at that time for color telecasts. LBJ abhorred them, with occasionally comic results. At a bill-signing ceremony, he urged Governors, Mayors and Congressional leaders to crowd around him for a picture, forgetting that he had ordered photographers barred from the event because of the lights they would require.

Johnson's confused handling of the Dominican crisis marked, in my view, the low point of his presidency, not because his actions there were more controversial than those in Vietnam, but because he appeared to lose his poise; to surrender command of the situation. His near-frantic rationalizations, replete with hyperbole and obvious falsehoods, were damaging to his cause, although I believe any President might well have made the same basic decisions that he did. Perhaps he flailed about because the crisis developed so quickly there was little time in which to build the sort of national consensus that he usually demanded before taking action.

"No President ever has a problem of doing what is right," Johnson told a labor audience during the Dominican upheaval. "I have never known one to occupy this office—and I have worked with five of them—that did not want to do what is right. The big problem is knowing what is right. This was no time for indecision, or procrastination, or vacillation. The American people hadn't elected their President to dodge and duck and refuse to face up to the unpleasant."

Acknowledging by then that "we don't propose to sit here in our rocking chair with our hands folded and let the Communists set up any government in the Western Hemisphere," Johnson went on to say that criticism of his intervention reminded him of a Huey Long story:

". . . everybody in the Senate was denouncing him because he had taken his sound truck into Arkansas and helped to elect the first woman elected to the Senate—Mrs. [Hattie] Caraway. . . .

"He sat there all afternoon and let one Senator after another denounce him for importing his sound truck and telling other people what to do, and dictating to them. He had this chocolate silk suit on—I'll never forget it—and his bright-toned brown and white shoes, and he was just marching back and forth.

"And it came his time to answer them and he got up and said, 'Mr. President, I have been denounced all afternoon.' He looked over at Senator [Joseph T.] Robinson, who was the majority leader and the most powerful man in the Senate—a very robust man, a very round man; he had a great big stomach.

"He walked right over to Joe Robinson, put his hand on his shoulder in a very affectionate and friendly way, and said, 'I wasn't in Arkansas to dictate to any human being. All I went to Arkansas for was to pull these big, pot-bellied politicians off this poor little woman's neck!'

"All we are in the Dominican Republic for is to preserve freedom and save those people from conquest."

Johnson ultimately was able to extricate his troops from Santo Domingo when the Organization of American States, for the first time, organized a peacekeeping force and sent it there. The President was jubilant and grateful, offering particular praise for Jose Mora, the OAS Secretary General. In one of his more memorable exaggerations, LBJ declared:

"That Jose Mora did a wonderful job for our country. He did such a wonderful job, he can have anything I've got. He can have my little daughter Luci. Why, I'd even tongue him myself!"

Controversy over the Dominican intervention coincided with the first sharp soundings of dissent over Johnson's course in Vietnam, and again LBJ was reminded of Huey Long and a tale the "Kingfish" told of a Louisiana farmer "that stayed awake night after night because of the frogs barking in the pond." Johnson told us that the farmer "got so irritated and angry and the way you-all describe me—those of you that never come around here— and he went out and drained the pond and killed both frogs." The President said he was not going to kill anybody, "but we recognize the frogs . . . and they keep us awake sometimes."

The number of frogs in LBJ's pond was increasing. "I am the most denounced man in the world," he lamented. "All the Communist nations have got a regular program on me that runs twenty-four hours a day. Some of the non-Communist nations just kind of practice on me. And occasionally I get touched up here at home in the Senate and the House of Representatives."

To one group, he urged that they communicate any advice, suggestions or differences "through Uncle Sam or Western Union or directly or through your friends; don't send them through my intelligence bulletin via Peking, or Hanoi, or Moscow." With some justification, he was convinced that public dissent served only to encourage enemy intransigence. "There never was a period in our national history," he remarked, "when unity, understanding, perseverance and patriotism would pay larger dividends than it would pay right now."

When Johnson's friend, Senator Russell, expressed the opinion that Ho Chi Minh would win any honest election in Vietnam, the President fumed, "Since when did Dick Russell become an expert on elections in Southeast Asia?" Another old Senate friend, J. William Fulbright, joined the dissenters and earned LBJ's label as "the stud duck of the opposition."

As criticism mounted, Johnson became more concerned than ever about what we were writing and broadcasting—and about the questions we were asking. Press Secretary Reedy had to assign one of his people to attend all news briefings to take notes on the identity of each questioner. The President received a prompt transcript that let him know which of us had asked which questions.

Then tiny microphones were installed on the walls of Reedy's office, where the briefings were held. We became convinced that "Big Brother" was listening, a conviction that was strengthened as Reedy began receiving mid-briefing phone calls as he was struggling to respond to pointed inquiries. Often he was able to put down the phone and produce replies that had eluded him theretofore.

Reedy often was besieged, sometimes exploding in anger but more often pausing to relight his ever present pipe and get a grip on his emotions. His position, caught between an inquisitive and demanding press corps and a secretive and demanding President, was not an enviable one. But occasionally he was given a respite, as when a reporter asked if he had once played a trombone in the Senn High School Band in Chicago:

Reedy: Those are the kind of queries I like. I can answer those. Yes. I also played the euphonium.

Q.: That is something that you blow, or bang on?

Reedy: A euphonium is a lineal descendant of a saxhorn, which is a sort of baritone horn, not a saxophone, and it is approximately a baritone version of a bass tuba, except that it has two bells. There is one bell which gives you the same effect as a valve trombone.

Q.: . . . What dates did you play the trombone and what dates did you play the euphonium?

Reedy: I would say the exact date would have been about . . . [long pause]

Q.: The year is enough.

Reedy: I am trying to recall. It would have been about 1931 to 1934. . . . I do wish it to be specified that that was the period in which the Senn High School Band was the national championship band. Please get that in. . . .

Q.: Do you still play?

Reedy: I still play but the difficulty with that is that you have to keep in practice because it requires the development of special lip muscles, and this week my lip muscles are wasted upon you rather than upon Bach, Beethoven and Brahms.

Q.: Your wind is all right?

Reedy: My wind is definitely in fine shape. . . .

Johnson sometimes contended that Reedy's mind was filled with more useless information than that of any man he ever knew, but I found George to be a delightful and learned friend. He took such a beating from both President and press corps that I was happy for him when he left the White House staff in 1965 following foot surgery. At six feet three, Reedy weighed 277 pounds when Johnson became President. He left weighing 202 pounds, partly the result of a low-calorie diet and partly, I suspect, because of other factors.

The increased monitoring of press corps activities during this period coincided with a renewal of the President's courtship of reporters. Following a back-yard stroll in April, LBJ lined up a group of us in front of his Oval Office desk and announced:

"I'm gonna help you-all become big men in your profession. I'll have each one of you in for a private lunch. You just see George and work out a mutually convenient time. Once you get settled on a date, you write to the six or seven people in your organizations that can do you the most good, and you say, 'Dear Joe, I am invited to have lunch with the President of the United States in the family quarters at the White House on such-and-such a day at such-and-such a time, and I would be most pleased if you could join us.' "

I hurried straight to Reedy's office and was assured that I was first in line for a luncheon date. Once the timing was fixed, I called my bureau chief, who was then William L. Beale, Jr., and related the entire plot to make me a big man in my profession. Inasmuch as the news business does not work like politics, Beale took it from there and arranged the guest list with the AP's general manager, Wes Gallagher, who retired in 1976.

On May 12, 1965, our delegation was escorted to an upstairs sitting room at the White House to have a preluncheon sherry with LBJ. Then we proceeded to the nearby dining room where we gathered around the table with an equal number of presidential aides: Reedy, Valenti, Bundy, Moyers, Busby and Cater.

Taking his place at the head of the table, Johnson directed Gallagher to sit at his right hand, then motioned for me to sit next to Gallagher.

"I'm kind of tired today," the President began. "I was up until four-thirty in the morning reading Jack Bell's book."

Bell had recently written *The Johnson Treatment,* which LBJ had told him in my presence had already been read and enjoyed. In retrospect, I suspect the President had planned his opening luncheon gambit in advance for reasons that may be gleaned from the dialogue that followed.

"How did you like it, Mr. President?" asked Gallagher.

Putting on a long face, Johnson replied:

"I found it rather entertaining but, unfortunately, it doesn't have any firsthand information. When I was up on the Hill, I used to see old Jack all the time, but since I've been President, I just don't get to see old Jack any more. So as a consequence, in order to write that book, poor old Jack had to rely on erroneous clips of things that Frank had written [a big fist was waved in my direction] that he in turn had gotten secondhand from somebody else!"

I thought this was a rather strange way of enhancing my professional standing, and it developed that the President had a more specific grievance against me, which he enunciated toward the end of the luncheon.

"You caught me by surprise with your first question at the last press conference," he told me, wagging a finger at me. "You tried to get me to make a damn fool of myself like Dean Rusk had done the week before!"

It had been my turn to ask the first question at a televised news conference on April 27, with the following result:

Q.:   Mr. President, do you think any of the participants in the national discussion on Vietnam could appropriately be likened to the appeasers of twenty-five or thirty years ago?
A.:   I don't believe in characterizing people with labels. I think you do a great disservice when you engage in name-calling. We want honest, forthright discussion in this country, and that will be discussion with differences of views, and we welcome what our friends have to say, whether they agree with us or not. I would not want to label people who agree with me or disagree with me.

I had asked the question because, privately, Johnson had repeatedly denounced his critics as latter-day Chamberlains who would lead the world to another Munich. Dean Rusk had nothing to do with my reasons for asking the question, and to this day I do not know what Rusk did or said to prompt LBJ's reference to him.

Staring at me across the table, the President clasped his hands in front of his chest, as if in prayer, and declared in a voice that trembled with apparent emotion, "Every night when I go to bed I kneel down and I thank the dear God that He didn't let Frank Cormier make a fool out of me!"

I do not believe that LBJ wanted to get me fired, although I cannot be certain. His maneuverings often seemed to contain wheels within wheels, and his mind and personality were complex. As he once told the editors of the Washington *Post,* tapping his forehead, "Sometimes I don't even know what's going on up there." Obviously, I was not fired. In fact I received a nice pay raise not long after the luncheon—so perhaps I can credit Johnson with doing just as he promised.

At the end of 1965 the President was arguing with us that his record in foreign affairs actually was more impressive than his success with Congress on domestic legislation, but he said we consistently downgraded his foreign policy achievements. In Southeast Asia, he contended, "things are a lot better," and if we thought American policy had not succeeded, look at China's efforts to line up client states in Africa—"name me one place where they've succeeded!"

Nevertheless, Johnson's policy of waging war to achieve peace seemed no closer to success than ever. His situation, in fact, seemed much like that of Mark Twain's in a story LBJ told about the writer visiting a friend in the country:

"Mark Twain was walking along the road and he asked a farmer, 'How far is it to Henderson's place?'

" 'About a mile and a half,' the farmer answered.

"He walked a while longer and he met another farmer and he asked the same question, 'How far is it to Henderson's place?' The farmer answered, 'About a mile and a half.'

"Mark Twain walked a little farther and he met a third farmer and he asked again, 'How far is it to Henderson's place?'

" 'About a mile and a half,' the farmer answered.

" 'Well,' said Twain, 'thank God I am holding my own!' "

14

"I Hurt Good"

Lyndon Johnson had planned the evening with care. The 1965 Congress had been so good to him that he would entertain the members at a Hollywood-style gala at the State Department, then have them over to the house for dinner. He even had a joke in mind for the occasion: "I was going to tell them I was reminded of that old song we used to sing in the hills of Texas: 'Keep on doing what you're doing to me, because I like what you're doing to me.'"

The President had to forgo the sure-fire laugh because, on the night set aside for celebrating, the House remained in session to act on beautification. Senators were free for the evening, however, and Johnson drove to the State Department to join them and their wives. When he arrived the cavernous auditorium was nearly empty and Fredric March and Hugh O'Brian were doing their best to stall the program without discouraging the few guests present.

"It was a challenge to begin with," O'Brian told reporters, "but this is getting a little ridiculous."

Eventually most members of the Senate trickled in and LBJ, setting aside his prepared speech, thanked them briefly for their efforts on behalf of the Great Society. Then, with Mrs. Johnson on his arm, he drove off at 11:15 P.M. to the Bethesda Naval Hospital where he was scheduled for surgery at 7:30 A.M.

When the announcement had been made a few days earlier that Johnson was about to lose his gall bladder, it attracted considerable attention because no President had undergone surgery while in office since Dwight Eisenhower had an ileitis operation in 1956. Those of us in the press corps mobilized for around-the-clock coverage at the hospital. The big theater-auditorium again was reserved for our use, and telephone and television camera cables were strung around it like spaghetti.

Bill Moyers, who had succeeded Reedy as press secretary, provided prompt word that the surgery was a success, adding a surprise announcement that a ureter stone had been removed at the same time. In the tradition of James C. Hagerty, Ike's press secretary who had made history of sorts by discussing the General's bowel movements during hospitalization, Moyers produced color slides of LBJ's stone and gall bladder. Projected onto the theater screen, they were guaranteed to upset the squeamish. We dutifully reported that the ureter stone was a rough-looking brown object and that the gallstone imbedded in the reddish-tan bladder looked like a giant raisin.

The President himself also wanted a complete record of his hospital stay. Barely recovered from anesthesia, he sent an aide to fetch a White House photographer. When none could be found, the AP's Harvey Georges was summoned to the sickroom.

Georges found LBJ stretched out on a reclining lounge with a variety of tubes for feeding and drainage attached to various parts of the anatomy.

"I want some pictures of me walking," Johnson announced, and laboriously shoved aside the covers to reveal that he was wearing a shortie nightshirt. A medical corpsman, looking somewhat alarmed, hurried over to lend assistance. Motioning him away, the President snapped, "I can get up by myself."

Johnson inched himself to the side of the lounge, eased his feet to the floor and, grimacing with pain, slowly hoisted himself to his feet. The tubes continued to dangle from him.

Georges stood staring in disbelief at the Chief Executive, whose private parts were fully exposed below the hem of the nightshirt.

"Get on with it," LBJ demanded.

Georges tried to aim his camera so the resulting negatives would be appropriately cropped, but Johnson wanted proof that he was able to stand without assistance. The negatives revealed all.

"Get me the biggest prints you can make," the President ordered, "and get 'em back to me as quick as you can."

The negatives were developed and printed in the AP darkroom, with a White House aide standing by to make certain that every negative and print found its way direct to LBJ.

Johnson had an easy relationship with Georges and other White House news photographers, so long as they snapped his "good side" and got his picture in the papers. An independent and sometimes irreverent lot, the photographers did not hesitate to kid around with LBJ, and he enjoyed it.

During the lunch hour one day the President decided on the spur of the moment that he wanted to have a news picture taken in his office. But the Press Office had declared a lunch "lid" and no photographers were around. Johnson waited and fumed and when they returned demanded, "Where in the hell have you-all been?"

"It's Friday, Mr. President," announced Frank Cancellare of UPI, "and there were an awful lot of bones in the fish."

Johnson immediately forgot his anger.

Like the rest of us, the photographers never knew what to expect next. On a winter morning Charles Tasnadi of AP and Roddey Mims, then of UPI, were intercepted as they came to work by Tom Johnson, a young man from Georgia who was serving as a press aide. No kin to the President, Tom Johnson later became associate press secretary.

"Hurry up!" Tom exhorted Tasnadi and Mims. "The President wants to see you right away."

Giving them no chance to shed their overcoats, Tom led them at a trot directly to the front door of the mansion, inside and up the stairs, two at a time, straight into the President's bedroom. A startled LBJ looked up and demanded, "What's this all about?"

"But, Mr. President," Tom began, "you asked for a—"

"Tom," interrupted LBJ in a patient tone, "how many times do I have to tell you to pay attention when I talk to you. I asked for a stenographer—not a photographer!"

Tom never was convinced that it wasn't a practical joke. Although the President was not known to be a practical joker, there was a prankish side to his nature. One of his tricks was played on Cleve Ryan, a colorful lighting technician who has worked for years at the White House with network cameramen.

Because Ryan had to light up the Cabinet Room for two

ceremonies a few minutes apart, the press secretary suggested that
Cleve leave his hand-held spotlights plugged into a baseboard out-
let after the first event and save himself some work. Finding this
agreeable, Ryan left the room and returned on schedule to hold
the two spots aloft for the second ceremony, which involved the
President and members of the Atomic Energy Commission.

"My God!" Johnson exploded. "We erect nuclear power plants
all over the country, we send men orbiting in space—but we can't
light up the Cabinet Room!"

A puzzled Ryan looked up and discovered that neither flood-
light contained a bulb. The President had removed them while he
was out of the room.

Ryan and LBJ had another confrontation, but of a different
sort, in Texas one Father's Day. Standing outside the tiny Catholic church in Stonewall, where Johnson was worshiping with his
daughters, Cleve was approached by a Secret Service agent who
announced, "The boss wants you to ride back to the ranch with
him."

Puzzled, Ryan readily climbed into the front seat of the presidential Lincoln beside Luci. As they drove along a back road LBJ
inquired why Cleve did not bring his family to Texas with him.

"My family is grown up," Ryan replied. "I have two boys in the
service."

"I know," said the President, "and that's why I want you to
spend Father's Day with me."

When they reached the ranch LBJ ushered Ryan to a table
under the live oaks on the front lawn and sat him down for coffee
generously laced with Bourbon. The longer they chatted and
drank, however, the more restive Ryan became, because he knew
that network reporters would be waiting for him to light up their
"stand-uppers"—the reports filmed for broadcast on the evening
news programs. He told his host that he should get back to Stonewall and retrieve his rented car.

"I'll send one of the boys after it," said Johnson. "Where are
the keys?"

Fumbling in his pockets and finding nothing, Ryan said, "They
must be in the ignition."

"Don't worry," the President told him, "the Secret Service will
find them."

Then Ryan discovered that the keys were attached to his belt. "Just put them on the table," said LBJ, summoning an agent to go get the car.

When the bodyguard appeared the keys were gone. Johnson immediately suggested the agent must have stuck them in his pocket. Protesting, the Secret Service man said they must have dropped into the coarse grass, perhaps when the Father's Day celebrants had gone to the house to fetch fresh cups of "coffee."

Johnson dropped onto all fours and Ryan and the agent joined him. Ryan actually found the keys but, saying nothing, surreptitiously tossed them back into the grass near Johnson.

"I found them!" exclaimed the President.

LBJ's own photographer, Okamoto, contributed to an amusing episode during the President's recuperation from the gall bladder surgery. While LBJ slept, Okamoto, smoking a pipe, was in an adjoining hospital room with Moyers and Valenti, who puffed on cigars, and Press Office secretary Sammy Bear, who was smoking a cigarette. Abruptly, a noisy smoke alarm was triggered. Knowing what Johnson's reaction would be if awakened, Moyers grabbed a pillow and blankets and jumped onto a swivel chair, muffling the sound while Valenti supported him. Moyers had to maintain his position until firemen arrived and turned off the alarm.

Although the President always insisted that his own health was superior, he often told us that his doctors were worried about Moyers and Valenti.

"Moyers will die before he's forty," said Johnson, "because he stays with it twenty-four hours a day. His heart is reflected in everything. He takes things too hard, and he's got stomach trouble."

In fact, Moyers had a duodenal ulcer.

As for Valenti, LBJ noted, "He's got pouches under his eyes, and he looks terrible. I can't get him to go home at night. I shoo him out, but he always comes back."

Johnson also reported that George Reedy "can't do anything he enjoys—he can't chase women, he can't drink and he can't eat."

Two days after the gall bladder operation four reporters were summoned to Johnson's room, where they found him visiting with Hubert and Muriel Humphrey. Straightaway, Johnson began lecturing the reporters that they shouldn't write that he was pressuring Congress. Asked if he was not pushing for action on home rule for the District of Columbia, he replied:

"I haven't insisted on a single bill. There is not one bill I consider a 'must' bill. I don't believe in must bills. I never wanted the President to tell me it had to be done. If there is a must bill, the Congress can see it. You fellows make those priority lists and build them up."

Twice the newsmen thanked Johnson and started to leave. Each time he called them back, once to regale them and the Humphreys with one of his stories. It seemed that a White House secretary, Vickie McCammon, brought a boy friend to Camp David who bowled a score of 165 "while we were shooting eighty or ninety."

"I offered Vickie some advice," he related. "I told her that when I was in the hospital with my heart attack Homer Thornberry used to come in and play dominoes with me. He let me win every game. He never won a game, and now he is on the Circuit Court. I told her to tell her man that if he wants to get ahead in this world he better quit doubling our score!"

When the reporters inquired if Johnson would go home to Texas when he was released, his reply was typical: "I have no plans to do so. I will be right at the White House for a while."

So after thirteen days in the hospital, and only one full day at the White House, LBJ flew to Texas where he spent much of the rest of the year.

On the flight to Austin the President complained of hurting and of being thirsty for a touch of alcohol, saying he hoped to get his weight down to 187 pounds because that would give him leeway to have a cocktail or two before dinner.

"I haven't had a drink since the last of August—not even wine," he reported, adding that he had complained to Mrs. Johnson about his dietary restrictions but she had informed him, "You can't run the country if you can't run yourself."

Shortly after we got to Texas, LBJ invited me into his ground-floor bedroom at the ranch and proceeded to shed his shirt. Before I could wonder what was happening, he hoisted his undershirt and bade me inspect his abdominal scar. I had been on the fifth-floor terrace at the hospital when Johnson opened his pajama top to display the broad bandage across his belly, but I hadn't really made very much of it. I regarded the episode as a typically Johnsonian gesture and did not refer to it until well down in my account. I realized my error of news judgment after photos of the impromptu exhibition caused a national stir.

The President did not hark back to the incident as we stood in the bedroom, but what he did do caused me to understand better why he had shown off the bandage at the hospital.

Moving his left hand down to the site of the incision, LBJ told me, "Those doctors came down here with their knives and they cut from here to here [gesturing and making a cutting motion]. Then they reached in [his right hand moved down by his left] and they cut out the gall bladder. And then they went a little deeper [more hand movements] and they dug out the stone." He paused, then looked me in the eye and declared, "I want to tell you that everywhere they touched it hurts!"

LBJ welcomed love and affection. By the same token, it seemed apparent that when he was hurting he craved sympathy. That was why he showed off the scar. He wanted all of us to know that it was no small thing.

"I hurt good," he had told the press pool during the flight to Austin.

Quite naturally, Johnson did not welcome or profess to understand the negative reaction to his display of his scar; he had simply sought to be informative. A year later he remained sensitive about it. On a Sunday morning in November 1966 we were gathered up by Bill Moyers for an after-church news conference at the Municipal Building at Fredericksburg, Texas. This was three days after we had been told that the President would undergo fresh surgery to remove a throat polyp and to repair an abdominal hernia at the site of the gall bladder operation. LBJ gave us his feelings about the polyp and the unhealed scar, then added in a sarcastic tone:

"I don't want to get into too much detail about that for fear it might arouse your sensibilities, or it might not be considered in good taste."

Johnson suggested that he was worried lest the polyp prove cancerous, although that possibility seemed unlikely. The surgeon who was to remove it had told us, when we asked what had caused it, "In this instance, excess voice usage." No one was surprised to hear that.

Once again the press corps gathered in the Bethesda theater, and again a pool of reporters was called to the President's bedside. This was my account:

WASHINGTON, Nov. 16 (AP)—President Johnson came through surgery today looking amazingly fit—but able to talk only in a hoarse whisper.

Just four hours after he underwent twin operations at the National Naval Medical Center in suburban Maryland, Johnson invited half a dozen newsmen to his room so they could see for themselves how he was faring. . . .

The visitors—they stayed 17 minutes—found Johnson's color good and his spirits high.

The President attempted to use his voice only a couple of times, however. Gesturing once toward his throat, from which surgeons had removed a benign growth, the President whispered:

"Just a sore throat, that's all—sore and very painful."

Johnson experienced evident discomfort at another point as he coughed involuntarily, raising some fluids from his throat and chest.

A drop of moisture glistened at the corner of his eye and he held his right side, where surgeons made a two-inch incision to repair an abdominal hernia.

Johnson made the best of his coughing attack, even so. Grabbing a felt-tipped pen, he scribbled on a piece of paper, for the benefit of his visitors, that it was good for him to cough—it helped clear the throat and chest. [The note read: "Good cough clears throat gets rid of phlegm clears the chest."]

The President was propped up in bed, a sheaf of papers on his lap. When the reporters were ushered into his comfortable beige-walled room, he was being given an intravenous feeding from a bottle suspended at the left side of the bed. On the right side, an electric vaporizer wafted jets of steam toward him.

Three large television sets, each turned to one of the major networks, were turned on but silent in front of him.

Johnson motioned to several television reporters present, to indicate he had seen them on the screen earlier in the morning.

Mrs. Johnson, wearing a floor-length gold robe, stood beside the bed with their married daughter, Luci Nugent, who wore a sweater and skirt. A couple of aides and secretaries also were in the room.

Johnson wore his glasses most of the time as he shuffled through papers in a folder marked "Action Items."

Most were messages expressing the good wishes of old friends. . . .

Johnson passed all these papers in front of the newsmen, sometimes with written comments.

He also made certain, through gestures, that they looked at three oil paintings on the walls—all scenes from his native Central Texas Hill Country. Done by Texas artist D. Harvey Jones and given to him by his staff on his 58th birthday, they show his birthplace, boyhood home and present ranch home. . . .

At that point, Johnson still hadn't been out of bed, nor had he taken any soft foods by mouth.

He did suck on a throat lozenge. . . .

Mrs. Johnson later told us that she had never known her husband to be speechless before, "and we're going to make the most of it."

But Johnson had found his voice by the following day and was overusing it to the despair of the doctors. He chatted with Dwight Eisenhower for forty-five minutes, met for an hour with economic and budget advisers, and visited with another reporting pool for twenty minutes.

"I'm sore as if I was beat with a baseball bat," he told the newsmen. Complaining of pains in his side, throat, right arm and legs, he declared, "It hurts all the time."

The press contingent suspected that he felt better than he was letting on, however, because he had the energy to lecture them. Noting a published report that he weighed 220 pounds, he insisted, "I haven't weighed that much since 1955. My normal range is 200 to 214. I don't think that's bad for fifty-eight and six foot three." Then he rolled up a pajama leg.

"That is not a fat leg!" he snapped.

Next he rolled up a sleeve.

"That is not a fat arm!"

As the bemused reporters left, he further admonished them, "I don't want anyone to report I made a speech—I'm prohibited from making public speeches."

Johnson was in the hospital on his thirty-second wedding anniversary, and reporters were invited in as he and Mrs. Johnson were presented with a fancy cake prepared by the White House pastry chef.

"It is pretty," said the President, "but I think I will have to have tapioca." LBJ loved cakes, but he claimed to enjoy tapioca almost as much.

"Tapioca has less calories than any other dessert that you can get," he related, "and it has great advantages when it is made with skim milk and Sucaryl. It's easy to make, and it's satisfying and it's filling. Zephyr Wright [the family cook] makes the best. She makes it in big batches and puts it up in containers, so I can have some when I want it."

Calling for a dishful, he motioned the reporters forward and fed each of them a spoonful.

LBJ talked with such enthusiasm about tapioca pudding, and got so many Americans interested in it, that Mrs. Johnson's office felt obliged to make public Mrs. Wright's recipe:

3 cups whole milk
5 tablespoons tapioca
1 egg beaten

Mix together and let stand 5 minutes. Then cook until "it boils up." Remove from stove immediately and let set until completely cold. Add 1 tablespoon sweetening (instead of sugar), ⅛ teaspoon salt, 3 beaten egg whites. Mrs. Wright prefers to add ¼ cup powdered sugar or less to make it stand up.

Deputy Press Secretary Robert H. Fleming was taken aback one evening at the White House when Johnson told him, "Get me a wooden spoon." Fleming did as directed but only found out much later why the spoon was needed. It seemed that LBJ had raided the refrigerator one night and used a metal spoon to scrape tapioca from a pan. The noise had awakened Mrs. Johnson, who lectured her husband about snacking between meals.

Johnson relished just about everything that Mrs. Johnson and his doctors tried to keep him from eating. I once saw him snatch a piece of chocolate cake off the plate of Muriel Dobbin of the Baltimore *Sun* while she had her back turned. He wolfed it down before she could catch him at it.

Another *Sun* reporter, Ernest B. (Pat) Furgurson, was associated in Johnson's mind with rich chocolate cake. While LBJ was whistle-stopping through Virginia in 1960, Furgurson's mother came to the train at Danville with a belated birthday cake for her son. The reporter set it out on a table in one of the press cars and was preparing to dig in when Johnson came down the aisle. Spying the cake, the vice-presidential candidate sat down across from Furgurson and exclaimed on the thoughtfulness of whoever had been kind enough to bake him, LBJ, a cake.

"Have a piece, Pat," he urged, never dreaming that the cake

belonged to the newsman. The two men enjoyed generous helpings, then Furgurson reported that his mother had baked it. Johnson continued to believe that she had baked it for him.

For years thereafter, even as President, Johnson would see Furgurson and automatically roll his eyes, rub his tummy and make "yum-yum" noises.

Cakes were not alone in tempting Johnson's appetite, either. During a visit to Australia in 1966 he leaned across a table on Air Force One and speared slices of bacon from the plate of the Prime Minister's wife. And while attending a black-tie reception at the State Department he at first refused proffered salted nuts, then scooped the dish almost clean with both hands. Quickly devouring the treat, the President placed his salt-covered hands on the backs of the men beside him and proceeded to wipe them clean on their tuxedos.

Johnson seemed oblivious to food much of the time, not caring when or if he ate. But when his diet rankled, food was very much on his mind. During one such period the President was touring his ranch with a group of reporters when he began exclaiming about the wonders of a vegetable soup that he reported Mrs. Johnson made to perfection. The more he talked the hungrier he became, finally inviting the group to return to the ranch house with him for generous helpings. After the feeding, one sated reporter offered effusive compliments to Mrs. Johnson for her wonderful soup.

"Yes," she answered, "Campbell's does very well."

Following his polyp-hernia surgery, Johnson once more headed for the ranch to recuperate. His doctor, James C. Cain of the Mayo Clinic, had told him he should not drive for "maybe three weeks," so we were not surprised when Mrs. Johnson drove her husband to church the first Sunday they were home. After the service, however, LBJ took the wheel.

A reporter telephoned Cain and the physician acknowledged that he had advised Johnson against driving.

"But he drove home from church," the newsman announced.

Pause.

"I meant," said Cain, "President Johnson should not drive a car over rough ranch roads where a sudden stop might be necessary."

15

"That Would Be Inaccurate"

The reception that Congress gave Lyndon Johnson's 1966 State of the Union Address pleased him mightily. "Any time that you receive the welcome we received and the some fifty-odd applauses that you receive—it makes you feel good," Johnson told us the next day. He even was able to joke about the fact that the applause was not universal, saying, "One fellow amused me by saying he thought he would leave the country, and I asked Billy Moyers to check up and see if that was the same fellow that was going to leave last year."

It was a guns-and-butter speech in which LBJ asserted: "This nation is mighty enough, its society is healthy enough, its people are strong enough, to pursue our goals in the rest of the world while still building a Great Society here at home."

Even so, the lingering war in Vietnam continued to claim an ever larger share of the nation's limited human and material resources. Expansion of the fighting force deployed in Southeast Asia even threatened to force a call-up of reservists, a measure that the President resisted because it would inevitably diminish his slowly eroding consensus and balloon the war effort beyond the limits he considered appropriate. Declaring at a March news conference that he had no plans to put the reserves on active duty, he added:

"I will tell you a little story about a boy I asked one time to come stay all night with me. His mother said no, he couldn't go. He had a little brother that was overweight and we nicknamed him 'Bones.' Cecil was the one I wanted to spend the weekend with me and his mother said, 'No, Cecil, you can't go.' Cecil kind of whined a little bit and said, 'Mama, I don't think that's fair. Bones done been two wheres and I ain't been no wheres.'

"So there have been some people that have been called before and already served. There are some people that haven't served at all. We are asking some to give their service for the first time. But when and if it becomes necessary to call the reserves, we will do it."

Unfortunately, spending for both guns and butter was giving a new push to inflation, putting the President under increasing pressure to do something about the economy. Cautiously, he called for voluntary wage-price restraint and decried mandatory measures:

"I lived through the OPA, the War Labor Board and the WPB in two periods of my life, World War II and the Korean War. I remember going home one time and going out to see a farmer neighbor. I told him I wanted to bring back a ham. Lady Bird wanted to serve a Sunday night buffet and hams were hard to get. I bought the ham and I said, 'How much?' He said, 'Three dollars.' I pulled out my wallet and gave him three dollars. Then I said, 'How many stamps?' He said, 'How many which?' I said, 'How many [ration] stamps are required for this?'

" 'Oh,' he said, 'you are talking about the OP&A. . . . Well,' he said, 'we just never did put that in down here!'

"Now, we don't want to go through that period again. We don't want to put them in down here."

Of course, raising taxes was another possibility, and LBJ gave that a lot of thought but he did not want the public to know it was a live option. We found out about it anyway, and I wound up in Johnson's doghouse once more as a result.

On the afternoon of March 29 the President held a reception in the State Dining Room for the White House Fellows, the most prestigious group of youthful government interns. The Press Office gathered up a pool and sent us into the room to watch and listen.

Johnson apparently did not know we were there, however, and he launched into a lengthy question-and-answer session that he must have thought was off the record.

Discussing the economy, he expressed an opinion that Congress would rather impose "a modest tax increase—five, six or seven per cent—corporate and personal—of our tax bill than to see inflation, and the value of the dollar go down." He added that he had not come to a decision and wanted to see another month or so of economic indicators before making up his mind. But he said that if inflation was to be resisted the choices were higher taxes, sharp spending cuts or price controls. A couple of hours earlier the Labor Department had announced the largest February increase in living costs since the Korean War, so the problem was a serious one.

In the news business, any hint of higher taxes is a priority item. I hurried back to the press room and dictated a bulletin account of what Johnson had said. Within a minute or two my report was appearing on the AP teletype machine behind LBJ's desk.

The AP and UPI tickers were "must" reading for the President, and he kept an almost constant watch on them. When UPI reported that his boyhood home in Johnson City would be open to the public for "fee tours"—a typographical error—he called the UPI desk to complain loudly that the tours would be "free." Minor ticker items from abroad prompted LBJ to telephone the CIA director so often that a special desk was set up to keep the intelligence chief informed about any CIA knowledge of any conceivable foreign development that we reported.

I had hardly finished dictating my tax story when Jack Valenti steamed into the West Wing reception lobby with my bulletin in his hand. How did I get such a story? I told him. Valenti argued that it gave the clear impression the President would ask for higher taxes. I pointed out three qualifications in the first two sentences. Seemingly satisfied, Valenti retreated toward the Oval Office and I presumed, wrongly, that I would hear no more about it.

On that same afternoon Murray Marder of the Washington *Post* was writing a report that U. Alexis Johnson, a top-ranking diplomat, was "understood to be scheduled to replace Edwin O. Reischauer as Ambassador to Japan."

The *Post*'s banner headline the next morning proclaimed that LBJ was thinking about asking for increased taxes, while Marder's account appeared next to a liquor ad on page twenty-two.

The President sent Congress a special message that day, March 30, on food aid for India and the press corps assembled in the Fish Room to be briefed on the subject by Secretary Orville Freeman. After the proceedings were well under way Johnson stepped into the room and took a seat in our midst. As we questioned Freeman, LBJ would crane his neck or turn in his seat to survey each questioner.

Felix Belair of the New York *Times* was present, smoking a cigarette in a long holder. Johnson sat right beside him. Belair, intent on his note-taking, did not notice the lengthening ash that was beginning to droop from the end of his cigarette, but the President did. LBJ had found two cigarette burns on his office carpet following a recent news conference, and only a week before had ostentatiously, for our benefit, picked up a crushed butt from the rug in the lobby. Without saying a word to Belair, Johnson got up and rearranged some chairs so he could lug over a pedestal ashtray. As he did so, Belair's ashes fell to the rug. In an instant the *Times* man was on his knees, using his notebook as a dustpan.

As the questioning of Freeman continued, the Secretary said he thought the President could better respond to some of the inquiries. Johnson did so, and the briefing came to a close. As we stood to leave, however, LBJ brought us up short, saying:

I think I might make an announcement. I do not know whether to do this or not, but I do not want any of you to take seriously some kid's statement over at the State Department that we have named a new Ambassador to Japan, because I've just read about it.

Q.: Mr. Reischauer is going to stay there?

A.: I don't know. I guess in the good old days that was the way they named Ambassadors. Those days are gone and forgotten.

The President then recited a verse: "The bridge of the railroad/ Now crosses the spot,/And the old diving logs/Lay sunk and forgot."

We supposed he was finished and again began to file out. But the President walked straight over to me, stuck his nose a few inches from mine and declared: "If any of you are interested in knowing, we have reached absolutely no decision on wage and price controls, taxes or cutting expenditures. The only man I know who has his mind made up on it is not in the White House executive department." With that, he gave me a derisive military-type salute and stalked out.

The story did not end there, either. Flying to Texas a few days later with Representative George Mahon, the President introduced me as his "tax adviser." Then, in front of a large group of generals in San Antonio, he said: "Gentlemen, I want you-all to meet Frank Cormier of the Associated Press. He endeavors to give me advice on tax policy." He pursued the heckling so persistently that after a few weeks I told one of the press officers that it had ceased to be a joke to me, particularly since I had not advocated or advised a tax policy of any kind. Johnson never raised the subject again—until four years later.

Out of office, citizen Johnson returned to Washington in the spring of 1970. Leonard Marks, a former USIA director, and his wife Dorothy held a cocktail party for the Johnsons at their home, inviting the reporters who had been White House "regulars" during LBJ's presidency.

I was standing by the dining table, sampling enticing hors d'oeuvres, when Johnson arrived. He walked straight to me and wanted to know how his "tax adviser" was getting along.

Later in the evening the former President sat on a living-room sofa and regaled us with plans for his forthcoming memoirs, while Mrs. Johnson kept urging him to leave and get some rest. LBJ had only recently emerged from a hospital stay that seemed to have been occasioned by heart disease.

"In a minute, Bird," he would say, and continue talking.

Around 10 P.M. the Johnsons left the house and entered their waiting limousine. But LBJ got out again almost immediately and climbed a steep flight of steps to the lawn where I was standing with Frank Reynolds of ABC. Addressing me, and poking at my chest with a forefinger for the last time, he said, "Frank, when my memoirs come out I want you to be sure and read the chapter called 'Bite the Bullet.'" Then he said good night and departed.

I presumed the chapter had something to do with Vietnam, but it did not. Rather it recounted why LBJ felt that he had to wait until 1967 to call for a general tax increase.

The *Post*'s Murray Marder, incidentally, was not a prophet

without honor for very long. U. Alexis Johnson was nominated to be Ambassador to Japan four months after Marder wrote that it was expected. But LBJ contended the *Post* report, which almost certainly caused him to delay the nomination, had destroyed any chance of persuading Reischauer to remain in the diplomatic service in another assignment.

The President's abhorrence of advance speculation extended beyond nominations and tax policy to simple matters, like the timing of trips to or from Texas. Nominations probably gave him as much trouble as anything, however. If they were leaked, he often canceled or delayed them. Occasionally he managed to preserve his personnel secrets, though, and make them known at a place and time of his own choosing. A 1966 example:

WASHINGTON, Sept. 21 (AP)—President Johnson played the question-and-answer game with reporters for nearly 20 minutes today before dropping the news bombshell he was holding.

He dropped it almost casually, in reply to a question that reporters had asked with wearying frequency for weeks: "There are a number of vacancies in the State Department—can you give any indication of when those will be filled?"

"Well," the President remarked, "one became vacant yesterday, the Under Secretary, Mr. Ball. That will be filled as of right now with the Attorney General."

A shout of surprised laughter rang through the Cabinet Room, where Johnson held today's informal briefing as a stand-in for Press Secretary Bill D. Moyers.

When the laughter subsided, Johnson went on matter-of-factly, but with a twinkle that betrayed his huge enjoyment of the situation.

Nicholas Katzenbach would resign as head of the Justice Department, he said, and would succeed George W. Ball . . . when confirmed by the Senate. The new Attorney General has not been chosen.

Over at the Justice Department, where the news also came as a complete surprise, the first reaction was one of sober shock. Katzenbach was talking at a meeting of the National Crime Commission when an aide passed him a note telling of the President's announcement.

The Attorney General paused to read it. He finished his interrupted sentence, then said:

"I guess there's something I ought to digress for a moment to tell you. I'm no longer Attorney General."

The faces of his hearers froze. Katzenbach went on:

"I guess the President wanted me to go over to the State Department to take George Ball's position. At least it was just on the radio, and to the best of my knowledge it's true."

Johnson held a more formal news conference the next day and was asked if Secretary Freeman might be considered for Attorney General. This exchange followed:

Johnson: When you see on the ticker that Oshkosh says that Bob Pierpoint [of CBS News] may be chairman of the Joint Chiefs of Staff, you don't necessarily need to give much credence to it, because the very fact that it is on there is the best indication that it is not likely to happen. Are there any other questions?
Pierpoint: Yes sir, Mr. President. I am glad I am not going to be chairman of the Joint Chiefs.

We often complained that Johnson filibustered at news conferences by reading lengthy opening statements that often concerned low-level appointments. So when Max Frankel of the *Times* asked, three weeks after the Katzenbach announcement, if the Justice Department vacancy had been filled, the President shot back:

"No, I have given a good deal of thought to it, but I guess you wouldn't feel it was appropriate for me to announce it publicly here at a conference like this. If the New York *Times* will be content to give me a little more time on it, I will have a mimeographed, full statement for you and we will give it to you in a 'handout' sometime."

The President was not always so churlish. When a reporter started to ask about "a little bit of a personal matter," which turned out to be not very personal, Johnson grinned and interrupted, "Do you want to go into it here?" Asked what could be done about complaints by women in service that they were barred from duty in Vietnam, Johnson responded, "There is always a chance of anything taking place when our women are sufficiently distressed." At another news conference LBJ remarked: "I would say we all ought to be commended for our good spirits and jolly frame of mind. I appreciate the good humor you are all in. I don't know how to account for it!"

But credibility problems persisted. When asked if he thought Congress could adjourn by June of 1966, for example, LBJ replied with some heat: "I came there thirty-five years ago, and the first thing I learned was never to predict when they would adjourn during the day or during the week or during the year. . . . I have never done it. I have never made any such prediction. And I do get a little bit sensitive sometimes when I see presidential decisions and predictions being made that I never heard of!"

Less than five months earlier, however, Johnson had said publicly: "We look forward to the Congress being able to get out of here early next year—I would say certainly far ahead of the fiscal year in June. . . ."

Forgetfulness may have accounted for this, but stubbornness seemed involved in some other cases. When LBJ announced the appointment of Walt Whitman Rostow as a special assistant, he was asked if it could be said that Rostow would assume "all or many of the duties and assignments handled by McGeorge Bundy." He replied: "It could be, but that would be inaccurate. It would not be true. . . ." In fact, Rostow *was* the new Bundy.

On another occasion Johnson announced that Bob Fleming, chief of ABC News in Washington, was being named deputy press secretary, although "I will want to call him my press secretary." When a reporter asked if Moyers did not have the title of press secretary, LBJ responded: "Special assistant to the President. It has always been that. You can call him press secretary, though, if it gives you any thrill." We were astounded and confused, the more so when it became apparent that Fleming would not function as press secretary and that Moyers was continuing in the position.

Of course the President did have occasion to grumble about our conduct, too. He was hurt, for example, by our distaste for briefings following cabinet meetings, which we tended to regard as propaganda exercises. After one fifty-minute walkathon, Johnson invited all of us to enter the Cabinet Room and observe the meeting for which he already was tardy. We dutifully did so, grabbing all available chairs and every inch of standing room. If we expected to witness a genuine cabinet meeting, however, we were doomed to disappointment.

The President began the proceedings by announcing that he wanted each department head to report to the press on current projects. Then, without apology or explanation, he retreated to his

office with Rusk and McNamara, leaving Cabinet Secretary
Horace Busby to preside. What followed was adequately summarized in one sentence by Tom Wicker of the *Times:* ". . . seldom before have so many told so little to so many." Cabinet
members "recited like pupils" when called upon by "schoolmaster" Busby, the height of something being reached when Orville Freeman launched into an incredibly enthusiastic discourse
on eradicating the screwworm in the Southwest. We were embarrassed, and I feel sure most members of the Cabinet felt the same
way. But Johnson was hurt by our indifference and, in fact, our
scorn. He told a subsequent news conference:

". . . I don't want you to feel that I am giving you more information than you want to take. At the same time, it looks like
when I talk with you after these cabinet meetings you say it is a
snow job if I tell you what happened. If I don't tell you, you say
your feelings are hurt because you say we won't let you in on the
knowledge."

Johnson went on to tell a story about the young son of Hobart
Taylor, director of the Export-Import Bank. The boy was studying Finland and asked his father to bring home some materials
about that country. Taylor brought back a briefcase full of books
and pamphlets, only to be told, "Well, Daddy, that is really more
information than I want on Finland."

So the President turned our complaints into a joke, as he did on
another occasion in 1966 when he felt he was damned if he did
and damned if he didn't. Having helped to work out a tentative
settlement between the airlines and striking members of the International Association of Machinists, he lamented:

"One of the editorials said that I was a dictator, and I had an
arrogance of power, and I twisted arms, and I had brought about
an agreement. That made me sad, because I don't like for people
to say ugly things about me and I don't want to be a dictator.

"And then the next day [the union] didn't ratify the contract.
They turned it down and a week went by. Some of the editorial
writers had to ride a train from New York to Florida instead of
being able to go by airplane. So then they said, not that he was a
dictator, but they said, 'Why doesn't he show some leadership?' "

On at least one occasion LBJ lectured us in dead earnest, and I
felt guilty because he certainly was right. We were at a federal

housing project for the elderly in San Antonio where the President was to sign a Medicare extension bill. Representative Henry B. Gonzales got up to introduce Johnson, and it seemed for a time that he never would sit down. Gonzales also introduced a sizable portion of the audience before he got around to introducing the President. We nudged each other in the ribs and snickered as the Congressman droned on—and Johnson saw us. He began his speech:

"First, I want to explain that the reason Henry took so much time was because I asked him to. Henry said that he had a little statement of about two and a half minutes, and I told Henry this was my day off. . . .

"I remember what my father said to me about public service when I was a little boy walking around, following him barefooted and standing there in the hot sand of Blanco County, and squeezing the dirt up between my toes. He used to say to me, 'Son, if you are to speak for people, you must love them.'

"Now sometimes among our more sophisticated, self-styled intellectuals—I say self-styled advisedly; the real intellectuals I am not sure would ever feel this way—some of them are more concerned with style than they are with mortar, brick and concrete. They are more concerned with the trivia and the superficial than they are with the things that have really built America. . . .

"So I told Henry I wanted him to take whatever time he needed. If any of you want to leave, you can leave. If any of you are in a hurry, you can go on. I stay in a hurry all the time. I am back home now and I am not going to hurry. I am going to do what I like.

". . . I thought that some of our sophisticated folks might say this morning that Henry was introducing too many people. . . . But that just shows you how he feels about human beings. He didn't want one single person to be neglected. He wanted to recognize the dignity of every person here, because they might be pretty unimportant to a stranger but they are not unimportant to Henry or to me.

". . . I hope that the years . . . will show that we moved ahead, that we made progress, that we weren't just concerned with what was in our platform, but we were concerned about what we did about it. . . .

"Well, here is what we did about it, just one little place."

Johnson did care about people. As Jack Bell wrote in *The Johnson Treatment:* "The President remembered birthdays and anniversaries. He was a quick man with the flowers and a cheery note if any friend went to the hospital or encountered some other misfortune. More than one newsman, overtaken by a serious and costly illness, got a discreet and personal offer from Johnson of financial assistance."

After Army Captain Albert M. Smith, Jr., the son of Merriman Smith, was killed in Vietnam, the Johnsons stood in the rain at Arlington Cemetery during the burial. And as long as he remained in office LBJ made it a point to frequently invite the elder Smith to lunch or dinner or to movies in the White House theater.

If the President had a mean streak, it was balanced by an expansive spirit, by a gentle side of his nature. And if he tended to be impatient, he admired patience in others.

"Dean Rusk is a great man," Johnson once told me. "We were up in the family quarters the other evening and we had to hurry over to the Situation Room for a very important meeting. We got in the elevator and the operator pushed the wrong button. We headed up instead of down. The fellow was upset and embarrassed but the Secretary told him, 'Don't think anything about it— I push the wrong button all the time over at the State Department.' Now anybody who can act like that is a great man, a really big man."

I feel certain that Johnson was impressed because his own instinct at the time was to give vent to anger. I saw it happen a number of times, often with no greater provocation.

I was with him in the bedroom on Air Force One when he erupted at his personal steward, Master Sergeant Joe Ayres. The President was drinking one glass of diet root beer after another, belching loudly and calling for more. Finally Ayres entered the room rather tentatively and announced:

"I'm sorry, Mr. President, but we don't have any more diet root beer. I can offer you diet Fresca, diet Pepsi, diet orange or diet ginger ale."

"Sergeant," Johnson shouted, "how many times do I have to tell you that I want diet root beer on this plane at all times! It's not a very difficult transaction. You can buy the fuckin' stuff anywhere. Sergeant, I want an order sent out to all Air Force bases: stock root beer!"

"Yes, sir," said Ayres, departing hurriedly. When the plane reached Andrews Air Force Base the sergeant went directly to the headquarters of the Special Air Mission. He sought and obtained a new assignment.

The unpredictability of Johnson's moods was made manifest during a chance encounter he and Mrs. Johnson had with me and my family. It was Easter and I had taken the family to Texas with me for the holiday stay. On Sunday, after attending the same church as the Johnsons, we drove to the boyhood home to take a public tour. We were on the back porch with other tourists, inspecting the mementos kept there under glass, when the President and his wife came up the back steps.

With LBJ in the lead, the Johnsons made a complete circuit around the porch, shaking hands with everyone. Almost everyone, that is. When Johnson came to my youngest son he pulled back his hand, then marched past the boy, my three other children, my wife and myself without so much as a nod. Mrs. Johnson followed his example. I did not have the foggiest notion what I had done to prompt this, and I never found out.

One child who never was snubbed by LBJ was Courtenay Lynda Valenti, who was taught by Johnson to respond to his invitation of *"besito"* by kissing him on the cheek and proclaiming, "I love Prez."

On a May Sunday in 1966, when Courtenay was two years old, the few reporters on duty at the White House were summoned to the Oval Office, where they found the President holding Miss Valenti in one arm while restraining a leashed beagle with the other. LBJ's future son-in-law, Pat Nugent, also was present.

"Who do you love?" Johnson asked Courtenay.

"I love Pat," she replied, looking over her shoulder in Nugent's direction.

Dutifully reporting this momentous development, my colleague Karl Bauman wrote that LBJ usually described Courtenay as his favorite girl friend, "but she turned out to be fickle."

When Bauman entered the White House the next morning Jack Valenti was waiting for him and announced, "The President is very upset about you misquoting Courtenay!" LBJ was certain she had said, "I love Prez."

Later in the morning the AP's Frances Lewine emerged from an

Oval Office event and told Bauman, "Oh, what he didn't say about you. I hate to write it."

"You just write any damn thing he said," Karl responded, "but let me write the first paragraph."

Bauman thereupon went to the AP typewriter in the press room and wrote: "President Johnson insisted today that his favorite girl friend remains faithful to him."

What Johnson had told Lewine was that Courtenay had made her customary "I love Prez" statement, and then had turned to Nugent and said, "Come on, Pat." The President reported that he already had telephoned Miss Valenti to inform her that Bauman had done her a grave injustice. Grinning, he said it was "humiliating" to have Vietnam servicemen read that their Commander-in-Chief no longer came first in Courtenay's affection.

Merriman Smith had been present for Sunday's exchange and also had heard "I love Pat." But when Johnson, still troubled, asked him about it in Bauman's presence, Smitty could not resist heckling his competitor by replying, "Mr. President, it came through loud and clear: 'I love Prez.'"

Johnson continued to carry on about the episode for several weeks, telling anyone who would listen that "old Karl needs a hearin' phone."

Perhaps such zany sideshows offered LBJ a diversion from larger troubles. As the Vietnam War dragged on, the forces that produced the 1964 landslide started to come unstuck, but not to the extent that one might imagine. In 1966, Johnson still enjoyed majority support, with those approving of his performance in office having nearly a two-to-one edge over his detractors.

"Now that's what you reported as a landslide during General Eisenhower's period," he observed.

Dissent from his Vietnam policies showed steady growth, however, until Johnson complained that he felt like a mongrel bitch set upon by a pack of males: "If I run, they chew my tail off. If I hunker down, they fuck me to death."

Those responsible for the President's safety began to worry about the forms that dissent might take, with results that often made our lives more difficult. On a balmy March morning, with eighty-degree temperatures predicted, many of us went to work in summer suits. But those of us picked for a surprise pool assignment wound up in New York City where the temperature was below fifty degrees. The following dispatch pretty well sums up the difficulties we faced—not to mention those that confronted LBJ:

NEW YORK, March 23 (AP)—From start to finish, President Johnson's brief trip here today for the funeral of a Congressman's wife was a study in tight security.

Veteran White House observers described the precautions taken to safeguard the President as unprecedented in peacetime.

White House reporters did not learn where the President was going until after his plane was airborne from Washington.

The small group of pool reporters aboard the craft were told then that the President was en route to New York to attend the funeral of Mrs. Emanuel Celler. . . .

Even then, they were cautioned against revealing the President's plans until they were given such permission after landing at Kennedy Airport.

Newsmen and photographers were barred from the ramp area at the airport for the presidential arrival and departure, something never done before at the airport in peacetime.

Not once did newsmen and photographers assembled hurriedly at the airport see the President leave the plane on arrival. They did get a glimpse of him boarding to leave.

A city police helicopter hovered over the hangar area as the presidential jet taxied to a halt after coming in. Another helicopter was parked on the apron nearby.

About 20 automobiles, including police and Secret Service vehicles, were in the heavily guarded motorcade that carried the President, his wife and government officials from the airport to the Jewish temple in Brooklyn where the funeral service was conducted. . . .

In the vicinity of the temple as well as at the airport, armed police and FBI and Secret Service men stood on the alert atop buildings and in the streets.

About 100 Secret Service agents saturated a four-block area surrounding the temple and some 80 security police stood guard inside the temple during the service. . . .

In Washington, a White House spokesman indicated the secrecy that marked today's New York visit would be the pattern for similar trips by the President in the future.

Strange stratagems were devised, to save Johnson not only from harm but from embarrassment. After the Secret Service learned that an economics professor planned to leave the platform in protest as LBJ began a speech at the University of Rhode Island, the White House recruited two nurses to rush up to the man as he left to make it appear he was ill.

This was a far cry from the glorious, ebullient, flesh-pressing campaign against Goldwater, although Johnson did manage a few campaign-style appearances from time to time. He went to Maine in August, mixing amusing stories with exhortations. To a crowd in Lewiston, he told of Franklin D. Roosevelt meeting a friend during the 1940 campaign and asking how he would vote.

"Republican," the man said.

"How come?" asked Roosevelt. "Is the third term bothering you?"

"No," the friend answered, "that's not it at all. It's just that I voted Republican the first time you ran . . . and I voted Republican the second time you ran . . . and I am going to vote Republican again, because I seem to have never had it so good!"

More often, as he became increasingly a prisoner in the White House, Johnson's attempts at humor had a bittersweet quality. When Mona Dayton, the Teacher of the Year, visited him, LBJ said:

"In Miss Dayton's class, I am told that there are six-year-old scientists who know how to build a sundial and know how to construct a model volcano. That is very impressive. When I was six years old I knew little about model volcanoes. But I have learned a lot since then from sitting on top of the real thing."

It got so that Johnson was finding an analogy between his plight and that of victims of Hurricane Betsy in Louisiana:

"One farmer was wiped out. The wind took his home, his barn, his livestock, his car, and a great deal of his topsoil. Finally the farmer looked over at his wife and family and laughingly said, 'Well, honey, we have lost everything—but we do still have the mortgage!' "

16

"Come Home with That Coonskin"

The law of averages told Lyndon Johnson that the Democrats would lose strength in Congress in the 1966 off-year election, since the party that scores a landslide in a presidential race almost always suffers a setback two years later. The President, of course, could try to counter the trend by putting his own sagging prestige on the line and waging a personal campaign in behalf of Democratic candidates.

"I want very much to go to every state that I can go to," LBJ told a news conference less than a month before the election. "But," he added, "that depends entirely on the White House business. That will come first."

In this instance, White House business included plans for the first great overseas odyssey of the Johnson presidency, a seventeen-day journey to South Vietnam—although that stop was not announced in advance—and six other Asian and Pacific nations. There were many motives for the 31,000-mile trip, and politics provided one of them. The President hoped to dramatize the fact that the United States was not alone in Vietnam, that it had Asian allies participating in the struggle. He also was hopeful that his journey would flash a signal to Hanoi: "We shall not quit."

In a buoyant mood, Johnson threw a pre-departure cocktail party for the press corps that would travel with him, then showed us a twenty-minute home movie of his wartime service in Australia, "in my young man days." We hooted and whistled, and Mrs. Johnson teased, when the thirty-three-year-old Navy officer appeared on screen with a very attractive Australian woman on his arm.

"They made you feel wanted, made you feel liked, made you feel cared for," he commented about Australians in general.

A crowd of more than 100,000 turned out as Johnson passed through Honolulu, and he reacted like the LBJ of 1964. An abundance of flesh was pressed and babies were chucked under the chin. After putting his hand on the damp chin of one teething infant, the President adroitly slid the hand down and dried it on the child's diaper.

"We do not expect to pull any rabbits out of the hat . . . ," he declared. "We are taking no magical wands and no instant solutions. We know all too well that this is a long road of many miles. But we will walk it mile by mile with free Asia."

The next stop was spectacularly beautiful American Samoa, never before visited by an incumbent President. Walking down a tapa-cloth carpet at Tafuna Airport, with Old Rain Maker Mountain towering in the distance, Johnson was greeted by dark-skinned Samoan chiefs in sarong-like lava-lavas and was escorted to a raised platform for a royal kava ceremony. The President was bidden to drink a cup of bitter juice brewed from the root of the kava tree, but he contented himself with merely touching it to his lips. Mrs. Johnson took a healthy swig, however, and later reported that the brew had "a slightly medicinal taste."

Driving through the jungle-like Samoan countryside, LBJ went to a new consolidated elementary school equipped to use educational television as a teaching aide. Cutting a ribbon, he dedicated it as the Lady Bird School.

For the aging schoolmaster's benefit, youngsters in one classroom demonstrated how they learned English—by aping the lip movements and sounds made by a face on the classroom TV screen. Taking a small boy by the arm, the President pointed to the press pool and had the boy repeat many times, "Noisy boys" —"noy-zee boyzzz."

At Wellington, New Zealand, no hotel had enough empty rooms to accommodate the large traveling press corps so the White House chartered a cruise ship for the overnight stay. Tied up at a dock, it was called the "Tiltin' Hilton."

Johnson's welcome was a warm one, but here he did encounter his first anti-war demonstrators. Making light of them, he told a luncheon crowd in the Parliament building: "We had some pickets carrying some signs saying, 'We Want Peace.' I did not consider them unfriendly. We want peace too."

In toasting Johnson, the Governor General, Sir Bernard Fergusson, declared: "The President is not tired. He is supernatural!" And the assembly responded with "Hear! Hear!"

A larger, more enthusiastic crowd awaited LBJ in Australia's capital city of Canberra. Even the minority of demonstrators seemed in fine spirits, some quixotically hoisting placards with such legends as "I Like Beer," "Eat at Joe's" and "God Save Ireland."

At a Parliament luncheon there Johnson recalled with fondness his brief wartime stay and reported, "There was a sign over a tavern yonder in Melbourne which read, 'U. S. Colonels Under Twenty-one Will Not Be Served Unless Accompanied by Parents.'"

Australia was due for its own election in barely a month and, with 4,500 Aussies fighting in Vietnam, the war was a major issue. But Johnson offered hope on that score, saying, "I believe there is a light at the end of what has been a long and lonely tunnel."

Later in the day, in Melbourne, LBJ was given a massive welcome—the largest he had ever seen anywhere up to that point. Hundreds of thousands turned out, filling broad streets from one building line to the other in many places and forcing the motorcade to a crawl. Responding as he would have done at home, the President used his limousine's public address system to shout:

" 'A' is for America. 'A' is for Australia. Long live 'A-A'!"

Then he harked back to the war and indulged in a bit of enthusiastic hyperbole: "I was in the trenches with the Aussies and the Japs were just thirty miles away over the Owen Stanley Range in New Guinea!" And he also talked about "that Japanese ace that was shootin' at me!"

As Johnson drove away from the home of a wartime friend

after dark, a young man tossed two paint bombs at the presidential limousine, smearing it from stem to stern and drenching three Secret Service agents. But the incident was insignificant compared to the size and warmth of the welcoming reception—and the paint proved to be water soluble. As Mrs. Johnson commented, with mild exaggeration, "In the perspective of two million people or so, it was just like a grain of sand."

More typical of Australia's reaction to LBJ was the behavior of weekend pub patrons as we drove back to the airport that evening to return to Canberra. Attracted by the sound of motorcade sirens, they swarmed into the street, still holding glasses and bottles. Unable to applaud thus encumbered, they simply dropped the glassware. The President's triumphal progress was marked by the tinkle of smashing glass and curbside renditions of "For He's a Jolly Good Fellow."

"If they ever do away with the United States," he enthused, "I know where I'm coming."

Back aboard Air Force One, I began to suspect that LBJ had been neglecting diet root beer in favor of something stronger. Snatching up the Australian newspapers laid out for his perusal, he read aloud the lead paragraph of one account: "Canberra last night gave President Lyndon B. Johnson a welcome that eclipsed even that given to Queen Elizabeth II."

Facing the wife of Prime Minister Harold Holt, who sat beside me, the President continued: "Miz Holt, don't you think anybody that did that deserves another drink?"

"If you say so, sir," she replied primly, pronouncing it "sigh so."

The newspapers certainly made good reading for Johnson. The Melbourne *Age* devoted nearly six pages to accounts and pictures of the visit and carried a page-one headline: "Melbourne Goes Wild for LBJ." The tabloid *Sun* proclaimed: "What a Day!" And a *Sun* commentator wrote: "In twenty years of covering arrivals, I have never seen another like this. . . . It was . . . a royal visit, Moomba [carnival] Day and the Beatles all rolled into one. Not at any other city function or arrival has there been such chaos, such carefree disregard to barriers and clamoring around official cars."

The *Age* characterized the welcome as "a thoroughly frightening—if affectionate—demonstration. . . . Civic dignitaries were crushed by the surging crowd."

"In many ways," I wrote, "each stop was a personal triumph for the President. His open-handed friendliness and his zest for mixing with crowds was a new experience for many in this part of the world—and they responded with enthusiasm."

"You're a beauty, mate!" one man cried out.

"LUV U LBJ," read a sign.

But another placard read, "L.B.J. Bloodfinger." Spotting it, Johnson leaned across the roof of his limousine toward the youth who held it and said in a soft voice, "Aren't you ashamed of yourself?" The sign was lowered immediately.

Australia's largest city, Sydney, provided the biggest reception, with more than a million people on the streets. Nearly half the crowd never saw the visitor, however, because Sydney also provided the most threatening anti-war demonstrations. Twice the motorcade was diverted to alternate routes to avoid young protesters, as well as many thousands of friendly citizens.

To ride in the press pool car, close behind the presidential limousine, was at times a rather frightening experience. At one crowded intersection demonstrators threw themselves into the motorcade's path as black crepe paper rained down on us and black balloons soared into the sky. I felt sure some of the prone figures would be crushed beneath our wheels.

Shielding Johnson from missiles and fist-wavers, Secret Service agents hustled the President out of his bubble-top car and into a nondescript black sedan that sped off on a zigzag course. We later were told that the limousine's air intake ducts had become clogged with confetti, but we noted that it had continued to navigate the entire route with a strange man occupying the seat that LBJ had vacated.

We could have done with some armor plating ourselves. Protesters sought to throw punches at us through our open windows, so we closed them and ducked low as objects of all sorts bounced off the car's roof, sides and hood.

After enjoying a barbecue-banquet in a ranch setting near Canberra that evening, we flew to Brisbane and another massive welcome. A crowd that had waited nearly seven hours slowed the motorcade so that it took almost an hour to drive a mile and a half from airport to hotel. Although he obviously was tired, Johnson called the people to his side for handshakes, and at one point surrendered his car's microphone to a drunken bystander who used it to shout: "Mr. President, welcome to Queensland—the home of fast horses and beautiful women!"

The next morning we stopped briefly at Townsville, where LBJ had lived for a short time at Buchanan's Hotel during the war. The President went to Sunday services and heard an Anglican bishop deliver the kind of sermon he could enjoy:

"There are those who would achieve peace by grabbing a placard and marching somewhere. But history would suggest that if they grabbed a prayer book and kneeled down, their efforts would have more lasting results."

Flying on to Manila and a summit conference with leaders of other nations participating in the Vietnam War—South Vietnam, Australia, New Zealand, the Philippines, South Korea and Thailand—Johnson talked to us of his hopes for both Vietnam and the elections back home. We could not quote him directly but I doubt that any reader was puzzled about the source of my account:

President Johnson hopes that his Asian journey and other developments will combine soon to persuade Hanoi to take a new look at possibilities for Vietnam peace talks.

. . . He is hopeful that the Asian summit conference, coupled with other developments, will demonstrate that the United States does not stand alone in Vietnam, that America and its President have the respect of Asians, and that Johnson policies are supported by the voters back home.

If all these factors converge as the President hopes they will, he thinks North Vietnam might decide to take a new look at the possibilities for a negotiated peace. However, he concedes there are big elements of doubt in all this. . . .

As for the U.S. elections, Johnson is convinced Hanoi expects his Vietnam policies to suffer repudiation at the polls. He sees this as a complete misreading of the American scene and declares that if all Republican congressional candidates won and all his fellow Democrats lost, there would be no reason to expect any softer attitude toward the war.

However, he believes Hanoi is making this mistake and, in view of that, he thinks the leaders there will have to reappraise their attitudes when the election returns are in. . . .

In fact, the Manila Conference produced nothing of enduring significance, and the President's visit to the Philippines provided fresh evidence that dovish Americans were not alone in questioning the wisdom of the war.

I was chatting with the President in his suite at the venerable Manila Hotel, along with the late Stuart Hensley of UPI and a small group of foreign reporters, when a din erupted in the street below. Anxious to find out what was happening, we broke off the conversation as quickly as we decently could and went to a window in the corridor outside LBJ's living room. An angry mob was attempting to storm into the central courtyard and enter the hotel through the main doors. Police fired shots into the air and the protestors fled to a park across the street, leaving the courtyard littered with their sandals.

Curious, I went downstairs and into the park, where youthful orators were denouncing Johnson, the United States and the war. No one bothered me, although I obviously was an American and hardly inconspicuous at six feet four.

What I took to be a string of firecrackers exploded a hundred yards away and I walked in that direction. Several young men were carrying a friend to a taxi. A bullet had passed through the man's neck. I did not care for that kind of firecracker so I retreated to the safety of the hotel.

On our final day in Manila a press pool followed the President to Corregidor, site of the U. S. Army's last stand against invading Japanese in 1942. I carried a typewriter along, having embraced a hunch that our final destination would be elsewhere. That evening I filed the following account:

CAM RANH BAY, Vietnam, Oct 26 (AP)—President Johnson, who likes surprises and drama, made a top-secret flight to this war zone bastion today and told the American fighting men here: "We depend on you."

Johnson spent exactly 2 hours 24 minutes on Vietnamese soil. He capped his historic visit by exhorting Gen. William C. Westmoreland and his top field commanders to "come home with that coonskin on the wall."

The President got closer to an actual battlefield than any President since Abraham Lincoln.

Johnson ate with the troops, visited the wounded, pinned medals on the brave, signed scores of autographs, shook hundreds of hands and delivered an emotional speech.

Several thousand of the 330,000 U.S. troops in Vietnam are based here. Men in battle dress grinned broadly and cheered lustily as Johnson moved among them on foot and standing erect in an open jeep, grasping a roof brace to steady himself in the vehicle.

The soldiers, who got almost no advance notice of Johnson's visit, sometimes appeared at a loss about how to react. Some seemed to think he should be treated like a general—until he extended his hand. Then they rushed forward, almost like any street corner crowd back home.

But there was an undertone of discipline and decorum.

On his arrival the President said:

"I came here today for one good reason: simply because I could not come to this part of the world and not come to see you.

"I came here today for one good purpose: to tell you and through you to tell every soldier, sailor, airman and Marine in Vietnam how proud we are of what you are doing and how proud we are of the way you are doing it. . . .

"Make no mistake about it: the American people who you serve are proud of you. There are some who may disagree with what you are doing here, but that is not the way most of us feel and act when freedom and the nation's security are in danger. . . ."

Johnson left Manila secretly in mid-afternoon, and headed back there after dark. No official announcement of his journey was made until he was safely back in the Philippines.

A fighter escort accompanied the presidential jet part of the way from the Philippines to Vietnam. While Johnson was here, he was guarded by only eight Secret Service agents—an unusually small number.

When one agent tried to get into a jeep with Johnson and Gen. Westmoreland—a routine precaution back home—the general told him to shove off. . . .

This supply base and airfield has burgeoned in the past year to a vast complex of runways, tents, quonset huts, supply shacks and hospital buildings. Within the last 24 hours fighting had taken place within a few dozen miles of the sandy bayside strongpoint.

But only the presence of the wounded attested . . . to the nearness of the war.

About 90 minutes before Johnson's arrival, however, there was a grim reminder of the difficult conflict in the rugged countryside nearby. All Vietnamese stationed or employed here were required to leave the base for the duration of the President's visit because, the commanders felt sure, Communist sympathizers were among them. . . .

A three-man guitar combo made music in the enlisted men's mess hall, where Johnson dined on pork chops, mashed potatoes and apple pie. . . .

"I don't believe they feed you that good all the time," said Johnson.

The GIs laughed and Westmoreland was quick with assurances that it was a routine meal.

But Johnson went on to recall that, as a boy, his brother Sam Houston Johnson once exclaimed after the preacher came to lunch at their house:

"Preacher, I wish you'd come every Sunday 'cause mama doesn't feed us that good all the time."

Johnson visited the Officers' Club too, walking past eight slot machines that had been inadequately camouflaged under white canvas. There he met with Westmoreland and his top field commanders—the men Johnson urged to bring home the coonskin. . . .

After resting for a day at the resort community of Bang Saen on the Gulf of Siam, Johnson and his party helicoptered to Bangkok for a two-day visit heavy with ceremonies and protocol. On the second evening there the President had an aide fetch me and others in the press pool and bring us into the other-worldly palace where the Johnsons were staying.

Following the aide up a ceremonial staircase, I encountered the First Lady and naturally said, "Good evening, Mrs. Johnson." Instead of responding as I would have expected, she snorted an abrupt "humph" and, tossing her head in apparent disdain, stalked away.

Passing through a series of antechambers, we came to a sitting room where we found LBJ and Jack Valenti, who had left the White House staff to become president of the Motion Picture Association of America.

"Sit down, boys," Johnson invited. "Kick off your shoes, prop up your feet and let's have a drink."

At this point I began to suspect the reason for Mrs. Johnson's displeasure. The President had been drinking more than usual during the trip, it seemed to me, and he was to host a state dinner for Thailand's King and Queen in less than two hours.

One of Johnson's valets took drink orders, then LBJ launched into a lively, relaxed monologue about his travels and his dreams for a postwar Asia. After many minutes had passed, he interrupted himself and, turning toward Valenti, demanded:

"Where in the hell are those drinks?"

"I'm sorry, sir," said Valenti, "but apparently they can't find any clean glasses."

Inasmuch as Valenti had been with us all the time since drinks were ordered, I decided that he was conspiring with Mrs. Johnson to cut off the President's supply of scotch. Further evidence of this was forthcoming when the normally efficient valet returned with an array of beverages that bore no relationship to the orders we had given him. Without comment, LBJ settled for a soft drink.

Visits to Malaysia and South Korea completed the journey, with officials in Seoul turning out more than a million greeters. Welcoming signs read: "We Love Big Shot of Free World . . . Great Texas Giant . . . Welcome Bluebird . . . You Are Sunlight of All Free Nations."

Buoyed by the reception, Johnson next day went to a U. S. Army base near the border with North Korea and, in delivering an impromptu patriotic speech to the troops, invented a bit of family history in his enthusiasm: "My great-great-grandfather died at the Alamo!"

While in Korea, LBJ also befriended a chin-whiskered village elder and took him for his first helicopter ride. "It's just like going to heaven," the sixty-five-year-old man told Johnson, who asked if he would like to go to America. "I cannot go today," the old farmer said gravely.

During the long journey Bill Moyers had acknowledged that, once we got home, the President would be undertaking a strenuous schedule of pre-election campaign appearances. But it was not to be, as the AP's Hal Cooper reported from New York four days before the balloting:

Leading Democrats from coast to coast busied themselves today unplanning plans for unplanned campaign visits by President Johnson.

Really caught short was Boston's Police Commissioner Edmund L. McNamara who had 1,100 uniformed men standing by to protect the President on an unplanned appearance planned for today.

Faces fell as far south as Memphis, as far north as Chicago and as far west as Los Angeles.

The President was asked at his news conference today whether his campaigning plans were off.

"First, we don't have any plans so when you don't have plans you don't cancel plans," he said. "The people of this country ought to know that all these canceled plans primarily involve the imagination of people who phrase sentences and write columns, and have to report what they hope or what they imagine."

Hopers and imaginers in Chicago had included Mayor Richard Daley, leader of the city Democratic machine, who had arranged for the President to address a party rally this afternoon. . . .

Among the planners of the unplanned plans, said an aide to a Utah Congressman, were "a dozen Secret Service men we had here in Salt Lake City and three advance men from the White House. . . ."

On to Los Angeles, where a press aide to Gov. Edmund G. (Pat) Brown had told newsmen plans for an LBJ visit Monday were being made "under the cloak of the White House secrecy which is routine whenever there is a visit by the President."

Also unplanning on the West Coast were Democrats of Oregon. There, Rep. Robert Duncan's press secretary said the party faithful had been advised from the White House "you should proceed on the assumption he will be coming Saturday afternoon."

In Phoenix, Ariz., a Democratic state official said he had been making arrangements for an unplanned presidential visit to the State Fair on Saturday but had made no advance announcement of any such plan.

"You know how Johnson likes to announce these things himself," the official explained.

In Memphis, aides of Rep. George Grider had passed the word that the President would appear there Monday. Unplanning there had advanced to the point where communications workers were setting up extra telephones at the airport for use by newsmen.

In Montana, Sens. Mike Mansfield and Lee Metcalf had announced that LBJ would make a weekend trip to dedicate the state's new Yellowtail Dam. . . .

Cooper went on to cite other examples of the plans that the President had attributed to our imaginings. In the final analysis, Johnson made only one pre-election appearance, at his old school in Cotulla, and it was more of a homecoming party than a political rally.

Election day found the President and Mrs. Johnson showing up at their Johnson City polling place thirty-nine minutes before it was supposed to open; they had gotten confused about the time. But, as I reported, "the election judges and clerks were already on hand when Johnson arrived . . . and they made no move to stop him from casting his premature ballot."

After announcing that he had voted for the full slate of Democratic candidates, the President surveyed us and declared, "You know, everybody's in fine humor this morning and I guess that indictates a Democratic sweep."

Obviously in high humor himself, he invited us to trail him back to the ranch where he had some new animals to show off. One of them proved to be a very large and fearsome-looking buffalo that the President tried to stare down, edging to within a few yards of the beast. Clarence Knetsch, chief Secret Service agent at the ranch, appealed to him to retreat and, amazingly, Johnson did so. But no one could dissuade him from entering a pen full of bulls and waving a big stick at them from a few feet away.

Safe behind a tall wire fence, however, was LBJ's mean, cigarette-eating red buck, also named Clarence. While a bodyguard quartered an apple to offer the animal, Johnson fed Clarence three cigarettes—then ate the apple himself.

The Democratic sweep that the President hoped would help move Hanoi to the peace table did not materialize. The Republican Party gained four seats in the Senate and forty-seven in the House, an impressive victory. The law of averages had been upheld.

17

"A Little Less Dangerous Place"

Lyndon Johnson looked out the french doors leading from the Oval Office to the Rose Garden on a balmy morning in 1967 and was horrified to see a workman on a ladder start to remove a nest, with three small birds in it, from one of the trees. Moving quickly to the doors, the President ordered the man to restore the nest to its original position.

On another occasion, in Texas, LBJ spotted a harmless armadillo and began blasting away at it with a gun. "Run, little creature, run!" cried Mrs. Johnson as the small animal scuttled to safety.

Although the President loved animals, his concern for them was not always consistent—and his attitude toward the press corps was no more constant. He avoided Douglas Kiker for months, then abruptly granted him an exclusive interview. "It's been a long time between drinks," Kiker joked to him. Similarly, the President could be incredibly candid, then indulge in unfathomable deceit. Asked if he was looking for a successor to Henry Cabot Lodge, serving a second tour as Ambassador to South Vietnam, Johnson replied, "No, there is no truth that I am looking for a successor." Ellsworth Bunker was nominated for the position a week later and

George Christian, who had succeeded Bill Moyers as press secretary, blandly explained, "The President was not 'looking' for a successor because he had already found him!"

Harboring a voracious appetite for titillating gossip, Johnson regularly included "my FBIs" in the stack of reading he took to bed with him each night; these were choice morsels served up to him regularly by J. Edgar Hoover. LBJ especially relished gossip about the press corps. During our trips to Texas he often called up his press aides to solicit reports about our after-hours conduct.

One night in San Antonio, which had succeeded Austin as our regular headquarters, I returned to our motel about 2 A.M. with a Washington *Post* reporter, a Press Office secretary and a Secret Service agent. The secretary decided that it would be fun to try catching, with her hands, the goldfish that swam in an artificial stream off the lobby. She had no luck. The *Post* man attempted the feat next, then I gave it a try. But the fish were safe from all of us.

At 9 A.M. that morning the press corps met with LBJ at the ranch, where the President announced to the assemblage, "I understand Frank Cormier is the champion fisherman of San Antonio!"

Before we moved to the Alamo city, Johnson heard of the arrival in Texas of a New York reporter who was partial to the ladies. "The price of whores is going up in Austin," he declared. When Associate Press Secretary Joseph Laitin informed him that columnist Robert Novak had been seen in the city LBJ snorted: "See him? You can smell him!"

We had, I suppose, something of a love-hate relationship with the President. Looking back, however, it seems clear to me that we coexisted amiably more often than not, and many of us had a genuine liking for the man. If you were to suppose that we automatically reciprocated his fits of pique, or met anger with anger, you would be wrong. Certainly we became angry at times. But more frequently our reaction to the President's outbursts was one of amusement. Flare-ups simply added to the legend of this extraordinary man.

On the morning of December 1, 1967, I was called to one of two pay phones that were attached to a pillar in the press room. Picking up the dangling receiver, I heard a pleasant voice announce, "One moment, please—the President." Then came a clicking noise and a near-bellow in my ear:

"Frank, I've got AP14 [a ticker item] in my hand and you say in the first paragraph that I felt powerless to stand in the way of Bob McNamara's resignation. Well, I'm President of the United States and I can do any goddam thing I want to!"

I was stunned. The night before, in the company of the late AP columnist James Marlow, Garnett Horner of the *Star* and George Christian, I had spent perhaps an hour in Johnson's private study next to the Oval Office, listening to his account of the background behind McNamara's forthcoming departure for the presidency of the World Bank. Now I could visualize the President standing over his AP teletype, waiting to see what I had written, then exploding and grabbing for the phone.

"But, Mr. President," I responded, "last night I got the clear impression that—"

The booming drawl interrupted and began a paragraph-by-paragraph dissection of my article, finding fault with virtually every sentence. After several minutes, which seemed longer to me, the volcano subsided.

"Now, Frank," said Johnson in a soothing tone, "you understand that I have the greatest respect for you, and I know you want to do the right thing."

I could only reply, "Mr. President, I don't see how you could in view of what you've just said."

"I mean it," he said, and hung up.

Hurrying to find my copy of AP14, I reread what I had written a few hours earlier:

Both in public and in private, President Johnson is saying Defense Secretary Robert S. McNamara's shift to the presidency of the World Bank reflected McNamara's own desire—and that Johnson felt powerless to stand in his way.

Moreover, no matter what others may think, Johnson seems satisfied McNamara is content with the way the President handled the situation and will depart the Cabinet with only warm feelings and appreciation for Johnson's role in the matter. . . .

In the chief executive's view, the Pentagon boss will be shifting from first base to shortstop when he resigns to become president of the 107-nation bank.

And Johnson insists that, had the decision been the President's alone, McNamara would have remained on first base indefinitely. . . .

I continued with a recital of the views that Johnson had provided, then ended with a chronology of McNamara's progress from first to short. For the life of me, I could not see that I had done anything more than accurately reflect what Johnson had told us. Wearing the armor of righteousness, I went to Christian's office more to marvel than complain at the President's stormy reaction. Christian was both amused and consoling, assuring me, "If you just hadn't used the word 'powerless,' he would have thought it was fine."

Surely Christian was right. The LBJ ego had been wounded.

Returning to the reception lobby, I had barely made myself comfortable on a green leather sofa—we called the décor "Dallas modern"—when I was summoned again to the pay phone. Johnson wished to volunteer a few additional pungent comments. I suspected they were a reaction to my suggestion that his respect for me was not as great as he professed.

You could not contradict Johnson with impunity, but you could offer him occasional advice and see it accepted. Jim Marlow once told LBJ, "Your speeches are like shopping bags—they've got everything in them." For a time afterward, the President confined himself to one or two themes per speech. Marlow also found occasion to phone Johnson to ask why he had not visited Dwight Eisenhower, who was a patient at Walter Reed Army Hospital. The next morning LBJ phoned the columnist, announced that he was driving out to see Ike and asked Marlow to ride along.

Jim telephoned the White House switchboard one evening and asked to be connected with LBJ. This was something few newsmen would ever dream of attempting. The startled operator assured Marlow that it would be impossible to make the connection, but she promised to have a press officer return the call. Joe Laitin responded.

"Joe," said Marlow, "I've got to talk to the President. There are a couple of questions I need to ask him for a column I've got to write tonight."

"Well, Jim, I don't know," Laitin replied. "The President had a pretty busy day and he's gone to the living quarters for the night."

Marlow persisted and Laitin promised to do what he could.

Within the hour Joe called back and said the President would see
Marlow at 10:30 P.M.

Arriving at the White House, the AP writer was ushered to
LBJ's bedroom, where he found the President lying naked on a
rubdown table getting his nightly massage from a medical corpsman. Asking his questions, Marlow got the answers he needed,
then was invited to remain with Johnson to watch the 11 P.M.
news programs on a triple-screen TV console in the room.

As the massage continued, the two men chatted and watched
TV. Then Mrs. Johnson entered, wearing a bathing suit. "Oh, I
didn't know you had company," she said and retreated. She had
just come from the White House pool.

Marlow tried to excuse himself following the news shows, but
Johnson told him to wait. Leaping off the table, still naked, the
President went to a bedroom closet and bent low to search around
on the floor. His bare fundament was almost in the writer's face.
Straightening up, Johnson handed his visitor a hard-bound vol-
ume of presidential speeches as a souvenir.

There was no way of predicting what LBJ might do next. If he
went to a party he might invite you inside to share the refresh-
ments. If he was driving somewhere, even in a formal motorcade,
he might ask you to hop in.

From the outside, presidential limousines—there are several of
them—look very big. Inside, with the jump seats in use, they are
cramped, as I discovered when Johnson invited Merriman Smith
and me to ride with him and the mayor of Kansas City.

"For God's sake, Smitty," snapped LBJ, "lean forward a bit.
You're diggin' into my knees!"

The President and his wife once made a helicopter pilgrimage to
Karnak, Mrs. Johnson's home town in East Texas, to visit her
stepmother and some of the first lady's girlhood friends. There
was a reunion party at one home, with coffee, tea and cookies,
and LBJ invited the entire press pool inside to eat, drink and meet
the folks. Then he took us out on the front steps to pose for a
group photo. I was standing near him.

"Move down a step, Frank," he commanded. "I don't want you
to look taller than I am."

I have the picture. Everyone is lined up in a row on the same
step, except me. I guess LBJ begrudged my extra inch of height.

On another occasion Smitty and I were summoned to the Oval Office without notice and introduced to Lieutenant General Stanley R. Larsen, just returned from Vietnam where he had commanded II Corps. Resting on an easel in front of the President's desk was a large map of the corps area.

"General," Johnson commanded, "give these fellows the same briefing you just gave me." Then he turned to us: "You-all ask him any questions you want to."

Pointer in hand, Larsen supplied a glowing assessment of the military situation in II Corps, but emphasized at one point that a particular bit of information was supersecret and should not be repeated. In any event the entire briefing was off the record.

About ten minutes after Smith and I had left the office Christian called the entire press corps into the Fish Room, where we found Larsen with his easel, map and pointer. The general proceeded to repeat the entire briefing, omitting only the secret item he had given us. I concluded that Johnson had wanted to see how Larsen would respond to press questions and had used Smith and me to test him.

The general's sanguine assessment was published in some newspapers, of course, but within six months II Corps was ravaged by the Vietcong during the 1968 Tet offensive, giving me fresh cause to wonder if anyone ever provided Johnson with a realistic appraisal of the situation in Vietnam.

Certainly the President had some naïve ideas on the subject. After a ranch visit he told me:

"Judge Moursund came up with an idea last weekend that we're gonna try out in Vietnam. You know, cowboys on horses aren't used much any more on the big Texas ranches. They use airplanes nowadays to do the roundups. So the Judge said, 'Why not use small planes in Vietnam to herd the Vietcong into bunches, so the troops on the ground can get at 'em?' It's a good idea and we're gonna get some small planes and try it."

In a sense, every day was an adventure for those covering the Johnson White House. Some reporters were invited, on the spur of the moment, to go skinny-dipping in the pool. Others were summoned to lunch in the family dining room. I found myself a guest at several state luncheons, invited on five or ten minutes' notice to fill in for someone who could not be present.

Back-yard strolls and conversations over coffee in the Oval Office continued, although less frequently than before. Karl Bauman was in one group that met with Johnson in the Oval Office, then departed via the canopied walk beside the Rose Garden. The President chased after them.

"Karl," he barked, "you left your overcoat in my office."

"I'm sure I didn't, Mr. President," said Bauman.

"Oh yes, you did," LBJ insisted. "You know, I'm reminded of the time Harry Truman went out to California and a heckler yelled at him, 'What about Earl Warren?' And Truman said, 'Earl Warren's all right and doesn't know it.' That's the way with Karl. His coat's in my office and he doesn't know it."

The coat belonged to Joe Laitin.

One evening Laitin asked the AP and UPI photographers to remain at the White House after their colleagues had been dismissed, offering no explanation. Around eight o'clock the UPI man, Roddey Mims, went to Joe and announced that if something did not happen soon he and his AP colleague would go home to dinner. Laitin asked for patience.

Finally the press officer came for the two photographers and took them to the Oval Office, where the President was holding a Vietnam-related conference with Walt Rostow and Averell Harriman. Mims and his competitor got some pictures, but they were not satisfied because the three conferees were sitting far apart.

"If you could just move closer together, Mr. President, we might get your picture in the papers," Mims suggested.

"Walt, Ave, move closer," ordered Johnson. "I guess he wants a football huddle." The trio put their heads close together. "How's that?" asked LBJ.

"That's fine, sir," said Mims. "Now if you could do it just once more for an 'insurance' picture, we'll be okay."

Johnson obliged, then turned to Rostow and Harriman and announced, with a nod toward Mims:

"I'm President of the United States—but *he's* runnin' the country!"

Mims and the AP man headed for the door. "Hold on a minute," said Johnson, then turned to Marvin Watson, who also was present. "Marvin, is that Mexican Ambassador still waiting?" Told that the envoy was standing by, Johnson sent for him.

After warmly greeting the diplomat with the traditional Latin *abrazo,* or bear hug, the President suddenly began waving a finger in his visitor's face.

"I guess," Johnson said to Mims, "you want it to look like I'm givin' him hell."

"That's just fine, sir," said Roddey.

"Don't forget the insurance picture," said LBJ.

Mims and the AP photographer started for the door once more.

"Wait just a damned minute," snapped Johnson, stopping the lensmen in their tracks. Eying Mims, the President asked:

"Can I have my country back now?"

Johnson enjoyed teasing Mims, a fellow Texan from Odessa. He did it again during a holiday stay at the ranch, when the UPI man persuaded him to pose for family pictures following an expedition to church. The President instructed the photographer to follow him back to the ranch house, but a Secret Service agent barred him from crossing the tiny Pedernales bridge near the Stonewall end of the property.

"The boss wants you to cross at the dam," the agent announced.

On the downstream side of the dam, and butting against it, is a single-lane of concrete that crosses the river. There had been heavy rains in the area and Mims discovered that water was rushing over the dam and down onto the narrow roadway. What's more, Lyndon Johnson was parked on the other side, waiting to witness his crossing.

The photographer eased his rented car down onto the semi-submerged concrete, then gunned it through the swift-flowing water, fishtailing all the way.

Johnson fixed him with a beady eye when Mims reached the safety of the far shore.

"What the hell are you tryin' to do, tear up my dam?" LBJ demanded. Mims sensed that Johnson had expected him to fishtail across the slippery concrete; surely that was why the President had insisted that the photographer cross at the dam, while taking the dry route himself.

"I didn't touch the dam, sir," said Mims.

LBJ beckoned to a Secret Service agent and instructed him to go down and make a close inspection of the dam to determine whether the UPI man's car had scraped against it. The hapless bodyguard removed his shoes and socks, rolled up his trousers and waded into the water. Johnson waited until the agent reported he could find no damage, then permitted Mims to proceed to the house for the picture-taking.

In April 1967, I was installed as president of the White House Correspondents' Association. But I could not persuade LBJ to attend my inauguration at our annual dinner, a black-tie affair attended by more than 1,100 reporters, government officials and diplomats. Vice-President Humphrey agreed to be the guest of honor in his place.

Shortly after 10 P.M., while Victor Borge was entertaining the diners and Humphrey was waiting to speak, Johnson arrived unannounced. Through emissaries sent backstage, I silenced Borge, then introduced the President.

Johnson began by paying tribute to me, in mock fashion, as "real presidential timber: larger than life, thin-skinned, and full of surprises." He recommended that I launch my administration with a "Correspondents' War on Poverty Act" that would raise reportorial salaries to a level above a poverty line that he defined as "the amount of money required for a family of four to live in Chevy Chase next door to a lobbyist."

Also urged upon me was a pollution control campaign to "be waged, and won, out where the action is—in the Press Club bar in Washington, at the Headliners in Austin. . . ."

Poking fun at both himself and the press corps, Johnson claimed to have visited the White House press room and discovered "stray notes of stories" already written about my tenure:

—"Unpredictable President Frank Cormier canceled a long-standing dentist's appointment this morning. When questioned, Cormier retorted that a President . . . receives many invitations to visit dentists' offices but does not always go."

—"It's too bad President Cormier doesn't come across to the American people the way he does face to face. He isn't really a wheeler-dealer at all, he only does the right things in the wrong way."

Hubert Humphrey never got to deliver his speech, but he promised to deposit the manuscript with the Lyndon B. Johnson Library.

The months that followed our dinner brought a big lift to LBJ's spirits and prospects. June was especially good to him.

The Six Day War between Israel and four Arab neighbors was not exactly good news but it produced the first crisis use of the Washington–Moscow "hot line," which the President and Soviet Premier Alexei N. Kosygin used in co-ordinating successful efforts to win adoption of a cease-fire resolution by the United Nations.

Two weeks later, on June 21, LBJ had more personal cause for celebration. At 6:59 A.M., Patrick Lyndon Nugent was born in an Austin hospital.

"The pace of change in our time is almost too swift for men to comprehend," said Johnson a day later. "Two days ago, I was a parent—only a parent. Yesterday, my role changed drastically. I became a grandfather. I did not seek that high office, but now that I have been chosen, the path of duty is clear—and I shall serve."

Kosygin was in New York on June 21, taking part in a continuing UN debate on the Middle East. It seemed logical that he and Johnson should get together, but a meeting was not easily arranged. Neither man was willing to risk losing face by traveling an extra mile to greet the other. Kosygin declined to visit Washington, and LBJ was equally reluctant to journey to New York.

An unusual compromise finally was arranged. Governor Richard J. Hughes of New Jersey suggested as a meeting site a 118-year-old stone mansion occupied by the president of Glassboro State College, located in South Jersey near the midway point between Washington and New York. The President and the Premier agreed to meet there on June 23.

In seventeen hours the turreted house called Hollybush was transformed into a place for summitry. Workmen installed sixteen air conditioning units, a new dishwasher and a refrigerator-freezer. The New Jersey Bell Telephone Company installed 750 phones in and near the mansion, strung 200 miles of cable, and erected a 146-foot tower to beam television signals to Philadelphia, seventeen miles away.

The Washington end of the "hot line" also was installed in the big house, although we could not understand why that was deemed necessary since the two leaders would face each other in the same room.

Johnson and Kosygin conferred for more than five hours, while several hundred of us milled about on the lawn in ninety-degree heat. In late afternoon the two men emerged and surprised us by announcing that they would return to Glassboro two days later for another meeting.

The President had to hurry across the continent to address a Democratic dinner in Los Angeles that evening, then fly to Texas for a one-day stay before joining Kosygin again.

On the return flight to the summit, from San Antonio, Johnson regaled us with an enthusiastic account of his first meetings with Kosygin. While talking, he doodled on a scratch pad that bore the presidential seal and a gilt heading, "Aboard Air Force One." At the end of the conversation, a fellow pool member grabbed the doodle.

"Hey," LBJ admonished him, "you shouldn't be the only one to have that. Maybe the others would like one too."

Grabbing the pad, he penciled three identical doodles and handed them to us. They looked like this:

> Preparation—
> Memorize—
> Lady Bird—
> P.L.N.—

These notations represented, he told us, his formula for a successful summit. He had made careful preparations, had memorized a lot of background materials and had called upon his wife for "general counsel." Finally, he felt he had broken the ice with Kosygin, a fellow grandfather, by talking about Patrick Lyndon Nugent.

The second round of talks at Hollybush in no way undermined the President's ebullience. He described the conversation as "helpful in achieving what we all want more than anything else in the world—peace for all mankind." More restrained, Kosygin said the talks had been useful because they permitted a comparison of the differing positions of the two leaders and their governments.

Knowing that Kosygin planned to make an 8 P.M. television appearance from New York, Johnson was determined to get on the air first, direct from the South Lawn of the White House.

To save precious minutes, the Air Force One crew obtained

special permission to land at Washington National Airport, closer to the White House than Andrews Air Force Base, but normally barred to 707 traffic.

The flight took twenty-two minutes but there was a last-minute hitch. Unfamiliar with the President's habits, the ground crew at National wheeled the only available ramp to the plane's front door. Waiting impatiently at the rear, Johnson cussed when he learned what had happened and led his aides past us at a dogtrot as he hurried to the front.

The presidential helicopter landed on the South Lawn at 7:42 P.M. Live TV cameras were waiting. The Glassboro talks had "not solved all our problems," Johnson reported, but they had made the world "a little less dangerous place."

The Glassboro summits helped boost LBJ's popularity rating to fifty-four per cent, a development he certainly welcomed barely eight months before the first of the 1968 primary elections. Kosygin's rating was unaffected. As the AP reported, "a 37-word item in *Pravda* and a post-midnight broadcast on Radio Moscow were all the Russians ever heard about Glassboro."

18

"*All the Way——*"

At 12:02 P.M. on December 20, 1967, Lyndon Johnson left Andrews Air Force Base on the most bizarre presidential journey ever recorded. The President was bound for Australia to pay a final tribute to Prime Minister Harold Holt, his friend and Vietnam ally who had vanished three days earlier while swimming in shark-infested waters near Portsea, south of Melbourne.

Holt, whose body never was found, had been the same age as Johnson—fifty-nine. LBJ said of the Prime Minister, in a taped interview with Peter Barnett of the Australian Broadcasting Commission: "We struck things off together. We spoke plain, unvarnished—without any dressing."

Barnett interviewed Johnson at the White House before departure and on the spur of the moment the President told him, "I want you to go with me as my personal guest." LBJ also invited the late Roy McCartney of the Melbourne *Age*.

Before any of us could leave, however, we had to report to the White House to be given five painful inoculations against a variety of oriental plagues—evidence, we thought, that the journey would take us to Vietnam at some point. With arms bared and shot records in hand, we lined up in the West Wing lobby. As we paraded forward to be jabbed, a door opened and the President entered. He surveyed us in silence but grinned broadly, then vanished.

There would be no press pool aboard Air Force One, we were told. All reporters and photographers would make the trip aboard a 707 jet chartered from Pan American World Airways. Even Barnett and McCartney, the "personal guests," were directed to a backup Air Force jet filled with Secret Service agents. Except for one leg of the long flight, into their own country from American Samoa, the two Australians remained with the agents—"drinking milk!" a disgusted Barnett later reported.

Some five hours after leaving Andrews, Johnson made his first stop at Travis Air Force Base, California. While his plane was being refueled he paid a quick, unscheduled visit to the base hospital, then headed for Honolulu. The traveling press corps was ignorant of the President's activities; we refueled in San Francisco.

The stop in Hawaii, for an hour and thirty-seven minutes, was too long for most of us because a tropical downpour drenched us. Once we returned to our Pan Am "mother ship," many in our group stripped and huddled in blankets, waiting for their dripping clothes to dry.

Another five hours found us back in American Samoa, where half-clad natives waited in darkness to honor the President at another kava-juice ceremony. For a long time it seemed they would be disappointed and, no doubt, insulted. About half an hour after arriving, however, LBJ finally appeared, looking sleepy, and made another pretense of drinking the bitter brew. As he left, he took Barnett and McCartney with him for the flight to Canberra.

The two Australians were in the President's cabin when Jack Valenti, borrowed again from the Motion Picture Association, appeared. Barnett introduced himself.

"What in the hell are you doing on here!" Valenti exclaimed. The Aussie broadcaster was taken aback, and offended. It took him a few minutes to discover that Valenti had mistaken him for the AP's Peter Arnett, who remained among LBJ's unfavorite reporters of the Vietnam War.

Johnson arrived in Canberra at 4:34 A.M., Australian time. We had been traveling for more than twenty-five hours and were ready to collapse. This was our first opportunity to file copy since Honolulu, however, so most of us were up until dawn, finally falling into hotel beds for a very few hours of sleep.

Upon awakening, we were distressed to learn that one of our

group, a representative of RCA Global Communications who was along to help arrange filing facilities, had collapsed and was hospitalized. It proved to be a case of simple exhaustion.

We spent about thirty-six hours in Canberra and Melbourne while LBJ conferred with world leaders assembled to honor Holt, then attended the memorial service for the missing Prime Minister in Melbourne's Anglican cathedral. During the stay in Australia we did get one full night's sleep—our first and our last for some time.

When we left Melbourne we had no idea where we were going, although we assumed that we would head toward Southeast Asia. A dispatch I filed later that day, December 22, tells the story:

DARWIN, Australia (AP)—President Johnson made an unannounced refueling stop here today en route to a mystery destination.

Johnson's big jet landed at about 5:35 P.M., Australian Central Standard Time, for a stop that the White House had hoped would remain undisclosed. . . .

Assistant Press Secretary Tom Johnson told newsmen there would be a "complete lid" on presidential movements for the rest of the day and that no one would be permitted to disclose that the chief executive had landed at Darwin.

Communications liaison men from private companies told their potential customers that although they had set up special facilities at the North Australian airport, the White House would not permit them to be used.

Reporters suspected they would be kept aboard their plane when it landed. But they were permitted to go to the terminal where, as it happened, a hundred or more spectators somehow had gotten word of the secret presidential flight.

The newsmen were directed to the second floor of the terminal building where inviting telephones were in their regular positions for the use of commercial travelers.

Once one reporter lifted the receiver to place a call, there was a mad scramble as all newsmen hurried to pass word that the President was at this point . . . and was heading north—rather than east toward the United States.

The assumption was that, before another 24 hours had passed, he probably would visit the troops in South Vietnam.

But there was no guarantee of that.

After we were airborne from Darwin, where we stopped for less than an hour without setting eyes on Johnson, we were told that our next destination was Korat, Thailand, some 120 miles north-east of Bangkok, where the U. S. Air Force maintained a large base for F-105 Thunderchiefs, used for missions over Vietnam.

As the press plane approached Korat a technician for CBS News collapsed in the aisle. Quickly we doused cigarettes as a White House medic, who always flies with us, began administering oxygen. When we landed we remained in our seats while Air Force men in battle dress came aboard with a stretcher and hauled away our stricken colleague. It was another case of ex-haustion. At this point we had been traveling for about seventy hours on one night's rest.

Because the President arrived at Korat after dark, we looked forward to a second night of sleep. Assigned to rooms in new brick huts built to house officers, we got to our quarters after mid-night. It was about 1 A.M. when Merriman Smith and I, assigned to room together, climbed into our cots.

Just as we dozed off Tom Johnson pounded loudly on our door and told us to get up quickly. My first thought was that LBJ must have collapsed, too, for I could think of no other reason for rous-ing people who badly needed sleep.

Reporters in varying states of undress gathered around George Christian in a dusty areaway between two rows of huts. He in-formed us the UPI somehow had been able to report from Bangkok that the President was in Korat, so we all were free to disclose the fact. First, however, Christian wanted to tell us about an unannounced midnight visit by LBJ to the Officer's Club on the base, where the President delivered a speech, then talked indi-vidually with a number of fliers about the air war in Vietnam. The press secretary also reported there were no special filing facilities for us at Korat, since our presence was supposed to be a secret. But he suggested we might be able to commandeer phones at head-quarters.

Spotting a jeep and driver nearby, I raced over and asked for transportation. The driver agreed and we started off. Although UPI had "scooped" me from Bangkok, I was elated at the pros-pect of beating my UPI roommate to a telephone in Korat. Smitty, however, suddenly hurdled over the side of the moving jeep and landed on my lap.

Only a handful of phones were available at headquarters but I grabbed one of them. Quickly I tried to call AP bureaus in Bangkok, Tokyo, New York, Washington and San Francisco. Each time I was informed that I could not be connected. Approaching the point of desperation, I remembered that somewhere in my notebook I had a military phone number for the AP bureau in Saigon. Finding it, I was connected almost immediately.

My frustrations did not end with that, however. John Wheeler, on the other end of the line, told me the AP's teletype circuit between Saigon and New York had been severed, presumably to help ensure security during the President's expected visit to the war zone. Wheeler and Peter Arnett devised a solution of sorts. I dictated to Wheeler while Arnett telephoned Washington and relayed my words to an editor in my home bureau. The Saigon-Washington connection was a very poor one, however, so Arnett had to shout, drowning out my dictation to Wheeler. After much repetition of phrases, we got the job done.

By the time Smith and I returned to our "sleeping" quarters it was time to shower, shave and head for breakfast. Sitting on a folding chair at the entrance to the communal bathroom, I found John McSweeney of Pan Am, a veteran of many press charter flights. He had been there all night, ready to stand guard whenever one of his stewardesses had to use the facilities.

At 5:30 A.M. on December 23, the President appeared on a makeshift stage beside the floodlit flight line at Korat and addressed about three thousand Air Force men. We could not report the speech, however, because we had to take off at once for another unannounced destination. In talking to the troops, Johnson declared, "I must return to Washington." A puzzled George Christian told me he did not know what this meant, or when we might get home.

Less than two hours later we were back at Camranh Bay where George MacArthur, then with the AP, was waiting. The military had hustled MacArthur out of Saigon during the night for "a trip" of an undisclosed nature. I was able to give him typed copy, which he wove into a comprehensive account of LBJ's visit after we departed. We spent less than two hours in Vietnam, then "flew off to another unannounced destination."

The next stop proved to be Karachi, Pakistan, where we landed after a ten-hour flight from Camranh Bay. Now it was clear to us:

We were flying around the world—something no President had ever done before!

Waiting for Johnson at Karachi was Mohammed Ayub Khan, the Pakistani President, who had flown seven hundred miles from the capital of Islamabad for the occasion. The two men talked for more than an hour and a half in an airport reception room.

Jack Valenti, meanwhile, held a conference of his own on the tarmac near Air Force One. We crowded around him with complaints of secrecy and lack of sleep. Hugh Sidey of *Time* was particularly impassioned. Valenti, in his memoir of LBJ's presidency, quoted Sidey as exclaiming:

"This is a flying circus and you know it and the President knows it. The best damn thing you and the President can do is start up this airplane, turn it around and head back home right now, in the same direction we came from."

Valenti, unbeknownst to us, found a way to convey to LBJ our general displeasure. Shortly before take-off from Karachi, a group of us were summoned to fly aboard Air Force One on the next leg. Our number included Sidey, Merriman Smith, Frank Reynolds of ABC News, Garnett Horner of the *Star,* and John (Pat) Heffernan of Reuters.

Soon after we were airborne the President invited us to join him in his cabin. After some amiable preliminaries LBJ turned to Smith, directly across the aisle from him, and declared:

"Smitty, I know all about the five dollars you handed to that Air Force sergeant when the press plane landed at Korat, and I know about the note to have him call your Bangkok office and tell 'em, 'Smitty is here.' Well, I really don't think it was necessary to tell the Communists that I was in Korat last night. I don't believe that advanced the national interest at all. I'll tell you one thing, though: I'm gonna have that sergeant's income tax return audited next year, to make sure he declares that five dollars as income! And I'm gonna have yours audited to make sure you don't claim a dee-duct!"

I was astounded, the more so when Smitty said nothing in response. But further astonishment was in store for us.

"I know what you-all been sayin' about me," the President asserted. "You're sayin' I'm a murderer and I'm killin' you-all because you haven't had enough sleep. I've got a full report on what you've been sayin', and it quotes you all by name.

"Well, I'll make you a proposition, fair and square. We can fly this plane straight to Madrid and I'll see General Franco. Then you can spend the night in a hotel, and we'll fly to Washington tomorrow. Or we can fly to Rome, and I'll see the Pope, then fly straight on to Washington tonight.

"You make the choice. Take a vote and I'll abide by your decision!"

It was an incredible gesture, something only LBJ would have attempted. I am certain our mouths hung open in amazement, until one of my colleagues collected enough wits to say: "Mr. President, we can't make that decision. It's your responsibility to decide what's in the national interest."

"All right," said Johnson, "but since you're all so damned tired, I've told all my staff to stay out of the bunks on this plane. They're all made up fresh, and since you're so damned exhausted, climb up into them and get some sleep!"

While we slept the AP transmitted an urgent dispatch that began: "President Johnson flew over Tehran today en route to Rome and an audience with Pope Paul VI, Iranian officials reported. Tehran's Mehrabad Airport was on the alert to service the President's special Boeing plane in the event of a last-minute change of plans."

Then came another AP report that, although LBJ was expected in Rome, "an informed source in Madrid said Johnson's plane would refuel and he would spend tonight there on his way home."

Of course we knew nothing about the rumors and reports that were circulating on the ground. When I awoke I asked a crew member where we would land.

"He hasn't told us yet," came the reply.

Within the hour—eight hours after leaving Karachi—we landed at Rome's Ciampino Airport, where some worn-looking Navy helicopters awaited us. We subsequently learned that white-topped presidential helicopters had been flown to Europe aboard large transport planes—but they were in Madrid! The choppers at Ciampino looked positively decrepit, and it was with some amusement that we heard George Christian volunteer to remain at the airport when it was announced there were not enough seats for all of us.

Helicopters were being used because Italian Communists and other leftist opponents of American involvement in Vietnam were massing in the streets to demonstrate against the President. The city was plastered with wall posters reading, "Johnson, Christmas is not your day and '68 will not be your year."

So that LBJ could avoid potential rioters, President Giuseppe Saragat had been persuaded to open his summer estate, Castel Porziano, south of Rome, for a courtesy visit. Our helicopter's landing in a plowed, muddy field on the estate produced a moment of laughter.

Merriman Smith, having visited the Vatican with Presidents Eisenhower and Kennedy, had volunteered a lecture during the flight to Karachi on the proper attire for an audience with the Pope. Now, wearing what we called his "papal suit," Smith emerged from the helicopter in total darkness and set off on the run toward auto headlights visible in the distance. Unable to see the deep furrows underfoot, he took an abrupt header into mud that left him looking quite unfit for a visit to the Vatican.

We spent twenty minutes in the drafty Saragat house, then returned to the helicopters to fly to the Vatican, where the arrival was unforgettable.

Johnson's chopper landed first, providing history with a footnote that he was the first visitor to arrive by helicopter in the Vatican gardens. Two previous landings there had been demonstration flights and had taken place in daylight.

Because the wheels of the President's borrowed helicopter sank through the wet turf to their hubs, our pilot was instructed by radio to circle and burn up fuel before attempting to land. We circled for more than a half hour, directly around the floodlit dome of St. Peter's Basilica. The massive church was so close you felt you could reach out the open door forward and touch it. St. Peter's Square also was illuminated. In less then twenty-four hours it would be Christmas Eve, a circumstance that added to the awe we felt as we circled this great landmark of Christendom.

Johnson and the Pope had been together for nearly an hour by the time we reached the papal apartments. It was their second meeting since LBJ had taken office. Pope Paul had visited New York in 1965 and the President had met with him at the Waldorf Astoria. On that occasion I had been in a press pool that LBJ, with characteristic informality, had beckoned forward for individual introductions to the pontiff—a scene broadcast on live TV throughout the hemisphere.

This time Johnson summoned us into the Pope's private library, where he presented each of us to the pontiff, who then handed us silver medallions in Florentine leather cases. While we looked on, the Pope gave the President a sixteenth-century painting of the nativity. LBJ reciprocated by giving Paul VI a five-inch bronze bust —of LBJ.

A day earlier the leader of the Roman Catholic faith had urged a bombing halt in Vietnam and, in talking with Johnson, he called for mutual restraint and spoke of "profound anguish" and "deep and painful apprehensions." Said the President in response to the mention of restraint:

"If that principle were accepted by both sides, there would be rapid and solid progress toward peace. We would be willing to stop the bombings and proceed promptly to serious and productive discussions."

Upon leaving Rome, those of us who had flown with him from Karachi were sent back to the press plane, while LBJ flew away toward yet another unannounced destination.

The AP's take-off bulletin said, "The presidential plane was expected to make a refueling stop at Shannon Airport, Ireland, en route to Washington." But more than an hour later, while the press corps was flying to Shannon, another bulletin followed: "The Irish government was notified Saturday night that President Johnson has canceled plans for a stopover at Shannon Airport." The account said Secret Service agents had been standing by at Shannon and that LBJ had been reported eager to "do some shopping" at the duty-free store there. A member of the Irish Cabinet had been sent to the airport to welcome Johnson on behalf of Prime Minister Jack Lynch.

While we stopped at Shannon, the President set down for refueling at an American base at Lajos in the Azores, then flew to Andrews, where he landed at 4:18 A.M. on the day before Christmas.

Johnson had circled the globe in four days, fifteen hours, fifty-eight minutes. On a single marathon day—December 23—he had been in Thailand, South Vietnam, Pakistan and Italy. The journey set all kinds of records that are not likely to be soon challenged. Only one other presidential trip that I know about was comparable in any way—and Lyndon Johnson made it. In July 1968 he visited the five countries of Central America in a *single day.*

As commentators assessed the President's globe-circling journey, thoughts of a famed nineteenth-century novel kept recurring. *Die Welt,* an influential Hamburg newspaper, reported:

"It was a performance which degraded Jules Verne's hero, who had circled the world in eighty days, to a comic figure. It was a running, extravagant feat that mocked every rule of protocol."

One of LBJ's own assistants, Harry McPherson, subsequently came close to echoing Hugh Sidey by terming it "a last, mighty trip, a kind of Phineas [*sic*] Fogg adventure that proved little more than the speed of Air Force One."

Back at the White House, Johnson boasted that he even had found time while overseas to buy a red, white and blue suit for his six-month-old grandson. Taking a woman reporter aside to admire the purchase, he announced, "It cost only a dollar fifty-eight in the Post Exchange!"

With an election approaching, the President may have expected his dramatic journey to give a lift to his sagging popularity. Although he had enjoyed majority approval following the Glassboro summit, by late October the Harris poll had his popularity rating at twenty-six per cent and falling. Asked about this, he said privately that he would continue to seek "peace with honor" in Vietnam, although he acknowledged, "I may end up with a poll of one per cent before it's over with."

In any event, the President must have been pleased with his trip. Members of the press corps received from him belated Christmas gifts in the form of a large album of trip photos titled, "All the Way—"

It was appropriate, certainly, that Johnson's journey was climaxed by a Vatican visit, given his church going habits. In 1968, with LBJ in his congregation, Washington's late Patrick Cardinal O'Boyle could not resist suggesting from the pulpit that the President might merit a Vatican assignment after returning to private life.

"I read in the papers where you attend two services—not one—

and maybe three," said the Cardinal. "And it's just possible some-one might say, after you leave the presidency, you might take on a part-time job in Rome and inform them on the different ecumeni-cal rites, for I think you must be an expert."

During a Texas visit LBJ attended Catholic and Episcopal serv-ices, back to back, and was asked by a reporter if he also planned to attend his own church, the First Christian Church of Johnson City.

"All of them are mine," he replied with a broad grin.

After he had been in office nearly two months Mrs. Johnson noted in her diary that her husband had called for grace before each evening meal since the Kennedy assassination—"a custom I like and have tried to foster for twenty-nine years." The First Lady also took note of LBJ's regular attendance at Sunday worship, and on special occasions in between, and wrote, "I am not going to say how glad I am about all this for fear it might somehow evaporate, but I have a feeling that it's not going to."

Rather than evaporating, Johnson's interest in churches ap-peared to increase, particularly after he became bogged down in the no-win Vietnam War and began agonizing about his military-diplomatic options.

After ordering the first air strikes in the vicinity of Haiphong Harbor in 1966 the President turned up at a Catholic church in Washington long after dark and prayed there with his daughter Luci, a recent convert to that faith. Later he said privately that only one American plane had been lost in the raid, instead of a predicted ten, and no Soviet ships in the port were hit. He quoted his daughter as telling him that she "knew her little monks would come through."

In times of trouble, Johnson told us, he had been advised by a former business partner to "find comfort in heavy thinking and deep praying."

The President seemed at home in any church, although his demeanor during services was not always what one would expect of a worshiper. After we reported that he had combed his hair and clipped his fingernails during a service in Johnson City, he avoided all churches for several weeks—the only such hiatus that I can recall during his presidency.

Johnson also had a falling out over unwanted publicity with the lay minister of his Johnson City church. The preacher made the mistake of confiding to reporters that the President had donated a central air conditioning system for the tiny edifice. LBJ's reaction was to boycott his own church and go where the clergymen could keep their mouths shut.

Periodically Johnson expressed great displeasure that he could not attend Sunday services without being followed by a small army of reporters and photographers. By adopting a policy of not announcing his church plans in advance, he kept us scrambling, especially in Texas where he worshiped from time to time at a half dozen churches spread over an area that was as broad geographically as denominationally. The AP's Frances Lewine drove two hundred miles in search of him one Sunday. To help track Johnson, we set up our own walkie-talkie network that rarely failed us.

Of course LBJ knew that it was our job to cover his public activities, however distasteful that might be to him. He tacitly acknowledged as much when a photographer, busy with his cameras, dropped a pencil while the President and Luci walked up the steps of Washington's National City Christian Church, where he customarily worshiped when he was in the city.

"Pick it up," he directed Luci. "He's working."

Quixotically, Johnson sometimes seemed to welcome our presence and would joke to those of us outside the church door: "Come on in. You need this more than I do."

Whenever the President did not venture out to a church, it was his custom to invite a clergyman into the Johnson home to conduct a private service. One minister ran out of communion wafers while officiating in the ranch living room, however, and LBJ was so furious that he abandoned another custom and refused to invite the man to stay for lunch.

If the President had an unofficial chaplain, I suppose it was Billy Graham. Noting the Reverend Mr. Graham's White House visits, often as an overnight guest, Johnson said, "Dr. Billy Graham comes here frequently and gives me strength and comfort and prays over me. . . ."

The evangelist accompanied LBJ on a speaking trip to Atlantic City when the weather was so foggy and foul that we could not see Air Force One until it taxied to a halt directly in front of us. Surprised when Dr. Graham emerged as an unannounced passenger, Dick McGowan of the New York *Daily News* said of Johnson, "I knew he came in on a wing and a prayer."

The President was equally comfortable with a Billy Graham or a small-town pastor back home. When Konrad Adenauer died, Johnson took the German-born Catholic priest from Stonewall to the funeral mass in the magnificent Cologne cathedral.

Perhaps only LBJ would have urged, as he did at a National Prayer Breakfast, the establishment in Washington of "a fitting memorial to the God that made us all." Most clerics and laymen seemed to feel that God did not need a Washington Monument of His own, and nothing further was heard about the idea.

Virtually all the prayers and sermons that Johnson listened to were, if not pleasing, at least inoffensive. There was one noteworthy exception.

About five weeks before he set out to circumnavigate the globe the President spent a weekend at Virginia's Colonial Williamsburg. On Sunday he and Mrs. Johnson went to Episcopal services in the historic Bruton Parish Church and heard a sermon by the Reverend Cotesworth Pinckney Lewis, a descendant of a Revolutionary leader who signed the Declaration of Independence.

Head cocked to one side, LBJ seemed attentive as the rector declared:

"There is a rather general consensus that something is wrong in Vietnam. We wonder if some logical, straightforward explanation might be given without endangering whatever military or diplomatic advantage we hold. . . . While pledging our loyalty—we ask respectfully, why?"

Johnson emerged from the church with only the trace of a smile, which vanished as the Reverend Mr. Lewis saw him to his car. LBJ nodded curtly. Mrs. Johnson simply remarked, "Wonderful choir."

19

"I Shall Not Seek..."

Clerics of distinguished lineage were not alone in questioning Lyndon Johnson's Vietnam policies, in wondering about the "whys" of the war. A month to the day after the encounter at Williamsburg, I witnessed a scene in LBJ's native Texas that struck me as particularly ominous.

The occasion was the dedication of Central State College at Killeen, very close to Fort Hood. There were civilians in the President's audience, but many of his listeners were young enlisted men trucked to the site from the big Army base.

Because he was saluting an educational enterprise Johnson focused his remarks on the Great Society programs and the promise that he felt they offered for the future of the nation. Departing from his text, he flailed away at critics, complainers and doubters who challenged his social welfare efforts and questioned their cost. Then, in an impromptu line that reflected his concern for people, he thundered:

"With your stomachs full, has it pressed your heart out of position where you no longer care?"

Turning toward the khaki-clad troops, the President continued:

"Well, those men who wear the uniform don't think it is too expensive. They love liberty and they love freedom enough that they are willing to die to preserve it!"

A low moan that grew in volume escaped the lips of scores of the soldiers. The sound seemed to move like a wave through their ranks. I was stunned. It was the first and only manifestation of unrest among the troops that I ever saw, or heard, in Johnson's presence. I had to believe it was significant.

During this period the President often was in the presence of men in uniform, because military bases offered platforms safe from the growing numbers of anti-war militants who were eager to disrupt any public rally. Fourteen months had passed, in fact, since Johnson had attempted an old-fashioned barnstorming tour.

Dissent was not confined to the streets, either. At the Pentagon and in the State Department, some officials just below the topmost levels were asking questions, challenging assumptions. Even at the highest levels there sometimes was a new disposition to wonder if policymakers were being dealt a full deck of facts.

Late in 1967, shortly before we learned that Robert McNamara would be resigning, Johnson called Merriman Smith and me into a cabinet meeting without advance notice or explanation. Ushered to seats backed up against a window that overlooked the Rose Garden, we noticed a stack of colorful posterboard charts, about four feet by three in size, standing upright against an empty chair. The top chart, the only one we could see, clearly dealt with Vietnam.

Marvin Watson noted our glances—I suppose the charts may have been highly classified—and ostentatiously picked up the stack and turned it around so we could see only the dull gray backing of a single chart.

While Watson fidgeted, periodically looking in our direction, LBJ shifted the discussion away from domestic policy to Vietnam and ordered Walt Rostow to give a war briefing. An obviously discomfited Watson seemed unbelieving as a Rostow assistant carried the charts to a waiting easel without the President making a move to shoo us out.

Pointer in hand, Rostow launched into a professorial discussion of kill ratios, infiltration rates and force levels, flipping from chart to chart.

Interrupting, Johnson turned to McNamara and asked, "What do you think of that, Bob?"

"Mr. President," replied the Secretary of Defense, "it is evident to me that something is wrong with the figures. If the kill ratios and infiltration rates are correct, the force levels cannot be right. We would have destroyed the other side some time ago."

Without anyone saying another word, Rostow turned to the next chart.

A few days earlier McNamara had accompanied LBJ on the first leg of a cross-country military inspection tour that had ended with a demonstration of night operations aboard a carrier off San Diego. The President ended the cabinet meeting by giving a personal report on the trip.

"When we were down at Ft. Benning," he related, "I got a very good report on one of Bob's pet projects, where you take young men who can't meet the draft standards and you give 'em a little readin' and writin' and good, healthy food, and you make soldiers out of them. One company commander down here told us that he had fifty-six of these boys that were going to go to OCS. Isn't that right, Bob?"

McNamara did not hesitate.

"No, sir, Mr. President," he responded. "What he said was that fifty-six of these men were going to attend NCO School. Frankly, when I get back to the Department, I'm going to order a restudy of the entire program, because none of these men should even be going to NCO School. They're all semi-literates."

Johnson did not hesitate either. His eyes sweeping the long table, he said:

"You-all hear that? Fifty-six of these boys are going to go to OCS!"

There was no further discussion.

Perhaps the President's seeming obtuseness reflected his partial deafness in one ear, although the affliction often appeared to trouble him only on a selective basis. Whenever he thought the occasion demanded it he could become very deaf indeed. He would cup a big hand around an outsized ear and, leaning close to whoever had addressed him, announce, "I don't always hear too good." With each repetition of an offensive statement, Johnson would lean even closer, ostensibly to catch what was being said, until the speaker got the point.

In McNamara's case, I think it more likely that LBJ had been irritated by the Secretary's questioning of Rostow's statistics, particularly in a forum that included many who had no responsibility for war policy.

But perhaps he was beginning to have doubts of his own. As Hugh Sidey wrote at the time, "Lyndon B. Johnson runs a war machine that he basically distrusts and dislikes, and with it he fights a war that he hates."

The President made another inspection trip in February 1968, giving us less than two hours in which to go home and pack and get to Andrews Air Force Base. And we were given no guidance on what kind of weather conditions to expect.

"I think you're going to find most of my trips are going to be without much advance notice," Johnson told us. Unwilling to acknowledge the threat posed by demonstrators, he cited "military security" as the chief reason, adding that he was not always certain of his precise route and did not want to make irrevocable commitments.

Of course we realized that LBJ could not campaign for re-election in secret, and we wondered how he would manage to show himself to the voters—if he managed at all.

Weeks before Johnson circled the globe I wrote, "Some wonder . . . whether multiplying troubles and his slippage in some of the major polls might cause Johnson to decide against running for another term." But, I added, "the odds are long against voluntary retirement."

In late February the President entertained participants in the National Governors Conference. Addressing them, he began: "Distinguished Governors, charming ladies, friends—and favorite sons, I am delighted to welcome you to the White House—temporarily."

His apparent determination to be a candidate was underscored by the reappearance at the White House of George Reedy, who was assigned unspecified chores that we suspected were largely political, and Sam Houston Johnson, who was given a desk at the Democratic National Committee. The President's brother told Frances Lewine of the AP that "Lyndon will run rather than walk" for a second term. But we could not be certain.

On March 2 my nagging doubts were stirred anew. LBJ went to Marietta, Georgia, that day to witness the formal unveiling of the

C-5A transport. Present for the occasion was retired Representative Carl Vinson, who had been chairman of the old House Naval Affairs Committee when young Johnson was a member.

From Marietta we flew to Ramey Air Force Base in Puerto Rico, where the President planned to enjoy a weekend of sunshine and golf.

During the flight to the Caribbean, LBJ told us in Mrs. Johnson's presence that Vinson claimed he had "never felt more productive in his life" than he did in retirement. Turning to her husband, Mrs. Johnson countered in a quiet but determined tone:

"There is living proof that you *can* leave town."

Ten days later, as a write-in candidate, Senator Eugene McCarthy came within 230 votes of defeating the President in New Hampshire's Democratic primary, the first of the election year. It was an extraordinary "moral victory" but LBJ tried to make light of it, telling the VFW Convention:

"I think New Hampshire is the only place where a candidate can claim twenty per cent is a landslide, forty per cent is a mandate and sixty per cent is unanimous. The New Hampshire primaries are unique in politics. They're the only races where anybody can run—and everybody can win."

Four days later Robert F. Kennedy entered the race. And without having yet campaigned, Kennedy already was tied with Johnson in a Gallup poll as the popular choice for the Democratic presidential nomination. The forces opposing LBJ now were formidable, and perhaps unbeatable. Yet a few days later I felt justified in writing:

"Johnson seems to be relishing his new role as the challenged President. In short, he looks vigorous, acts vigorous—and obviously is spoiling for a fight."

Flying from Texas to Minnesota for a speaking engagement, LBJ acknowledged to the press pool that McCarthy might have picked up "two or three" more votes than the President had expected. As for Johnson's own plans, "I will make an announcement at the proper time."

Had Kennedy's candidacy surprised him?

"I haven't been surprised for many years."

Had he always felt that Kennedy would challenge him?

"I always felt that he wanted very much to do so."

What did he see as the major campaign issues?

"I see them as Vietnam, the cities, race problems, and the farm problem. I am going to deal with them. I have other things to deal with, too—two daughters with husbands away [in military service] and a wife who wants to plant trees. I also have to deal with primaries and the convention, and I also could have to deal with an election.

"But I've said, 'First things first.' I think you-all would feel better about your President giving his attention to the things that are most important, and in my judgment primaries and the convention and the election are not as important as the decision whether to bring about a wider war. . . .

"Do you walk off [from Vietnam decisions] and leave it all and slug it out in New Hampshire? I think campaigning is good for the country, and it's good for me. I don't accept the theory that campaigning hurts you. I like to do it. But I've got to think about other things first."

Johnson also discussed the Communists' Tet offensive in Vietnam:

"They [U.S. officials in Saigon] notified me January 24 that Hanoi was going to break the Tet truce, and I alerted every American. That truce was a decoy, but you see that some of your good Christian newspapers show little mention of that. Yet here was a case when you are asked to put down your pistol, undress and put on your pajamas, and as you're crawling into bed, they take out a gun and shoot you. That is what happened at Tet. . . .

"It must be significant that you see very few stories on Ho Chi Minh breaking the truce. That was a dastardly act, and if we had done it, it would have run [in the news media] for days and days. He has broken every truce—something every schoolboy ought to know."

The President argued that there was a pattern in efforts to discredit the nation's Vietnam policies, sometimes by "well-intentioned, patriotic people" but "sometimes by people on the other side of our viewpoint."

"It doesn't make any difference who causes you to jump out the window after you have jumped," he declared.

When Johnson spoke of decisions that could involve a "wider war," he was being completely candid. Since mid-February he had been wrestling with a request by General Westmoreland for 205,000 additional troops—over and above an authorized 525,-000. If LBJ agreed he would have to extend enlistments, increase the monthly draft calls and summon many thousands of reservists to active duty.

Dozens of meetings and many hours of thought produced a presidential decision to address the nation on March 31, at which time he would disclose a new peace initiative, one far bolder than any undertaken in the past. In a unilateral effort to de-escalate the war, he would halt all bombing of North Vietnam except for strictly defined staging areas for the movement of troops and supplies into South Vietnam. Meanwhile, Westmoreland would be given minimal reinforcements.

On the day before Johnson was to speak, daughter Lynda was in California bidding farewell to her husband, Marine Captain Charles Robb, who was bound for Vietnam. At 7 A.M. the next morning she returned to the White House and, with tears brimming in her eyes, asked her father the question that had been raised by the clergyman in Williamsburg. Wrote Johnson in his memoirs: "Why, she asked, was her husband going away to fight, and maybe die, for people who did not even want to be protected?"

After talking to his daughter and trying to console her, the President went to Sunday mass at the church of Luci's "little monks" with Luci and her husband, Airman First Class Patrick Nugent, who was himself destined to leave for Vietnam within days.

That evening Johnson stepped into his Oval Office and, after drinking from a glass of water, began addressing his television audience at 9:01 P.M. He announced his peace initiative and then, at nine thirty-nine, stunned us all:

"With America's sons in the fields far away, with America's future under challenge right here at home, with our hopes and the world's hopes for peace in the balance every day, I do not believe that I should devote an hour or a day of my time to any personal partisan causes or to any duties other than the awesome duties of this office—the presidency of the United States.

"Accordingly, I shall not seek, and I will not accept, the nomination of my party for another term as your President."

As soon as the red lights on the TV cameras winked off Mrs.

Johnson fairly leaped into her husband's arms, embracing and kissing him. There were tears in her eyes.

Barely an hour afterward the President met with reporters in the family quarters, in the Yellow Oval Room that leads to the Truman Balcony.

"How irrevocable is your decision?" he was asked.

"Completely irrevocable," he replied.

Other reporters tried in various ways to test Johnson's sincerity.

"My statement speaks for itself," LBJ declared, seemingly with strained patience. "I don't see why we should have these high school discussions about it."

The next day, flying back to Washington from a speaking date in Chicago, he talked for nearly an hour and a half in his Air Force One cabin with another group of reporters.

It seemed to him, he asserted, that he was becoming almost "the object of contempt," that he was approaching the point where he could be immobilized, unable to function as President.

"I felt that even if I signed the Lord's Prayer it wouldn't matter any more," he said.

Drawing an analogy that would be familiar to his listeners, he said a reporter might write an article he was proud of, only to see his editor put it in the second section of the paper without a by-line. "Pretty soon you say, 'Why do I keep on writing?' "

Musing about the presidency, he remarked, "Maybe other people can do it better." He said he bore more handicaps after four years in office "than if I were a new man coming in."

In January, he related, he had been prepared to disclose his disavowal of candidacy during his State of the Union Address; he even carried the announcement to the Capitol in his pocket.

"I didn't use it then," he added. "I thought it might hurt in getting the legislation I felt was vital."

He sought another opportunity, and found it in his peace-initiative speech.

"I don't think Mrs. Johnson believed I was going to say it until I actually read the line," he declared. "But *I* knew it."

The President confided that he hoped now to be able to shake people up and "get things done" without it being argued that he was only trying to win a primary in Wisconsin or California. He continued:

"As long as I live, I'll find plenty of satisfaction. My feelings are not hurt. People have been better to me than I deserve. . . . I've been happy doing everything I've done in my life. I'm not a crybaby. . . .

"I don't need the job . . . the salary. I don't need your approval. I'm going to live a full, happy life. I don't give a particular damn what you think!

"But I do think that this country is going to be better for you-all, for the things I've done. . . ."

The President's monologue, which was set down at the time by my colleague Clifford Evans of RKO General Broadcasting, seemed to have a rather plaintive, even whining quality that was absent from Johnson's public statements. As I wrote that same day, any private misgivings he may have had about his renunciation of a second-term bid "were totally camouflaged" from the public.

LBJ ostensibly was perfectly content to have his decision remain "completely irrevocable." He seemed at peace with himself and with the world. And the world, as represented by its leaders, continued to beat a path to his door. Proudly, the retiring President announced that the 201 foreign visitors he entertained during his tenure represented yet another record.

"It comes to about four fifths of a potentate a week," he joked.

While others vied for the Democratic presidential nomination, LBJ enjoyed greater freedom than ever to relax in his native hill country. He made so many trips there during the summer of 1968 that I began one dispatch: "President Johnson arrived at his Texas ranch Friday night, ending a four-day stay at the White House."

In August, Johnson went to his alma mater at San Marcos and told a summer commencement crowd, "I'm not a candidate for anything, except maybe a rocking chair."

The Democratic Convention that began in Chicago two days later was timed to coincide with the President's sixtieth birthday. Stacked and ready in the basement of the International Amphitheater were hundreds of placards that read, "Happy Birthday LBJ." We were in Texas that day and many of us half expected to make a birthday flight to Chicago. Instead we were invited to join the President and Mrs. Johnson at Luci Nugent's house in Austin to share a single-candle birthday cake. It was, I thought, a rather sad occasion, because Johnson surely would have gone to Chicago had there not been rioting in the streets. Even at that, he hinted that he might attend a later convention session, although that prospect subsequently was foreclosed by violence in Grant Park.

With the selection of Hubert Humphrey as the Democratic nominee, my own association with LBJ neared an end. My new assignment was to cover the Humphrey-Nixon campaign.

On October 1, I was reporting on the Vice-President's activities in Salt Lake City when I was summoned to a telephone outside the Mormon Tabernacle. My bureau chief was calling to order me back to Washington, where I would remain until I managed, if I could, to interview LBJ about his thoughts during the campaign season. I began to worry about sitting out the campaign itself while awaiting an appointment with the President that might never come.

Arriving home the next day, I called George Christian to explain my predicament.

"The President is very busy with a new Vietnam policy review," Christian told me. "I don't think he'll be able to see you right away."

Two days later I was in the Oval Office having my last interview with LBJ. I did not see him again until the day that Richard Nixon became President. This is how I began my final report from the Johnson White House:

President Johnson, on the inside looking out at the 1968 presidential race, insists he has not the slightest regret about his self-exile from the campaign.

Underneath, however, he's a bit restive. After thirty-plus years in public life . . . it isn't easy to retire to relative obscurity.

As Johnson sees it, his historic decision of March 31 not to seek reelection may have been his only means of keeping the nation whole.

The decision was not an easy one, although Johnson now contends he had it in the back of his mind from the moment he won his record 1964 victory. . . .

At that time, Mrs. Johnson began counting the days until the end of his four-year term. Periodically she would remind her husband of the precise time remaining.

Johnson definitely misses active campaigning this year but has no plans to become a stump speaker for Vice President Hubert H.

Humphrey, who has his endorsement. The President is reserving the option, however, to do some limited campaigning.

The President, looking back on nearly five years in the White House, expressed his greatest pride in his foreign policy record—precisely the area that has brought him the greatest measure of criticism both at home and abroad.

He likes to point out that, during his tenure, Communist countries did not succeed in altering a single boundary or engulfing any new territory. As he stated the case at one recent private meeting:

"The Communists have not made a gain—and they've got lots of trouble." . . .

As we chatted, with Johnson making no effort to hasten the end of our meeting, Patrick Lyndon Nugent played with his grandfather's several telephones and with the triple-screen television console across the comfortable room. Lyn, as the President called him, was a source of great pride and comfort in the pre-retirement months. On the child's first birthday LBJ wrote him a letter that read, in part:

You are my link to the future; you are also my link to the present. In you and through you I have an even deeper sense of responsibility to all the other children, their mothers and fathers and their grandparents, not just in America but throughout the world. And I devoutly wish for them the happy, fruitful and ennobling life I wish for you—a life free of war, poverty, disease, and inner darkness; an end to the conditions that separate fathers from their families on happy occasions like this.

The President's pride in his grandson was excessive. After the youngster teethed on a package of Juicy Fruit gum, LBJ, with a flourish, presented the damp packet to Richard Saltonstall of *Time,* announcing gravely, "Little Lyn chewed on this!" We got the impression that he expected Saltonstall to mount it under glass.

During an Air Force One flight Johnson stood the boy on a table around which the press pool members were seated. As the plane bounced through turbulence, we reached out to grab the child, who had only recently learned to stand up by himself.

"Let him alone!" the President commanded. "He won't fall down."

At Johnson's urging, Luci took Patrick Lyndon to witness the retiring President's final State of the Union Address. "He might not remember it," said LBJ, "but I would."

"You are my link to the future," the President had written, in what must have been a cry from the heart, because LBJ was returning to private life without a political heir.

When Johnson had turned from teaching to politics in 1931, his mother observed that "he was aided and abetted by his father, whose overwhelming ambition for his son was governmental position."

Similarly, when Lynda Bird reached voting age, her father told us, "I'd give anything in the world for her to have a political career—but I don't know what she'll do."

Lyndon Johnson spent much of his life searching for a substitute for the son he never had. Recruited to fill the role at various times were Bobby Baker, Bill Moyers and Tom Johnson. Finally there was Patrick Lyndon Nugent as the only young male in the family.

As LBJ walked out of the White House for the last time as President, his hopes and ambitions surely were focused on his grandson, his "link to the future." Otherwise, Johnson's horizons were quite limited. When Saul Pett of the AP asked him what he looked forward to in retirement, the President cited very simple desires:

"Freedom, I guess. Freedom to be my own man. To hike in the pastures fourteen or fifteen miles a day with no phones and no reporters. To sleep under the stars. To be able to take my wife by the hand and walk through the woods without forty Secret Service men around. I look forward to the day when the press won't give a damn about me as copy, when I can walk in and get a beer and a hamburger somewhere without it being regarded as outrageous."

That was our Lyndon, always and forever his own man. With the dignity of an elder statesman, he returned to Texas for the seventy-eighth time since taking the presidential oath in Dallas.

And we continued to give a damn.

Index